Ambassadors in Foreign Policy

AMBASSADORS IN FOREIGN POLICY

The Influence of Individuals on U.S.-Latin American Policy

EDITED BY
C. NEALE RONNING
ALBERT P. VANNUCCI

PRAEGER

New York
Westport, Connecticut
London

Library of Congress Cataloging-in-Publication Data

Ambassadors in foreign policy.

   Bibliography: p.
   Includes index.
   1. Ambassadors—United States.   2. United States—
Foreign relations—Latin America.   3. Latin America—
Foreign relations—United States.   4. United States—
Foreign relations—20th century.   5. United States—
Foreign relations administration.   I. Ronning, C. Neale.
II. Vannucci, Albert P.
E747.A677   1987   327.7308   87-2833
ISBN 0-275-92393-2

First published in 1987

Praeger Publishers, One Madison Avenue, New York, NY 10010
A division of Greenwood Press, Inc.

Printed in the United States of America

The paper used in this book complies with the
Permanent Paper Standard issued by the National
Information Standards Organization (Z39.48-1984).

10 9 8 7 6 5 4 3 2 1

Copyright Acknowledgment

The authors and the publishers are grateful to the following for granting the use of their material:

Excerpts from *Navigating the Rapids 1918–1971: From the Papers of Adolf A. Berle,* edited by Beatrice Bishop Berle and Travis Beal Jacobs. Copyright 1973 by Beatrice Bishop Berle. Reprinted by permission of Harcourt Brace Jovanovich.

To the memory of Bryce Wood
who was to contribute to this volume
and who provided a model and inspiration
for several generations of Latin Americanists.

Contents

Introduction

Albert P. Vannucci

> In our age of mass politics, it is popular to believe that collectivities, not individuals, determine political actions. Government bureaucracies, multinational corporations, and the masses are often viewed as the main forces that shape political life. . . . The age of mass politics has hidden heroes, namely the manipulative elite who are disguised and buried behind the bureaucracies, propaganda, and collectivist political theories.
>
> Individuals are the cutting edge of world politics. Nation–States and historical conditions present human beings with opportunities and limitations. But individual willpower and foreign policy decisions make a critical contribution to the outcome and direction of events. Man is conditioned, but at times he can also become a condition.
>
> Robert A. Isaak, *Individuals and World Politics*

The role of individuals in U.S. foreign policy seems to be given either central importance (as in biographies and psychohistories) or minimal attention (as in systems theories, "realist" analysis, or studies of organizations). Moreover, the individuals who do receive attention are virtually always presidents or secretaries of state or defense. And while the field is rich in studies of institutions such as the State Department, it is practically devoid of any assessment of individuals qua individuals at any level below that of secretary.

This study proposes to address that gap. It is an examination of six individuals who served as U.S. ambassador to an important Latin American country at a particularly determinative time. The individuals were both career Foreign Service officers and political appointees; the countries are of varying size; and the studies span more than 60 years. The criterion for selection was that, during the period of the posting, something of lasting importance occurred for both U.S. foreign policy toward the country and region and for the Latin country itself. The questions of whether the ambassador played a major role in the important developments, in what manner, for what reasons, and with what lasting consequences were left to each contributor.

Five of the six case studies are written by scholars who have studied U.S. Latin American policy, as well as a particular Latin country, and whose past work offers a diversity of viewpoints and methodologies. The final case study stands somewhat apart as a self-study written by the subject himself, Nathaniel Davis, who was U.S. ambasssador to Chile from 1971 to 1973.

Our preliminary expectation was that each study would reveal the existence of considerable conflict among often competing policy objectives: the "official" policy of the administration at the time, which may or may not have given the particular country adequate importance; the policy developed and promoted by the State Department in Washington, with all of the attendant considerations for bureaucratic competition that we have come to expect; the collective field policy of the embassy staff, who may or may not have had favorable impressions of the ambassador's abilities; and, finally, the ambassador's "personal" objectives, which most certainly would have included not only his perceptions of the most desirable policies and effective methods but also considerations about his future career and "place in history." What conflicts existed among these policies; what different perceptions; in what manner differences were resolved; and with what consequences, all seemed to be potentially fertile questions.

Additionally, we wondered how the ambassador's perceptions were shaped by his previous experiences; by his personality "needs"; and by his image of Latin America, of the particular country, and of his role there. Did he have a world view, and how did it affect his performance? Did he become an advocate for his host country, a lobbyist to the bureaucracy in Washington? What were his relations with superiors, peers, and subordinates? These and many other questions presented themselves as possible avenues of insight to orient and shape the studies.

Rather than ask each contributor to fit his or her study to a preconceived framework, each was left to determine what warranted examination and how best it should be analyzed. The common point of departure was that the studied individual was serving as ambassador at a time of important developments. Latin Americanists routinely treat the U.S. Embassy in any Latin country as one of the most significant actors. This study examines both whether that assumption was valid at the times and places studied and what role the official chief of mission played. Those who study the State Department have long observed that Latin America has not engaged the interest of the department's "best and brightest." This study also addresses the accuracy of this assessment and its impact.

Twenty years ago, James Rosenau offered a theoretical framework for the analysis of U.S. foreign policy. He proposed to investigate data in five different source categories: the external environment, the societal environment, the governmental setting, the roles played by key decision makers, and the individual characteristics of important policymakers. Although this formulation has been modified several times, by Rosenau himself and others, its original form captured the imagination of a great many foreign policy analysts and has come into widespread use. Perhaps its fullest treatment is found in Charles W. Kegley, Jr. and Eugene Wittkopf's *American Foreign Policy: Pattern and Process* (1979, 1982 and 1987). This much admired text has proven very satisfying to many, appropriate for both graduate and undergraduate courses.

However, those of us who study U.S. foreign policy toward Latin America have sometimes questioned Kegley and Wittkopf's conclusions and have wished to see their analysis applied to particular geographic regions. Latin Americanists, wonder about the way in which Kegley and Wittkopf rank Rosenau's five categories in degree of "relative potencies." In noncrisis instances, they conclude that the most powerful source of foreign policy behavior is the role variable, followed by the governmental, then the societal, next the external, and finally the individual.

Actually, U.S. foreign policy in Latin America has seemed most determined by the external environment, by developments elsewhere in the world that led us to view any Latin country in one or another way. We also wonder about the lowest ranking being accorded to the individual variable, and expect that this study may contribute to some modification. It must be noted that Kegley and Wittkopf alter their ranking for times of crisis ("characterized by surprise, limited response time, and perceived threats to high priority goals"), giving the individual variable the greatest potency then, followed by the role, the governmental, and the societal categories. (The external variable is not factored, because it is the source of the crisis.) It is also one of our tasks to consider whether our case studies are of true crises, and whether this modified ranking withstands scrutiny in the Latin context.

In a famous dictum, Hans Morgenthau declared. "International Relations is the study of contemporary history." It is that, and more. The purpose here is to offer more than a collection of case studies, although that would be a legitimate undertaking. Additionally, however, it is our hope that these studies will reveal some patterns, some consistencies, and some lessons applicable to U.S. present and future policies in Latin America. Our desire is to illuminate the past, so as to assist in the unfolding of a more felicitous future.

That the United States has been a true global actor only since World War II may serve as an excuse for many U.S. foreign policy misperceptions and failures. Unfortunately, the United States cannot claim innocence in its relations with Latin America. This is the one region in the world in which it has been actively involved for over a century. Yet, regrettably, U.S. policies in Latin America have been no more successful and may, arguably, present a record of less success than with regions and countries of much more recent interest. Past U.S. Latin American policy begs for closer scrutiny. We propose to contribute here to that effort.

Ambassadors in Foreign Policy

The Ambassador *Simpático:* Dwight Morrow in Mexico 1927–30

Richard Melzer

A special train sped through the United States en route to Mexico in the fall of 1927; it was bringing Dwight Morrow to his first diplomatic post. On October 21, accompanied by a small entourage of family members and aides, the newly appointed U.S. ambassador entered Mexico for the first time in his life. Morrow was met with great fanfare and considerable hospitality. Mexican dignitaries greeted the 53-year-old envoy's party at the border in Nuevo Laredo and further south in Monterrey. Two carloads of heavily armed Mexican soldiers were assigned to escort Morrow's train; and armed agrarians guarded the tracks to Mexico City, with strict orders to shoot anyone who might attempt to sabotage the ambassador's peaceful journey.[1]

Morrow received an even greater reception when his train arrived in the Mexican capital on October 23. Just over five feet tall, with uncombed hair, crooked tie, and a disarming manner, the foreign traveler looked more like a disheveled schoolmaster than a Wall Street banker (which he had been for 13 years) or a traditionally dapper diplomat. A large, enthusiastic crowd greeted the unimposing envoy in a "demonstration of welcome [such] as had never . . . been accorded to any diplomat" in Mexican history.[2] A Mexican official told reporters at the station that he felt "profound satisfaction" in Morrow's arrival, because he fully expected that "all matters now under consideration between the [United States and Mexico] will be settled satisfactorily."[3] Others in the government and the press shared his opinion. According to *El Universal*, "It is impossible that such a man as Mr. Morrow . . . could fail. What a . . . leader in the world of finance cannot accomplish, no one can do."[4]

Given this warm reception and high praise, an innocent observer in the depot crowd would have frowned in disbelief, had he been informed that all was not well between the United States and Mexico. Indeed, an innocent observer would have been shocked to learn that the United States and Mexico had not enjoyed peaceful diplomatic relations in at least three years and that the diplomatic air had been so charged with tension that there had even been talk of war between the neighboring nations, just ten months prior to Morrow's arrival.[5]

But unfortunately, such was the case. Complex issues involving nearly every aspect of diplomatic relations divided the two nations and begged for resolution. Mexico was caught in the whirlwind of a political and social revolution that had caused great changes in the critical concepts of national sovereignty and foreign property rights. Jealous of their authority to alter these concepts, revolutionary leaders clashed with foreigners, who recalled an earlier age when Porfirio Díaz welcomed them as harbingers of progress and allowed them extraordinary privileges in Mexico. Gone were the days when U.S. citizens could acquire huge land holdings, wantonly exploit oil and mineral reserves, dominate entire industries, and receive preferential treatment for the least complaint. The urgent need to pull in the reins on foreign influence and power had little meaning for conservative businessmen, who had come to Mexico with unbending views regarding private property and the limited role that government should play in a free economy. Spoiled by Díaz, these foreigners and their sympathetic allies in the U.S. Embassy were repulsed by the revolutionary ideas incorporated in the Constitution of 1917 and implemented (however gradually) by the revolutionary regimes of Venustiano Carranza (1917–20), Álvaro Obregón (1920–24), and Plutarco Elías Calles (1924–28).[6]

The United States earnestly sought to defend its citizens and their rights abroad, while discouraging disruptive, radical change in Mexico or any other country of Latin America. Dominated by business-minded Republican administrations in the 1920s, Washington was especially sensitive to complaints registered by conservative political supporters—such as Edward L. Doheny of the Pan-American Petroleum Company—who felt threatened by radical legislation enacted as part of the Mexican Revolution. Washington was also receptive to protests voiced by those with great influence on public opinion—such as William Randolph Hearst—or those who represented extremely large voting blocs—such as the Catholic Knights of Columbus, which objected to the cruel treatment of the church and its devout followers in Mexico. In addition, there were many in Washington who hoped for the return of a "responsible" government in Mexico, because they feared the effect of Mexico's revolutionary example on other Latin American nations. Officials led by Secretary of Commerce Herbert Hoover were seeking to create a new international order based on mutual cooperation and shared capitalist gains. The creation of such an informal empire was considered impossible so long as relations with our closest neighbor were characterized by strife, rather than harmony, in regard to nearly every diplomatic issue.[7]

The United States had implemented various tactics in its attempt to cut this Gordian knot: Diplomatic recognition had been withheld (1920–23); negotiated agreements had been attempted (at Bucareli in 1923); an arms embargo had been instituted (1923–29); a steady stream of diplomatic notes had been sent (1924–27), and unsubtle threats of direct military intervention had been made.[8] But nothing seemed to make a difference. By 1927, it was evident that, the more the United States attempted to pressure Mexico, the more Mexico—led by President Plutarco Elías Calles—would remain set on its revolutionary course.

Calles's reaction was politically predictable. Bending to U.S. pressure and compromising revolutionary principles would have meant political suicide for any revolutionary leader of the 1920s. Never the dangerous Bolshevik that he was pictured to be in the United States, Calles was, in fact, eager to control the revolutionary forces that had played havoc with Mexico's political, economic, and social stability for nearly two decades. Calles sincerely desired to harness these powerful forces to the wheel of constructive development, so that he could consolidate his power and lead his nation beyond the violent phase of its revolution.[9]

However, each time the president was about to control one or more of the revolution's most radical factions, reactionary elements surfaced—threatening his regime and its largely conservative goals. Faced with this recurring menace, Calles was frequently forced to rely on radicals in the ranks of labor and the agrarian reform movement to defend the revolution—albeit at the inevitable cost of satisfying more, rather than less, of their radical demands. Unfortunately, satisfying these demands often led to new crises, in which much of the work of the revolution (measured in material terms, at least) was trampled underfoot or destroyed beyond recognition.

Calles perceived reactionary predators on many fronts. The Catholic Church, foreign oil companies, overly ambitious officers, and a long parade of meddling U.S. ambassadors were all identified as major enemies of the revolution.[10] Ironically, each usually worked against their own best interest by attacking Calles and forcing him to rely on revolutionary caudillos—such as Saturnino Cedillo of San Luis Potosí and Adalberto Tejeda of Vera Cruz— to defend his regime, at the considerable cost of granting additional concessions to the masses and additional political favors to their powerful chieftains. Cedillo, for example, could be counted on to mobilize no less than 1,500 *ejidatarios* to help suppress the de la Huerta revolt of 1923–24 and 6,000 additional fighters to help crush the Cristero Rebellion of 1926–29, because he had granted nearly a million hectares of land to the peasants of San Luis Potosí in the course of the 1920s.[11] Armed and in search of tangible rewards for their service to the state, these agrarians pressed for the redistribution of new farmland or the protection of already divided estates. Although Calles personally opposed such radical land reform in an economically chaotic period, he nevertheless yielded to agrarian demands from 1924 to 1927 by resigning himself to the fact that these expensive political debts represented the high price he was required to pay for the safety of his extremely vulnerable regime.

Calles recognized the United States as his most formidable enemy. Aptly known as the "Colossus of the North," this powerful giant enjoyed so much power that it could readily assist any number of Calles's opponents in any number of ways. For example, it could relax its arms embargo, allowing a restless Mexican general to procure sufficient amounts of arms and ammunition to launch a major revolt against the government. In another instance, it could lend aid and comfort to conspiring reactionaries by allowing the U.S. Embassy or a convenient border town to serve as headquarters for their nefarious activities. Or Washington could easily "sow alarm" [12] in Mexico by making several blunt demands and then flatly stating that "The government of Mexico is now on trial before the world," as Secretary of State Frank B. Kellogg informed the press in mid-1925. [13] The list of such subversive strategies could go on and on. However, in nearly every case, threats posed by the United States and its reactionary allies were magnified several times over—because they usually led to new demands on the part of the revolutionary radicals, who were needed by the Mexican government to counter each new round of attacks. Faced with this vicious circle of threats and demands, it became increasingly evident that the best way to control not only the predators, but also the radicals of the revolution, was to make peace with the revolution's most powerful nemesis. Thus, in 1927, Calles recognized the great political need for peace with Washington.

Calles realized the key role of the U.S. ambassador in any such peacemaking endeavor. An amicable, cooperative ambassador could appreciate Calles's basically conservative nature, understand his political dilemma, be receptive to peace overtures, and convince officials in Washington of his sincere desire for détente. A hostile, less cooperative ambassador would continue to portray Calles as a power-hungry radical, turn a deaf ear to all talk of peace, and convey only negative dispatches to the U.S. government. Well aware of the explosive impact of some U.S. ambassadors—such as Joel Poinset (1825–29) and Henry Lane Wilson (1909–13)—on Mexican history, Calles hoped that an individual with amicable characteristics would finally be sent—someone to help chart a new course in U.S.-Mexican relations.

Calles had every reason to believe that Dwight Morrow was just such an individual. Educated at Amherst and Columbia, Morrow had served as a corporation lawyer in the prestigious New York law firm of Reed, Simpson, Thacher, and Barnum before joining J. P. Morgan on Wall Street in 1914. Morrow enjoyed great success in the financial world and reportedly earned a million dollars a year when he was a Morgan partner in the 1920s. [14] According to Calvin Coolidge, Morgan had recruited Morrow "not merely because of his [legal] talent, for such talent was plentiful and easy to buy, but . . . for his character, which was priceless." [15] Speaking in 1927, a fellow Morgan banker remarked that "There has never been any problem, however difficult, that we [have] had [at J. P. Morgan] which Morrow has not been able to solve."[16]

Morrow's methods were simple and direct. Having observed his negotiating skill in practice, an English author described the three steps that Morrow normally followed in solving a thorny problem. Sir Arthur Salter's observations read like a diplomatic handbook:

First find the facts—all the important facts that are relevant—before you let yourself even begin to form a policy; second, try to penetrate the real mind of the person you are negotiating with, to see the problem as he sees it, to understand what it is that is really important to him; third, try to evolve out of this a solution which will really be to the common interest and not [simply] a diplomatic score [for your side alone].[17]

Morrow had successfully employed these tactful methods in public as well as private affairs prior to 1927. The banker was awarded the Distinguished Service Medal for his fine work on the Allied Maritime Transport Council during World War I. In addition, Morrow had chaired the civilian board of inquiry that had investigated Colonel Billy Mitchell's highly publicized charges against the armed forces in 1925.[18] Few problems seemed beyond the banker's proven ability as a troubleshooter in a vast array of fields.

Despite the fact that he had never set foot in Mexico until the fall of 1927, Morrow had also become something of an expert on Mexican affairs through his work on Wall Street. Mexico ran a substantial foreign debt in the 1920s, and experienced great difficulty in repaying its international creditors in a timely fashion. Therefore, the Mexican government was in constant contact with foreign bankers led by Thomas W. Lamont, a senior Morgan partner and a major force on the International Committee of Bankers on Mexico.[19] Morrow was drawn into Lamont's dealings with the Mexicans and became acutely aware of the complex, interrelated problems that beset Mexico and its depressed economy. Morrow and Lamont soon established close personal ties with several Mexican leaders—including Mexico's former minister of finance, Alberto J. Pani, and the Mexican ambassador to the United States, Manuel C. Téllez. Known as the "national development faction" of the Calles regime, these important individuals shared Calles's strong desire for peace—for economic as well as political reasons. Impressed by Morrow's and Lamont's sincerity, Pani and his colleagues turned to the Morgan partners for advice and support at the height of the diplomatic crisis of 1927.[20]

Morrow was recognized as a particularly valuable ally because he enjoyed great influence in the Coolidge administration, as well. The banker had been a close friend and trusted advisor to Calvin Coolidge in the years since the two men graduated from Amherst College in the class of 1895. A fellow

Republican, Morrow worked so hard to have his former classmate nominated as the Republican vice-presidential candidate in 1920 that at least one observer called Coolidge's nomination "a great political accident, brought about by the imagination of Dwight Morrow."[21] In August 1923, Morrow's involvement in his friend's career grew even stronger when Warren Harding died in office and Coolidge assumed the presidency. Morrow was a frequent guest at the White House and was soon known as one of the president's most trusted lieutenants.[22]

At several critical junctures in the period 1923–27, Coolidge solicited Morrow's advice regarding Mexico. Counterbalancing the advice of hard-liners in the State Department and at the U.S. Embassy in Mexico City, the banker swayed Coolidge from raising the U.S. arms embargo (on at least three occasions in 1925 and 1926) and from "Cubanizing" Mexico through direct military intervention (in early 1927).[23] Morrow counseled the president against such dangerous actions because he adamantly opposed the use of military force in Latin America—especially as a means to collect international debts, regardless of their size and regardless of any delay in their repayment. Expressing his views in several public forums, Morrow argued that "when we need the sheriff to help collect a loan, we recognize that our venture has turned out a failure. We are then only trying to save some planks from a shipwreck."[24] Morrow hoped to avoid a shipwreck of this kind, because he and his Wall Street colleagues knew that only a financially sound Mexican government could ever afford to improve its economy and finally pay its international debt.[25]

Calvin Coolidge prudently followed his former classmate's advice and readily thought of Morrow as an excellent candidate to replace James R. Sheffield, when Sheffield resigned his post as the U.S. ambassador to Mexico in July 1927. In sharp contrast to Morrow's way of thinking, Sheffield had always insisted that a "firm policy" was needed to "protect the United States against the menace of extreme radicalism at our side door."[26] Although he continually denied that he sought U.S. military intervention in Mexico, Sheffield privately wrote that "There is a vast amount of policing to be done in this world, and as the greatest and the richest of the nations, we will have to do our full share of it in the interest of civilization and peaceful commerce."[27] Sheffield openly conspired with counterrevolutionaries and all but refused to deal with Calles's government, claiming that the only difference between Mexican officials and Mexican bandits was "the difference between success and failure."[28]

Calles was greatly relieved to hear of Sheffield's departure and Morrow's appointment as his successor. Based on optimistic reports from Pani and other members of the national development faction, Calles knew of Morrow's noninterventionist philosophy and of his considerable influence in high political and financial circles. The chief executive learned more about the new envoy by collecting newspaper clippings from across the United States.[29]

He also received a personal letter from Gerardo Machado in which the Cuban president praised Morrow for his great help in negotiating two international loans for Cuba in the early 1920s.[30] Calles could not have been more pleased by what he read. The president had at last found an amicable, cooperative ambassador to take the place of a hostile, uncooperative one. Calles eagerly awaited Morrow's arrival, so that he could get on with the important business of creating détente.

Washington clearly shared Calles's great faith in Morrow's diplomatic skills. With few Mexican experts to rely on for advice (only one State Department official had served in Mexico since 1910, and no one at the U.S. Embassy had served there for more than three years[31]), Morrow was trusted with carte blanche and given the president's sole instruction to do whatever was necessary "to keep us out of war with Mexico."[32]

Morrow's warm reception in October 1927 was quite understandable, in light of Calles's hopes for improved relations with the United States. Although some historians have suggested that Morrow's diplomatic service began under a cloud of doubt and mistrust, the contrary is a far more accurate description of the anticipation shared by high government officials in both the United States and Mexico. Thus, while some observers may have feared that "after Morrow comes the Marines,"[33] Calles and his top advisors knew enough about Morrow and his background to know that such fears were unfounded. Rather than waste their time in securing military defenses, the Mexicans made plans to welcome the new ambassador and brief him on the situation at hand.[34]

Therefore, only two days after his arrival in Mexico City, Morrow was greeted by Mexico's minister of foreign affairs, Genaro Estrada. Estrada was kind and gracious; but lost no time before telling the envoy just exactly how anxious Calles was to deal with him on a direct, personal basis. As Morrow later described this conversation in a dispatch to Secretary of State Kellogg, Estrada explained that, in Mexico, "the system of administration was a 'Presidential system' and that as the President alone had the authority to make decisions on behalf of the Government he hoped that I would at all times discuss with President Calles matters of difference" between the United States and Mexico.[35]

Morrow was to hear this message from various sources; but none of his new acquaintances emphasized the point more emphatically than did Calles himself. Not willing to let a single opportunity pass, Calles insisted on talking to Morrow immediately following the ambassador's formal presentation of his diplomatic credentials on October 29, 1927. The president cordially invited Morrow to "feel free at all times to come directly to him" with any problems that might arise as he "earnestly desired that [all issues] be settled amicably." Morrow concurred.[36]

Having taken the diplomatic initiative, Calles did not wait for the new envoy to seek him out for private discussions on diplomatic differences. In-

stead, the president extended an invitation for Morrow to join him at breakfast 48 hours after their first encounter at the National Palace. Sending a car
for Morrow at 6:15 in the morning, Calles had the ambassador driven to his
160-hectare ranch east of Mexico City. Calles gave Morrow an hour-long
tour of his modern ranch before proceeding to breakfast, where he described his many efforts to improve Mexico's rural economy. Pleased with
this session—but disappointed that no specific problems had been discussed—Calles invited Morrow to join him at another private meeting on
November 8.[37] These rather informal sessions were applauded as promising
signs that peace was around the corner. The leaders' unique approach to
international relations was dubbed "ham and eggs diplomacy" by reporters
who anticipated the easy solution of complex problems around Calles's
breakfast table.[38]

In yet another show of earnest goodwill, the president invited Morrow and
his aides on a 3,000-mile tour of northern Mexico, during the first week of
December 1927.[39] Although Morrow was rebuked for accompanying Calles
so shortly after the government's brutal execution of Fr. Miguel Pro Juárez
and three other Cristero leaders, Morrow dismissed this criticism by stating
privately that "I am accredited to General Calles and if I am to accomplish
anything in Mexico I cannot start by offending him."[40]

The ambassador's tactful response in this instance was typical of his new
approach to diplomatic relations in Mexico. Morrow privately felt that the
priest's execution was "terrible"; but, given his purely diplomatic status in
Mexico, he wisely labeled the affair a "domestic question" with legal justification derived from Article 28 of the Mexican Constitution.[41] Thus, while
Calles went out of his way to put Morrow at ease and earn the ambassador's trust in preparation for serious negotiations, Morrow went out of his
way to prove that he scrupulously respected Mexican sovereignty and customs as few U.S. ambassadors had ever done before.

The envoy attempted to demonstrate this respect in numerous additional
ways. On November 19, for example, Morrow addressed a U.S. Chamber
of Commerce luncheon and showered praise on the foreign business community in Mexico City. Then, when he felt that "they were in a good enough
humor to take it," the ambassador quoted a 1907 speech by Elihu Root in
which the former secretary of state had urged U.S. businessmen in Mexico
to remember that, "while you continue to be good, loyal American citizens,
you should [strive to] be good . . . loyal Mexican residents," as well. His
listeners were thus reminded of the need to respect the Mexican government and its laws if they hoped not only to prosper in Mexico, but also to
help ease diplomatic tension without resorting to arrogant insults or renewed
cries for intervention.[42]

The ambassador also demonstrated his deep respect for Mexico by making several significant changes in the U.S. Embassy itself. Morrow did not
purge the embassy of hard-liners left from Sheffield's diplomatic staff, but
worked patiently to control their excesses until they were either won over to

his way of thinking or gradually transferred to other Foreign Service assignments. Meanwhile, the sending of frequent diplomatic dispatches was discouraged, and U.S. consuls were reprimanded for filing derogatory reports regarding the Mexican government.[43] Morrow preferred to send many of his own reports over a recently installed telephone line to Washington, although it was rumored that his phone was tapped by Mexican agents. Undisturbed by these rumors of security leaks, Morrow told the State Department that "If we spend our time . . . feeling that the main object of our Embassy is secrecy instead of effectively carrying on the Government's business, we will become slaves of our suspicions, instead of servants to our Government."[44] In a symbolic but significant gesture, Morrow went so far as to change the name "American Embassy." Acknowledging that Mexico and all nations of the Western Hemisphere were American, the envoy renamed his residence "U.S. Embassy" and insisted on being called the "U.S. Ambassador to Mexico."[45]

Morrow made frequent visits to the Mexican countryside and purchased a beautiful summer home in Cuernavaca, to further demonstrate his interest in the people and culture of Mexico. Photographs showed Morrow mixing with the peasants and admiring their handicrafts.[46] Many of these handicrafts were used to decorate the ambassador's home in Cuernavaca, while others became part of an exhibit that Morrow personally sponsored and sent on tour to the United States in the spring of 1928.[47]

In another unorthodox step, Morrow refused to bring his own translator to meetings, trusting the government's interpreter to accurately translate even the most sensitive diplomatic discussions. In vain, the envoy attempted to learn Spanish by hiring a language professor to coach him at the breakfast table each morning. Unfortunately, a hearing disability seriously hampered his daily lessons. The Mexicans nevertheless admired his effort and easily forgave his linguistic errors, as when Morrow introduced their wives as Sonora (a state in northern Mexico) rather than Señora.[48]

On a more spectacular level, Morrow invited Charles A. Lindbergh to fly to Mexico as a goodwill gesture. Lindbergh gladly accepted the ambassador's invitation and, over Morrow's protest that it would involve unnecessary risks, insisted on making his journey the first nonstop flight from Washington, D.C., to Mexico City. Thousands of Mexicans awaited Lindbergh's arrival; they literally carried the Spirit of St. Louis to a hanger when the aviator landed in his famous plane on December 14, 1927. The Calles regime proceeded to honor Lindbergh in every imaginable fashion. Newspaper editorials across the United States shared Mexico's great enthusiasm; but the impact of Lindbergh's trip was best described in a personal letter to Calles from Bertram W. Edwards, a businessman from Buffalo, New York. Edwards stated that news of

the reception given our . . . Lindbergh by all of Mexico and especially by you . . . has opened our eyes and our hearts and caused practically a complete change of thinking. We like you immensely and personally and when two people are personal friends it is pretty hard for things to go wrong between them.[49]

President Calles quickly acted to resolve all major diplomatic problems, because he realized that the recent thaw in U.S.–Mexican relations could not last forever. The formation of U.S. policy in Mexico may be temporarily assigned to an envoy like Morrow, but the larger design of U.S. policy in Latin America was still shaped at the State Department in far-off Washington. Calles sought to move ahead in negotiations before an unexpected explosion might occur to suddenly wreck his carefully laid plans.

Even Morrow was "rather startled" by the speed with which Calles moved to resolve longstanding disputes. As early as their November 8 meeting, the president had brought up the controversial oil legislation of 1925, which made Article 27 of the Mexican Constitution retroactive against foreign oil interests. While carefully respecting Mexican sovereignty, Morrow pointed out that Article 14 of the same constitution provided that no Mexican law could be applied retroactively. Calles agreed with this legal reasoning and stated that only U.S. arrogance and radical political pressure had forced him to sign the oil bill, in the first place. It had been a classic case of a predator (in this instance, the United States) threatening the revolution (by questioning Mexican sovereignty) and forcing Calles to concede certain radical demands, despite the fact that the ruler recognized the potential loss of oil production and revenues as a sure route to economic suicide. With U.S. respect for Mexican sovereignty now assured, the president told Morrow that a Mexican Supreme Court decision in favor of the oil interests could be expected within two months. The court's favorable decision was handed down in less than two weeks. Details were ironed out in the ensuing months.[50] With Morrow's unfailing cooperation and Calles's dogged determination, other disputes—of which the church–state conflict is the most famous—were similarly resolved.[51] However, of all the diplomatic problems that received attention, the agrarian problem ranks as one of the most interesting, most complex, and (unfortunately) least studied by historians. The question of land reform clearly revealed both Morrow's great diplomatic skill and Calles's pragmatically conservative nature, in the period 1927–1930.[52]

Employing the diplomatic methods observed by Sir Arthur Salter, Morrow tackled the agrarian problem by first collecting "all the important facts that are relevant." The ambassador obtained this information with the help of two of the several aides he specifically recruited to assist him at the U.S. Embassy. Colonel Alexander "Sandy" McNab, Jr., the embassy's new military attaché, and George Rublee, a trusted friend since before World War I, were asked to collect all the data available so that, as in the oil dispute, Morrow "was certain that he had more facts in favor of the American case than the Mexicans could ever produce . . . in support of their [own]."[53] The embassy staff searched every bookstall in Mexico City, in pursuit of relevant volumes on Mexican law and customs. Two large rooms at the embassy were filled with materials, which were read, summarized, and translated "for the Ambassador to digest with the least loss of time."[54] An "old Mexican hand" with six years of U.S. Army experience on the Mexican border, Sandy McNab also spoke to many Mexican officials about the agrarian issue, while Rublee compiled a detailed list showing many of the U.S. property owners who had outstanding legal cases related to the land reform.[55]

Morrow and his aides traveled through much of rural Mexico to see the agrarian problem firsthand. McNab and Rublee thus accompanied Morrow and Calles on their 3,000-mile, seven-day train trip through northern Mexico in December 1927. Calles took great pains to show his foreign guests evidence of the modern improvements that were already underway in Mexican agriculture. The president's party stopped to inspect a credit institution specializing in loans to small farmers; an agricultural school for boys in Celaya; and two huge new dams, each built to irrigate more than 120,000 acres of farmland. Calles explained that schools, banks, new roads, and dams were all critical components of his "integrated solution" to the agrarian problem. Rather than favoring the carving up of property into communal or *ejido* landholdings, Calles favored a gradual redistribution of land in small private plots. These plots were to be granted to individual peasants who, with access to sufficient resources and a vested interest in national prosperity, could become productive yeomen and model citizens. Eager to institute this integrated solution, Calles told his traveling companions what he had told the *campesinos* on many occasions—that the "period of agitation" for more land was over and the "era of reconstruction" had begun.[56]

These words were very reassuring to Morrow, as he proceeded to the next stage of his problem-solving strategy: "to penetrate the real mind of the person you are negotiating with, to see the problem as he sees it, to understand what it is that is really important to him." Thus, the ambassador was encouraged by Calles's capitalist vision of a rural society led by productive, loyal farmers. Nonetheless, he had great misgivings about how soon Calles could control arbitrary land seizures, create his revolutionary "new man," and institute his integrated solution. In fact, Morrow's research had shown that Calles's attempt to create a new rural class of small landowners only served to compound the problems surrounding the agrarian reform. Credit institutions suffered from a lack of funds; what little credit was available usually went to either large landowners or political favorites, who seldom spent a peso on agriculture in Mexico. The production of essential foodstuffs declined because small farmers often lacked the money to plant their crops and large farmers often lacked the incentive to work their fields, fearing that their property might be overrun by peasants and confiscated at any moment.[57]

Morrow was also concerned about the impact of constant warfare in the countryside. Agricultural production suffered when campesinos were regularly called away to help suppress one or another revolt or when an unfortunate turn of events converted planted acreage into bloody battlefields. The critical need to finance the reform with equitable compensation for confiscated land was another major issue that troubled the banker-turned-diplomat. Morrow was particularly concerned about this problem, because he felt that the financial strain of paying large landowners was a major drain on the national budget and a major contributor to Mexico's growing public debt. Mexico could never hope to attract additional foreign investment so long as it was consistently unable to balance its budget with reasonable estimates regarding the annual cost of land reform.[58]

But Morrow could do little to alleviate these problems, short of waiting for opportune moments in which to discretely suggest solutions to Calles and other top officials. Usually, political exigencies precluded the implementation of this advice in all but one critical area: the confiscation of land belonging to U.S. citizens. Calles recognized this area as especially important, because it had a direct bearing on U.S.–Mexican relations and could conveniently be used as a camouflaged means to slow down agrarian agitation, in the larger interest of international peace. Few could accuse Calles of selling out the revolution to Yankee representatives in the U.S. Embassy so long as Morrow continued to respect Mexican law and work in conjunction with agrarian officials in his efforts to resolve individual agrarian cases.

The U.S. ambassador was willing to accept these circumstances because (to refer to Sir Arthur Salter's previously quoted words) they represented "a solution which [was] to the common interest and not [simply] a diplomatic score [for his side alone]." The Calles regime could thus begin to apply the brakes to radical land reform, while the U.S. Embassy could quietly work to protect the property rights of its landowning citizens in Mexico. With these goals in mind, Calles went so far as to place a National Agrarian Commission official in the Mexican Foreign Ministry, where he could "devote himself exclusively to the adjustment of [U.S.] claims" from December 1927 to February 1928.[59] Calles also instructed his compliant Supreme Court "to expedite the disposal of . . . *amparo* proceedings involving U.S. citizens with the least possible delay."[60] Given these extraordinary advantages, Morrow and the State Department were confident of favorable treatment when they regularly advised injured U.S. landowners to "exhaust all . . . judicial remedies before involving the aid of their diplomatic or consular representatives."[61]

Morrow was willing, nevertheless, to become directly involved in "special or emergency cases." Expanding on Calles's request that the ambassador deal directly with him on troublesome problems, Morrow sought out other high officials to assist him in the peaceful resolution of particularly difficult conflicts involving U.S. landowners. When confronted with such cases, Morrow was in the habit of requesting that National Agrarian Commission officials, state governors, and even Foreign Minister Estrada join him on fact-finding junkets to wherever the land in question happened to be. Once arrived, the group worked diligently to gather information, consider all sides in the dispute, and come to a mutually just arrangement. The ambassador and his staff reportedly traveled some 10,000 miles and visited nearly every state in Mexico in their great efforts to settle knotty land problems.[62]

Morrow and his staff found most of their traveling companions to be "very reasonable and fair minded."[63] As a result, of the 38 cases investigated in 52 trips from 1928 to 1930, 11 were settled in agreements that generally favored U.S. citizens, 11 were settled in compromises that satisfied all parties, and only 6 ended in unfavorable decisions for large landowners born in the United States. The remaining 10 were either not resolved or still under investigation in 1930.[64]

These were impressive figures in an era of widespread rural unrest, but 38 cases represented only a small fraction of the total disputes involving U.S. landowners. In fact, many who had hesitated to protest their cases for fear of retaliation suddenly stepped forward when they learned of the embassy's relative success in the countryside. So many new cases developed that one cynical observer reported to the former ambassador, James Sheffield, that "the material [the ambassador and his aides clear] away in front of [them] is about equalled by [the number of] new cases springing up behind [them]."[65] Morrow reconciled himself to this irony because he realized that most of these new cases were really old, unprotested ones, rather than cases of recent origin. In addition, the envoy and his staff believed that their work helped to discourage new land seizures involving U.S. citizens, because "all expropriations in the future will be much more carefully studied as to their real necessity."[66]

Calles was equally pleased with this development, because it contributed to a larger trend in which the entire land reform movement was curtailed in 1928. The president felt secure enough to take this politically dangerous step because nearly all of his enemies had been either reconciled with or largely emaciated by midsummer 1928. Without predators to disturb the peace, Mexico's radicals—in this case, its *campesinos*—could be controlled, at last. Land redistribution plummeted from a record high of nearly 1 million hectares in 1927 to less than 640,000 hectares in the following year.[67] Calles planned to further reduce the amount of land to be redistributed in 1929, by fixing a budgetary limit of 10 million pesos for compensation to large landowners who might lose their land as part of the scaled-down reform. Originally suggested by Morrow to Calles's young minister of finance, Luis Montes de Oca, this undertaking marked the first time that compensation for confiscated land had ever been included as a line item in the federal budget.[68]

These ambitious plans were suddenly torpedoed when a religious fanatic assassinated Álvaro Obregón on July 17, 1928. Obregón, Calles's preordained successor in the presidential election of 1928, drew much of his political support from Mexico's agrarian masses.[69] Calles was therefore obliged to select an interim president who could rally Obregón's agrarian followers, should the government be suddenly confronted with a new military revolt. In another case of a predator (in this case, the Cristeros) forcing Calles to unbridle his radical allies to defend the revolution, Calles faced the unwelcomed prospect of increasing—rather than decreasing—the amount of land to be redistributed in 1929.

Calles selected Emilio Portes Gil as Mexico's interim president. Portes Gil, a 37-year-old former governor of Tamaulipas and a well-known agrarian leader, quickly objected to Calles's previous plan to slow the agrarian reform in 1929; he fully expected still another predator—the military—to revolt in protest because an officer had not been selected for the coveted job of interim president. As always, armed agrarian support would be needed to defend the revolution, just as it had been needed in 1923–24 against Adolfo de la Heurta and in 1927 against insurgents led by General Arnulfo R. Gómez and Francisco R. Serrano.[70] Portes Gil went so far as to declare that he would decline the provisional presidency if he were unable to continue the land reform and count on thousands of campesinos to defend their practical benefactor in Mexico City.[71]

Dwight Morrow was disturbed by this reshuffling of priorities, but he appreciated Calles's difficult position in the new succession crisis. Morrow urged Calles to remain in office until a new presidential election could be held in 1929.[72] When Calles rejected this idea and appointed Portes Gil, Morrow dutifully accepted the decision and went to great lengths to support Calles's solution, in the interest of Mexican stability and international peace. The ambassador understood the political need for a new burst of agrarian activity, although he did everything in his diplomatic power to make sure that the government would need to rely on radical agrarians for only a relatively short, minimally destructive period of time.

Morrow attempted to assist Calles in the succession crisis of 1928 in four main ways. First, although he disliked making speeches and made very few of them while abroad, Morrow once again addressed the U.S. Chamber of Commerce in Mexico City. His purpose was to tell the foreign business community (and the world) of his admiration for the "fortitude and tranquility with which the Mexican people have withstood a stunning blow." Morrow asked his audience to share his absolute confidence in Mexico's ability to resolve its "great problem" by the "orderly process of law." Encouraged by these words, *Excelsior,* Mexico's largest daily newspaper, declared that the ambassador's confidence was the greatest aid that foreigners could extend to Mexico in its hour of need.[73]

Fifteen days later, Morrow departed on a tour of Puebla and Oaxaca to prove that the Mexican countryside remained peaceful, despite the "great problem" caused by Obregón's tragic death. Appreciating the impact of this trip on world opinion and internal tranquility, Calles made sure that Morrow was given "a reception equivalent to that accorded to a chief executive of the country." [74] Morrow's successful trip not only alleviated U.S. fears, but also helped to deter internal troubles; few rebels would dare to exploit the succession crisis so long as they knew that Calles could count on Morrow's confidence and the U.S. support it guaranteed.

Morrow also helped resolve the succession crisis by attending Calles's important address to the Mexican Congress on September 1, 1928. In perhaps the most critical speech of his political career, Calles declared that the time had come to create a government based on laws and institutions—rather than on strong personalities—so that Mexico could survive the loss of even the greatest of its leaders. Calles wanted to make his message especially clear to the generals in his audience, who might attempt to exploit this crisis to rebel and seize power—in the worst Latin American tradition. Morrow showed his support for Calles's words by ignoring the traditional rules of protocol and rising to his feet to heartily applaud Calles at the conclusion of the leader's address. Few failed to notice this conspicuous demonstration of international support. [75]

Most importantly, the United States assisted Mexico in its succession crisis by providing almost total support for the government when a group of jealous officers did, in fact, rebel on March 3, 1929. Led by General José Gonzalo Escobar and nearly a third of the Mexican officer corps, 30,000 troops took to the field, charging Calles with "imposing" Portes Gil on Mexico and betraying the revolution. [76] Delaying their revolt until Herbert Hoover's inauguration and a possible change of policy in Washington, the insurgents courted U.S. aid by sending agents across the border, mailing reams of propaganda to U.S. cities, exaggerating the extent of their mutiny, and confidently predicting victory within 90 days. [77]

But rebel overtures fell on deaf ears in Washington. Although the new Hoover administration was hardly pleased with Portes Gil's record as a radical agrarian, Morrow stressed the need to defeat Escobar so that the amount of rural unrest could be controlled and the presidential election of 1929 could be held on schedule. Moreover, a short, decisive war would do less damage to U.S. economic interests; it was no secret that the greatest share of U.S. investments in Mexico was in four of the five states involved in the revolt. [78]

The United States could not have done more to assist Portes Gil. Washington refused to grant belligerent status to the rebels and declared that they were legally "in no better position than ordinary outlaws." The U.S. arms embargo was strictly enforced, and rebel assets were frozen in U.S. banks. Surplus war material was shipped to Mexico in the form of 3,200 bombs, 5,000 rifles, 69 machine guns, 2,500 hand grenades, more than 3 million rounds of ammunition, and at least 32 airplanes. J. Reuben Clark, Jr., a former Morrow aide and now the U.S. under secretary of state, cut through miles of red tape to give this material "preferential treatment"; and Sandy McNab was sent to the United States to facilitate its rapid transport to the front. Other experts, including Charles Lindbergh, assisted in the training of Mexican pilots and aviation mechanics. In addition, Washington offered U.S. territory along the border as a haven for distressed federal troops. Moreover, three U.S. destroyers were sent to Mexico's west coast in a classic display of saber rattling in support of Portes Gil.[79]

Morrow kept close tabs on the war—making the U.S. Embassy look more like a general's headquarters than an ambassador's chambers. Military maps lined the walls of his office, as he followed the government's steady progress against the rebels. Portes Gil personally briefed the envoy between five and seven o'clock each evening, and McNab wired frequent reports from his post as a military observer in the federal army. Supplied with this abundant information, Morrow sent "reassuring advice" to the State Department— which, in turn, provided even greater support for the provisional government. Thanks to this aid and massive agrarian assistance, Escobar and his cohorts were defeated in less than two months.[80] The United States received a diplomatic bonus soon after the rebels' defeat, when the church–state conflict was finally resolved—due, in part, to Morrow's hard work on this extremely complex issue.[81]

The successful outcome of the Escobar revolt and the church–state conflict set the stage for the presidential election of November 17, 1929, and for the conclusion of Mexico's prolonged succession crisis. Stopping short of personally endorsing the government's candidate, Pascual Ortiz Rubio, Morrow labored behind the scenes in a manner that drew heavy criticism from the leading opposition candidate, José Vasconcelos.[82] With the indirect aid of Morrow, wholesale corruption, and excessive election-day violence, Ortiz Rubio won a landslide victory.[83]

Ortiz Rubio was considered a politically acceptable candidate to the United States because he maintained close ties to Calles (now the country's *Jefe Máximo*) and parroted conservative ideas on most issues, including the agrarian reform. Rather than favor small landowners or ejidatarios, he had thus declared in Toluca that "large-scale agriculture is a powerful factor of equilibrium in our economy and for that reason it will receive my decided support."[84] And, in a statement that Morrow welcomed with unabashed enthusiasm,[85] the Mexican leader had promised to create a special fund in the budget to compensate landowners in cash for the full value of their expropriated property.[86] As a result, the redistribution of land dropped to nearly as low a level in 1930 as it had dropped in 1928.[87]

Unfortunately, Morrow was denied the opportunity to enjoy the diplomatic euphoria he had labored so hard to create. Indeed, a wave of resentment against the ambassador had set in, just when many of his most important goals were finally realized. This "backfire of resentment" can be traced to two developments that badly damaged the envoy's reputation in

1930. First, it was rumored that Morrow had used his diplomatic post as a convenient stepping-stone in his own political career. At various times, Morrow was said to be destined for an important U.S. Cabinet post, a prestigious new ambassadorship, or a high elected position in the United States. Some foresaw "nothing less than the presidency" by 1936. Mexican suspicions were reinforced when the ambassador announced plans to run for the U.S. Senate in the New Jersey Republican primary of 1930.[88]

Next, the envoy's reputation suffered badly when Mexican leaders became increasingly sensitive to charges that Morrow had acquired too much influence in certain government offices and too little respect for Mexican sovereignty, despite his earlier demonstrations of overt respect in 1927 and 1928. It was commonly believed that Morrow had begun to exploit Calles's invitation to deal with problems directly, by spending as much as two hours a day closeted with one or another high official in the government.[89] Tragically, these rumors were given an air of credence when Sandy McNab delivered one of several political speeches in Morrow's behalf in New Jersey. As McNab indiscreetly told the Newark audience, Morrow had once informed him that it was their "task to put Mexico on its feet financially and to give it a strong government." McNab asserted that the ambassador had "gone a long way toward accomplishing this . . . task" by taking Mexico's young minister of finance "under his wing" and teaching him finance. McNab also claimed that Morrow was solely responsible for the church–state settlement of 1929 "merely because [all sides] wanted to please Mr. Morrow as they liked him personally."[90]

Few statements could have been more damaging. The disastrous speech caused nothing less than a great sensation, because many Mexicans concluded that Morrow's earlier display of friendship for Mexico was nothing more than a charade used to manipulate events to Washington's (and Morrow's) advantage.[91] Other laudatory statements in the U.S. press added insult to injury in Mexico.[92] Morrow easily won the Republican primary in New Jersey, but these terrible blunders destroyed his last bit of influence in Mexico. The ambassador was "cordially·detested" when he returned to Mexico for a brief two-and-a-half month period in mid-1930. At every turn, Morrow was rebuffed; few officials wanted to suffer the stigma of being taken under the envoy's "wing" and of succumbing to his personal influence. In the first year of the Great Depression, adverse Mexican reactions to new U.S. tariffs and stricter immigration labor laws served to aggravate the problems that Morrow faced in his final days at the embassy.[93] Although he made two final speeches extolling Mexico and its great potential, Morrow was "deeply wounded" by the erosion of his once substantial effectiveness.[94] The ambassador left Mexico City on September 17, 1930, and resigned his post on September 30—exactly three years and ten days after the announcement of his appointment in 1927. Despite his many triumphs, Morrow retired from diplomatic duty a sadly disappointed, but hardly bitter man.

There is a longstanding myth regarding Dwight Morrow's diplomatic role in Mexico. Ironically based on the same exaggerated notions that caused much of the Mexican resentment against Morrow in 1930, the myth has been perpetrated in nearly every history of this period—from Morrow's official biography to the most recent works on the Mexican Revolution. According to this myth, the diminutive envoy captivated Calles and his followers with his disarming charm, persuaded them to alter their evil radical ways, and gently moved them into line behind the United States on major issues—including the oil question, the church–state conflict, and the agrarian reform. Supposedly, the diplomatic impasse was broken when the Mexicans became pawns in Morrow's velvet-covered hands. It was said that the ambassador accomplished this remarkable feat with so much goodwill and so much easy success that "the Mexican Revolution died when Morrow smiled." [95]

This interpretation of events is quite misleading and—frankly—insulting to Mexico. It is more realistic to assert that the radical phase of the revolution (prior to 1930) died when Morrow nodded his support for Calles, the revolution's strongman and chief executioner. That is, by obtaining Morrow's valuable cooperation, Calles was able to enjoy U.S. support in defeating his reactionary enemies, co-opting his more radical allies, and consolidating his own power without appearing to compromise major revolutionary principles or succumbing to U.S. demands. But Morrow's assistance must not be confused with Morrow's control. Perhaps the best proof that Morrow did not kill the revolution with the force of his personality or the power of his official post came in 1929, when Calles reluctantly reopened the floodgate on agrarian reform in order to help suppress the Escobar revolt. Neither Morrow's behind-the-scenes maneuvers nor his consistently benign facial expression could alter Calles's decision to temporarily breathe new life into the revolution for purely practical political reasons.

Despite such temporary setbacks, Washington's Mexican policy in this period was successfully engineered by its astute envoy on the scene. While officially an ambassador, Morrow was actually an expert troubleshooter, who was sent to resolve a seemingly impossible situation when all other strategies had failed; the perplexed State Department virtually abdicated all policy-making authority to its envoy in the U.S. Embassy. [96] Fortunately for the United States, Calles had long hoped that an envoy of Morrow's high caliber and cooperative nature would be assigned to his problem-ridden government. Thriving in this ideally receptive environment, Morrow worked on complex problems with an enviably free hand and relatively few obstructions during most of his three years abroad.

But there were also disadvantages in sending a troubleshooter to play an ambassador's role for any length of time. Even the most talented troubleshooter could only hope to enjoy a receptive environment for a limited while, because his unorthodox negotiating style was bound to be misconstrued and resented once the diplomatic air was cleared. In fact, one can think of a troubleshooter as a clock that runs well for a time, but that almost inevitably winds down as a result of several possible national and international developments. In Morrow's case, these developments included a significant change in Mexico's political environment under Calles's stewardship. The United States (via Morrow) had contributed much to this development; but, having achieved their long-coveted political goals, the Mexicans no longer appreciated Morrow's intrinsically different style. Morrow had simply outlived his political usefulness.

The envoy's troubleshooting clock was also adversely affected by the exaggerated stories about what he was single-handedly able to accomplish in Mexico. U.S. policy shifts, including the raising of import duties and the creation of new immigration laws, only increased Mexican resentment and shortened the time left on Morrow's clock. Washington's decision to utilize his troubleshooting skills in other arenas (at the Sixth International Conference of American States in 1928, and at the London Naval Conference in 1930) caused Morrow to regrettably neglect his post in Mexico, thus adding weight to the rumors that he was using Mexico as a stepping-stone to advance his own career. A new wave of xenophobia caused additional hard feelings when Morrow was accused of profiting from the sale of Mexican securities, having a personal interest in the opening of a National City Bank branch in Mexico City, and buying up so much land in Morelos that the state was destined to be renamed "Morrow-elos." [97] Privately, Morrow dismissed these charges as "perfectly ridiculous"; [98] but the damage had already been done and could not be easily repaired. Final proof that Morrow's effectiveness was exhausted came when the Ortiz Rubio government scorned Morrow's opposition to the new foreign debt agreement signed with the International Committee of Bankers on Mexico, shortly after the ambassador's return to Mexico City in July 1930. A personal letter describing Morrow's objections to the pact was returned to the U.S. Embassy labeled *inconveniente* by President Ortiz Rubio. [99] In Mexico, Morrow's clock had finally run down.

Dwight Morrow never served in another diplomatic post, and he lived only a short while after his departure from Mexico; but his brief success in the world of diplomacy was to have a lasting impact on U.S. policy in Mexico, in particular, and in Latin America, as a whole. Although his work is still resented in leftist circles and when nationalistic fervor runs high, many in the United States and Latin America remember Morrow's early success and point to his demonstrations of goodwill and deep respect for Mexican sovereignty as qualities that all U.S. envoys should emulate in laying the groundwork for effective diplomacy. Others still praise Morrow's remarkable ability to place himself in his opponent's shoes and to sift out the most critical issues at stake for all parties in a controversy. Some have also detected the ambassador's imprint on the State Department's 1928 Memorandum on the Monroe Doctrine, which was authored by J. Reuben Clark, Jr., Morrow's top legal aide and confidant in Mexico. Written within six months of Clark's return from Morrow's side at the U.S. Embassy, the Clark Memorandum (as it is commonly called) was the only State Department document to effectively repudiate the use of U.S. military force in Latin America in the late 1920s.[100] Although Clark's memo did not alter U.S. foreign policy at the time,[101] its convincing argument against intervention has been generally acknowledged as an important factor that "helped to foster Good Neighborism" and a strong U.S. commitment to nonintervention after 1933.[102]

Given his probable influence on Clark's memorandum and his other admirable characteristics as an ambassador, several leading historians and statesmen have identified Morrow as a precursor of Franklin Delano Roosevelt's Good Neighbor Policy of 1933–45. No less an historian than Daniel Cosío Villegas referred to Morrow as "the genius of the new diplomacy",[103] and it was said that, "without Morrow's ushering in the first era of good U.S.–Mexican [relations] since [before] the Revolution," Josephus Daniels' work as Roosevelt's envoy in Mexico "would have been twice as hard."[104]

Morrow may well have been such a precursor to the Good Neighbor Policy, but it is essential to recall that Good Neighborism was predicated on feelings of reciprocal respect and cooperation among nations of the Western Hemisphere. As Bryce Wood put it in his *Making of the Good Neighbor Policy,* "the idea of reciprocity expressed that, if the United States did certain things desired by Latin American states, these states would respond by doing other things desired by Washington."[105] A former Wall Street banker could thus be considered a prototype of the Good Neighbor Policy not only because he respected Mexican sovereignty, opposed U.S. military intervention, and was eager to negotiate major issues in a cooperative manner, but also because his support and style of diplomacy were what the Mexicans really needed and desired at a critical moment in their history. Calles responded "by doing other things desired by Washington," because these actions were recognized as in Mexico's own best interest. In short, the United States finally experienced a major diplomatic breakthrough in Mexico, because the Mexicans themselves were ready and willing to grasp the olive branch of peace that Washington held out through the service of its ambassador *simpático,* Dwight Morrow.

NOTES

1. *Excelsior,* October 22, 1927; New York *Times,* October 24, 1927; H.F. Arthur Schoenfeld to Frank B. Kellogg, Mexico City, October 20, 1927, Archives of the U.S. Department of State, 812.00/28897; Genaro Estrada to Joaquín Amaro, Mexico City, October 13, 1927, Archivo de la Secretaría de Relaciones Exteriores (AREM), Expediente Nombre: Cuerpo Diplomático: Dwight Morrow, 3P/323(73)/1. (The Archives of the U.S. Department of State are hereafter cited as ADS.)

2. New York *Times,* October 24, 1927. Previous works on Dwight Morrow's service in Mexico include Stanley R. Ross, "Dwight Morrow and the Mexican Revolution," *Hispanic American Historical Review* 38 (November 1958):506–28; Stanley R. Ross, "Dwight W. Morrow, Ambassador to Mexico," *The Americas* 14 (1957–58):273–90; Richard Melzer, "Dwight Morrow's Role in the Mexican Revolution: Good Neighbor or Meddling Yankee?" (Unpublished Ph.D. dissertation, University of New Mexico, 1979). Mexican sources include Oscar E. Duplan, "Mr. Dwight W. Morrow," *El Universal Gráfico,* October 7, 1931; Genaro Estrada, "La gestión de Mr. Morrow," *Excelsior,* October 30, 1935; Mateo Podan, "Admonitorias: Y entonces llegó el Embajador Dwight Morrow," *La Prensa,* April 28, 1951.

3. Mexico's ambassador to the United States, Manuel C. Téllez, quoted in the New York *Times,* October 24, 1927.

4. *El Universal,* October 24, 1927.

5. This tense atmosphere is well described in James J. Horn, "Did the United States Plan an Invasion of Mexico in 1927?" *Journal of Inter-American Studies and World Affairs* 15 (November 1973):454–71.

6. See H.N. Branch, "The Mexican Constitution of 1917 Compared with the Constitution of 1857," *Mexico Commerce and Industry* 9 (March 1927):8–57. Díaz ruled under the Constitution of 1857.

7. See Joan Hoff Wilson, *American Business and Foreign Policy, 1920–33* (Lexington: University Press of Kentucky, 1971). Hearst was one of the three largest U.S. landowners in all of Mexico. On the U.S. reaction to Mexico's church–state controversy, see Mollie C. Davis, "American Religious and Religious Reaction to Mexico's Church–State Conflict, 1926–27: Background to the Morrow Mission," *Journal of Church and State* 13 (1971):79–96.

8. John W. F. Dulles, *Yesterday in Mexico: A Chronicle of the Revolution, 1919–36* (Austin: University of Texas Press, 1961), pp. 158–72 and 322–24. The extreme option of intervention was vetoed in the United States, because much of the nation could not imagine going to war in defense of the oil interests when these interests were still identified with the sordid Teapot Dome scandal. James J. Horn, "Mexican Oil Diplomacy and the Legacy of Teapot Dome," in *Dependency Unbends: Case Studies in Inter-American Relations,* ed. Robert H. Claxton (Carrollton: West Georgia College, 1978), pp. 99–112.

9. See Holland Dempsey Watkin, "Plutarco Elías Calles: *El Jefe Máximo* of Mexico" (Unpublished Ph.D. dissertation, Texas Tech University, 1968); Luis L. León, "El Presidente Calles," *Historia Mexicana* 10 (1960):320–31; Plutarco Elías Calles, "The Policies of Mexico Today," *Foreign Affairs* 4 (1926):1–5; Plutarco Elías Calles, *Mexico before the World* (New York: Academy Press, 1927).

10. See David C. Bailey, *¡Viva Cristero Rey! The Cristero Rebellion and the Church–State Conflict in Mexico* (Austin: University of Texas Press, 1974); Lorenzo Meyer, *Los grupos de presión extranjeros en el México revolucionario* (México: Secretaría de Relaciones Exteriores, 1973); Janet A. Lane, "U.S.–Mexican Diplomatic Relations, 1917–42" (Unpublished Ph.D. dissertation, Georgetown University, 1972).

11. Dudley Ankerson, "Saturnino Cedillo, A Traditional Caudillo in San Luis Potosí, 1890–1938," in *Caudillo and Peasant in the Mexican Revolution,* ed. D.A. Brading (Cambridge, England: Cambridge University Press, 1980), pp. 148–49 and 151–52.

12. Calles quoted in Dulles, *Yesterday in Mexico,* p. 317.

13. Quoted in ibid.

14. The standard biographies on Morrow are Harold Nicolson, *Dwight Morrow* (New York: Harcourt, Brace, 1935); Hewitt H. Howland, *Dwight Whitney Morrow: A Sketch in Admiration* (New York: Century, 1930); Mary Margaret McBride, *The Story of Dwight W. Morrow* (New York: Farrar and Rinehart, 1930). Nicolson's work was commissioned by the Morrow family, while Howland's and McBride's read like political campaign biographies.

15. Calvin Coolidge, Introduction to Howland, *Dwight Whitney Morrow,* p. vi.

16. Thomas W. Lamont, quoted in "The Reminiscences of Hilarion N. Branch," Columbia Oral History Collection (1966), p. 49. (The Columbia Oral History Collection is hereafter cited as COHC.)

17. Sir Arthur Salter, *Personality in Politics: Studies of Contemporary Statesmen* (London: Faber and Faber, n.d.) p. 161.

18. Nicolson, *Morrow,* pp. 280–87.

19. Robert Freeman Smith, "The Formation and Development of the International Committee of Bankers on Mexico," *Journal of Economic History* 23 (December 1963):574–86.

20. Melzer, "Morrow's Role," pp. 63–65.

21. "The Reminiscences of Guy Emerson," COHC (1951), p. 189.

22. New York *American,* September 21, 1927; Louis S. Levy, *Yesterdays* (New York: Library Publishers, 1954), p. 248; Ray Thomas Tucker, *The Mirrors of 1932* (New York: Brewer, Warren, and Putnam, 1931), p. 110.

23. *Christian Science Monitor,* September 21, 1927; San Antonio Express, September 25, 1927.

24. Dwight Morrow, "Who Buys Foreign Bonds?" *Foreign Affairs* 5 (January 1927):232. Morrow's speeches on this topic were made to the Institute of Politics on August 4, 1924; the American Bankers Association on September 20, 1924; and the Commercial Club of Chicago on April 23, 1926. Copies of these speeches are in the Dwight Morrow Papers, Amherst College, Amherst, Mass. (hereafter cited as the Morrow Papers).

25. Robert Freeman Smith, *The United States and Revolutionary Nationalism in Mexico, 1916–32* (Chicago: University of Chicago Press, 1972), p. 253. Morrow and Lamont were not the only U.S. businessmen who sought peace, rather than war, with Mexico. See *Excelsior,* January 19, 1927; and the Special Mexico Edition, *Pan Pacific Progress* 7 (July 1927). *Excelsior* of May 3, 1927, reported that the Mexico Property Owners Non-Intervention League had held a mass rally in opposition to war.

26. James R. Sheffield to Secretary of State Kellogg, New York, December 28, 1928, in the James R. Sheffield Papers, Yale University, New Haven, Conn. (hereafter cited as the Sheffield Papers).

27. James R. Sheffield to General James G. Harbord, New York, November 5, 1928, Sheffield Papers.

28. James R. Sheffield to Secretary of State Kellogg, Mexico City, July 1, 1926, Sheffield Papers. Sheffield served in Mexico from 1924 to 1927. His work abroad is best covered in James J. Horn, "Diplomacy by Ultimatum: Ambassador Sheffield and Mexican–American Relations, 1924–27 (Unpublished Ph.D. dissertation, State University of New York at Buffalo, 1969); James J. Horn, "El Embajador Sheffield contra el Presidente Calles," *Historia Mexicana* 20 (Octubre–Diciembre 1970):265–

84. Calles was so exasperated with Sheffield's refusal to work with his regime that he requested that Coolidge send a "personal representative" to Mexico, so that Calles could assure the United States of his "absolute sincerity and friendliness in all of his dealings with the American Government." Quoted in L. Ethan Ellis, "Frank B. Kellogg," in *An Uncertain Tradition: American Secretaries of State in the Twentieth Century,* ed. Norman A. Graebner (New York: McGraw-Hill, 1961), p. 159.

29. The Ramo Obregón–Calles in the Archivo General, Mexico City, Mexico (especially 104–L–28 and 721–I–6) and the Expediente Nombre: Cuerpo Diplomático: Dwight Morrow at the AREM are, in fact, the best sources for press clippings on Morrow to be found in the United States or Mexico. (The Ramo Obregón–Calles will hereafter be cited as RO–C.)

30. Gerardo Machado to President Calles, Havana, October 1, 1927, RO-C, 104–E–76.

31. New York *World,* March 13, 1927.

32. Nicolson, *Morrow,* pp. 313–14.

33. Quoted in ibid. p. 309; see also Howard F. Cline, *The United States and Mexico* (New York: Atheneum, 1973), p. 211.

34. H. F. Arthur Schoenfeld to Frank B. Kellogg, Mexico City, October 20, 1927, ADS, 812.00/28912. Feelings of cautious optimism were also reflected in many major newspapers, including *Excelsior, El Universal, La Patria, El Pensamiento, El Sol, El Universal Gráfico,* and *El Machete.*

35. Dwight Morrow to Secretary of State Kellogg, Mexico City, November 8, 1927, Morrow Papers. Estrada, who was Mexico's foreign minister from 1927 to 1932, is best remembered in diplomatic history for his Estrada Doctrine of 1930. The Estrada Doctrine asserts that foreign recognition of a new government should be automatic, because a declaration of recognition implies foreign judgment of each new regime.

36. Dwight Morrow to Secretary of State Kellogg, Mexico City, November 8, 1927, Morrow Papers.

37. Ibid.

38. New York *Times,* November 3, 1927. See also the *Christian Science Monitor,* February 27, 1928; and Carleton Beals, *Glass Houses* (Philadelphia: J. B. Lippincott, 1938), pp. 270–71.

39. Melzer, "Morrow's Role," pp. 206–15.

40. Quoted in Arthur Bliss Lane, "Memo on Dwight Morrow's Mission to Mexico," Box 4, Folder 91, Arthur Bliss Lane Papers, Yale University, New Haven, Conn. (hereafter cited as the Lane Papers). Will Rogers accompanied Calles and Morrow on this trip and sent many favorable reports back to the United States, via his popular newspaper and magazine columns. Rogers' column was carried in 150 newspapers and magazines across the United States. See, for example, the *Saturday Evening Post,* May 12–June 9, 1928.

41. Dwight Morrow to Robert Olds, Mexico City, December 9, 1927, Morrow Papers.

42. Dwight Morrow, "Address to the U.S. Chamber of Commerce," Mexico City, November 19, 1927, Morrow Papers. Morrow explained the reasons for his remarks in Dwight Morrow to Robert Olds, Mexico City, November 22, 1927, Morrow Papers.

43. Melzer, "Morrow's Role," p. 204.

44. Dwight Morrow to Robert Olds, Mexico City, May 22, 1928, Morrow Papers.

45. Will Rogers, "More Letters from a Self-Made Diplomat to His President," *Saturday Evening Post* 200 (May 19, 1928):10 and 108.

46. See, for example, the New York *Times,* November 4, 1929.

47. Elizabeth Cutter Morrow, "Our Street in Cuernavaca," *American Mercury* 23 (August 1931):411–18; Anne Morrow to Constance Morrow, November 5, 1928, in Anne Morrow Lindbergh, *Bring Me a Unicorn: The Diaries and Letters of Anne Morrow Lindbergh, 1922–28* (New York: Harcourt, Brace, Jovanovich, 1971), p. 228; *Excelsior,* March 11, 1928.

48. New York *Times,* May 13, July 4, and September 3, 1928; Elizabeth Cutter Morrow, *The Mexican Years: Leaves from the Diary of Elizabeth Cutter Morrow* (New York: Spiral Press, 1953), entry of March 27, 1928.

49. Bertram W. Edwards to President Calles, New York, January 21, 1928, RO–C, 104–L–28. On Lindbergh's flight, see Charles A. Lindbergh, "To Bogota and Back by Air," *National Geographic Magazine* 53 (May 1928):529–602; E.C. Morrow, *Diary,* entries of December 15 and 17, 1927; *Excelsior,* December 16, 1927. Lindbergh met Morrow's daughter, Anne, in Mexico City. The two were wed in 1929.

50. Dwight Morrow to Secretary of State Kellogg, Mexico City, November 8, 1927, Morrow Papers; *El Universal,* November 18, 1927; J. Reuben Clark, Jr., "The Oil Settlement with Mexico," *Foreign Affairs* 6 (July 1928):600–20; Lorenzo Meyer, *México y Estados Unidos en el conflicto petrolero, 1917–42* (México: Gráfica Panamericana, 1968). Government oil revenues had equaled 86 million pesos—or 30 percent of all federal earnings—in 1922, but had dwindled to 34 million pesos—or only 11 percent of all federal earnings—by 1926. H.F. Arthur Schoenfeld to Frank B. Kellogg, Mexico City, October 26, 1927, ADS, 812.6363/2412.

51. See, for example, Walter Lippmann, "Church and State in Mexico: The American Mediation," *Foreign Affairs* 8 (January 1930):186–207; L. Ethan Ellis, "Dwight Morrow and the Church–State Controversy in Mexico," *Hispanic American Historical Review* 38 (November 1958):482–505; Sister M. Elizabeth Ann Rice, *The Diplomatic Relations between the United States and Mexico as Affected by the Struggle for Religious Liberty in Mexico, 1925–29* (Washington, D.C.: Catholic University Press, 1959); and Edward J. Berbusse, "The Unofficial Intervention of the United States in Mexico's Religious Crisis, 1926–30," *The Americas* 23 (July 1966):28–63.

52. The following is a short analysis of Morrow's diplomatic work in relation to Mexico's land reform. It is hardly a complete review of Mexico's complex land problems of the 1920s. The latter is attempted in several able studies, including Eyler N. Simpson, *The Ejido: Mexico's Way Out* (Chapel Hill: University of North Carolina Press, 1937).

53. "The Reminiscences of James T. Williams, Jr.," COHC (1957), p. 704. J. Reuben Clark, Jr., and Captain Lewis B. McBride were Morrow's other two top aides in Mexico. Melzer, "Morrow's Role," pp. 187–91.

54. New York *Times,* May 13, 1928.

55. "Memorandum Giving [the] Names of American Properties Visited and Made the Subjects of Discussion with Agrarian Authorities during the Years 1928–29 and 1930 with Results of Visits," Mexico City, 1930, Morrow Papers.

56. Melzer, "Morrow's Role," pp. 112–15 and 210–13.

57. Ibid., pp. 291–95.

58. Dwight Morrow to Frank B. Kellogg, Mexico City, November 9, 1928, ADS, 812.51/1642; James Wilkie, *The Mexican Revolution: Federal Expenditures and Social Change since 1910* (Berkeley: University of California Press, 1970), pp. 111–12. For Morrow's thoughts on the Mexican budget in general, see Dwight Morrow to Captain Lewis B. McBride, Mexico City, March 19, 1929, ADS, 812.51/1497.5; Dwight Morrow to Henry L. Stimson, Mexico City, May 21, 1929, ADS, 812.51/1499.

59. Dwight Morrow to Robert Olds, Mexico City, December 9, 1927, Morrow Papers; H.F. Arthur Schoenfeld to Frank B. Kellogg, Mexico City, January 26, 1928, ADS, 812.52/1483.

60. Dwight Morrow to Frank B. Kellogg, Mexico City, February 14, 1928, ADS, 812.52/1487.

61. Dwight Morrow to Frank B. Kellogg, Mexico City, December 3, 1927, ADS, 812.52/1518; Robert Olds to Edward P. Lowry, Washington, D.C., April 16, 1928; ADS, 812.5200/782.

62. Melzer, "Morrow's Role," pp. 298–301.

63. Colonel Alexander McNab, Jr., "Memorandum on Trip to Tamaulipas," Mexico City, May 19, 1928, Morrow Papers.

64. "Memorandum Giving [the] Names of American Properties," Morrow Papers.

65. Alexander W. Weddell to James R. Sheffield, Mexico City, June 8, 1928, Box 9, Sheffield Papers.

66. McNab, "Memorandum on Trip," Morrow Papers.

67. Simpson, *Ejido,* table 17, p. 609; Alan Knight, *The Mexican Revolution: Counter-Revolution and Reconstruction* (Cambridge, England: Cambridge University Press, 1986), p. 517.

68. Emilio Portes Gil, *Autobiográfia de la Revolución Mexicana* (México: Editado por el Instituto Mexicano de Cultura, 1964), p. 425.

69. Linda B. Hall, "Alvaro Obregón and the Agrarian Movement," in *Caudillo and Peasant in the Mexican Revolution,* ed. D.A. Brading (Cambridge, England: Cambridge University Press, 1980), pp. 127–29; Dulles, *Yesterday in Mexico,* pp. 167 and 355.

70. Edwin Lieuwen, *Mexican Militarism: The Political Rise and Fall of the Revolutionary Army* (Albuquerque: University of New Mexico Press, 1968), pp. 76–77 and 99.

71. Portes Gil, *Autobiográfia,* pp. 425 and 650. Portes Gil armed 40,000 agrarians during the first three months of his fourteen-month regime.

72. Dwight Morrow to Secretary of State Kellogg, Mexico City, August 14, 1928, Morrow Papers.

73. *Excelsior,* August 2, 1928. Morrow's speech was printed in this edition of *Exelsior.*

74. New York *Times,* September 3, 1928.

75. Dulles, *Yesterday in Mexico,* pp. 384–86. See Dwight Morrow to Frank B. Kellogg, Mexico City, September 3, 1928, ADS, 812.00/29309, for the text of Calles's speech.

76. Quoted in Jones, "Memorandum on Amilcar Zentella," San Antonio, April 5, 1929, ADS, 812.00 Sonora/637. Also see Lieuwen, *Mexican Militarism,* p. 103.

77. New Orleans *Times-Picayune,* April 6, 9, 11, and 17, 1929.

78. New York *Times,* March 6, 1929.

79. Melzer, "Morrow's Role," pp. 386–87 and 390–403.

80. A total of 1,084, 370 hectares of land, the largest annual sum during Morrow's three years in Mexico, were redistributed as the payoff for this important agrarian aid. Simpson, *Ejido,* table 17, p. 609.

81. New York *Times,* March 6, 1929; Dwight Morrow to Henry L. Stimson, Mexico City, March 5, 1929, ADS, 812.00 Sonora/71; Dwight Morrow to Stimson, Mexico City, April 7, 1929, ADS, 812.00 Sonora/539; Dwight Morrow to Stimson, Mexico City, April 11, 1929, ADS, 812.00 Sonora/714.

82. José Vasconcelos, *El Proconsulado* (México: Ediciones Botas, 1946), pp. 109, 112, 176, and 330; José Vasconcelos, *A Mexican Ulysses: An Autobiography* (Westport, Conn.: Greenwood Press, 1972), pp. 223–24, 229, 235, 238–39, and 270.

83. Melzer, "Morrow's Role," pp. 449–75.

84. Quoted in Stokeley W. Morgan to Henry L. Stimson, Mexico City, June 2, 1929, ADS, 812.00/1549.

85. Dwight Morrow to Henry L. Stimson, Mexico City, October 15, 1929, ADS, 812.52/1576.

86. *Excelsior,* September 1, 1929.

87. Simpson, *Ejido,* table 17, p. 609.

88. Melzer, "Morrow's Role," pp. 515–21.

89. W.R. Castle to Arthur B. Lane, Washington, D.C., December 30, 1930, Box 4, Lane Papers.

90. The text of McNab's speech appeared in the Newark *Evening News,* May 5, 1930.

91. Melzer, "Morrow's Role," pp. 523–29.

92. See, for example, the New York *Times,* June 22, 1930. Ambassador Tellez underscored several offensive parts of the article and sent it to his superiors in the Mexican Foreign Ministry.

93. *Excelsior,* June 21, 1930; Lawrence B. Mann, "Foreign Reactions to the American Tariff Act," *Foreign Policy Association Information Service* 6 (October 1, 1930):261–73; Melzer, "Morrow's Role," pp. 529–44 and 598–608.

94. E.C. Morrow, *Diary,* entry of August 18, 1930. Dwight Morrow spoke to the U.S. Chamber of Commerce on September 12, 1930, and to the U.S. public via a nationwide radio broadcast on September 14, 1930.

95. The Morrow myth is examined in some detail in Melzer, "Morrow's Role," pp. 1–26.

96. L. Ethan Ellis, "Frank B. Kellogg," pp. 158–61. This was not the first time that Coolidge and Kellogg had abdicated policy-making authority to an envoy in the field. Henry L. Stimson, Kellogg's eventual successor in the State Department, enjoyed this authority in Nicaragua after April 1927. Like Morrow, Stimson was simply instructed to "straighten the matter out": Coolidge, quoted by Ellis, p. 158.

97. Newark *Star-Eagle,* March 10 and 12, 1930; James R. Sheffield to Madison Grant, New York, June 6, 1930, Box 10, Sheffield Papers; Alfonso Taracena, *Mi vida en el vértigo de la revolución mexicana* (México: Ediciones Botas, 1936), p. 673.

98. Dwight Morrow to H. Johnson, [no location cited], March 17, 1930, Morrow Papers; Beals, *Glass Houses,* p. 277.

99. Dwight Morrow to Ortiz Rubio, Mexico City, August 20, 1930, Morrow Papers. See also Robert Freeman Smith, "The Morrow Mission and the International

Committee of Bankers on Mexico," *Journal of Latin American Studies* 1 (1968):149–66.

100. Frank W. Fox, *J. Reuben Clark: The Public Years* (Provo, Utah: Brigham Young University Press, 1980), pp. 517–21.

101. Robert H. Ferrell, "Repudiation of the Repudiation," *Journal of American History* 51 (1965):669–73; Gene A. Sessions, "The Clark Memorandum Myth," *The Americas* 34 (1977):40–58.

102. Thomas A. Bailey, *A Diplomatic History of the American People* (Englewood Cliffs, N.J.: Prentice-Hall, 1974), pp. 680 and 682; Harold Eugene Davis, "The Origins and Nature of Latin American Foreign Policies," in *Latin American Diplomatic History,* eds. Harold Eugene Davis, John J. Finan, and F. Taylor Peck (Baton Rouge: Louisiana State University Press, 1977), p. 20.

103. Daniel Cosío Villegas, *American Extremes* (Austin: University of Texas Press, 1964), p. 40.

104. Joseph L. Morrison, *Josephus Daniels: The Small-d Democrat* (Chapel Hill: University of North Carolina Press, 1966), p. 177.

105. Bryce Wood, *The Making of the Good Neighbor Policy* (New York: W.W. Norton, 1961), p. 7.

2

In Defense of Hegemony: Sumner Welles and the Cuban Revolution of 1933

Louis Pérez

Let me explain to you that the United States, until the advent of Castro, was so overwhelmingly influential in Cuba that . . . the American Ambassador was the second most important man in Cuba; sometimes even more important than the President.

Earl E.T. Smith
U.S. ambassador to Cuba, 1957–58

The mid-1920s were good years in Cuba. Sugar prices were rising, and production was expanding. The year 1924 was an election year, and economic good times favored the ruling Liberal party. Liberal candidate Gerardo Machado won election by promising four more years of prosperity and economic growth, a promise he partially kept. He pursued industrial development through tariff protection, promoted agricultural diversification through credit subsidies, and supported economic growth with new communication and transportation facilities.[1] The government enacted the Customs–Tariff Law, easily one of the most important pieces of economic legislation of the early republic, whereby the state provided support and subsidy for the expansion of national industry and agriculture. Duties on raw materials decreased, as a means to promote local manufacturing; tariff imposts on manufactured goods increased, as a way to protect local industry.[2]

Beginning in 1926, however, the world price of sugar began to fall, and the Cuban experiment came to an abrupt halt. The government responded to the crisis with the Verdeja Act, an effort to arrest declining world prices by decreasing Cuban supplies. A quota system allotted a fixed share of the total crop to each province and all mills. The 1926 crop was fixed at 4.5

million tons—a 10 percent reduction from the 1925 harvest—while the length of the harvest season was shortened from 136 to 87 days.

Cuban efforts to reduce national production as a way to raise prices had calamitous local repercussions. The Cuban economy slumped and stopped expanding. All sectors of the economy suffered from the decline of sugar production. Imports declined and internal consumption dropped. Sugar workers, especially, faced hard times. In effect, the shortened *zafra* meant less work for tens of thousands of Cubans who were already suffering underemployment. Professionals lost clients; merchants lost customers; and white collar employees lost jobs. Living standards that had increased steadily since 1923 faltered, and declined.

The year 1928 was not the best of times for an incumbent to seek reelection. The administration that appeared incapable of resolving the economic crisis of the previous two years could hardly be expected to win a mandate for another four. Machado knew this; and, in 1928, he arranged his reelection through a mixture of co-operation and coercion.

Machado was not without opposition. Some of it originated with members of the old-line parties. The Conservative and Popular parties denounced reelection. Even in the president's own party, opposition to a second term for Machado was widespread. In 1927, rival Liberal candidate Carlos Mendieta broke with Machado and established a new party, the *Unión Nacionalista*.

But opposition did not originate exclusively, or principally, from the old-line parties. New forces were stirring in Cuba. By the late 1920s, the first republican-born generation had come of political age. National disillusionment first found expression in the marketplace of ideas: in university reform, in new literary and artistic currents. Disillusionment quickly gave way to disaffection, and hopes for cultural regeneration fused with visions of political redemption. New items were added to the expanding political agenda, which soon included antiimperialism, political reform, and social justice. Intellectuals, students, and workers pushed dissent beyond the limits of traditional partisan politics and into the realms of reform and revolution. The very content of the national debate had changed; politics now turned on systems and ideology, not on personalities and cults. The republican generation was possessed of a peculiar redemptive mission, one that had as its goal the total regeneration of the republic—one, too, that challenged the assumptions upon which Machado governed as much as it challenged Machado's government.

To be sure, the palpably specious mandate for a second Machado term in 1928 served to deepen the opposition and give a focus to political dissent. In the end, however, it was the depression after 1929 that wrought utter havoc to the already ailing economy and plunged Cuba into crisis. In mid-1930, conditions further deteriorated when the United States passed the Hawley–Smoot Tariff Act, a protectionist measure that increased the

duty on Cuban sugar. The Cuban share of the U.S. market shrank from
49.4 percent in 1930 to 25.3 percent in 1933.[3] Cuban exports declined by
80 percent, even as the price of sugar decreased by 60 percent. Sugar producers struggled to remain solvent by lowering wages and cutting production through labor layoffs. The harvest was reduced again, this time to 62
days—that is, only two months' work for tens of thousands of sugar workers.[4] The value of tobacco, the island's second largest export, declined from
$43 million in 1929 to $13 million in 1933. Salaries and wages were reduced, workers laid off, and businesses and factories closed. Unemployment
soared. Some 250,000 heads of families, representing approximately 1 million people out of a total population of 3.9 million, found themselves totally
unemployed. Pay for agricultural laborers fell by 75 percent. In the sugar
zones, wages fell as low as 20 cents for a 12-hour workday. On one large
estate, workers received 10 cents a day—5 in cash, and 5 in credit at the
company store. In some districts, laborers received only food and lodging
for their work. "Wages paid . . . in 1932," one wage survey commented
tersely, "are reported to have been the lowest since the days of slavery."[5]
As wages fell in absolute terms, the value of the *peso* decreased in purchas-
ing power. The peso was worth 28 *centavos* less in 1928 than in 1913.[6]
Profits plummeted everywhere. Commerce came to a standstill. Local industry and manufacturing reduced production, in response to reduced pur-
chasing power of the population; this, in turn, sparked a new round of unemployment and new wage cuts. The cycle seemed to have no end.
Commercial, banking, and manufacturing failures reached record proportions. Business failures produced another spiral of unemployment and new
rounds of shortages and price rises.[7] Between 1930 and 1931, the government inaugurated a policy of drastic salary cuts for all public employees
except the armed forces. Pay reductions of as much as 60 percent were not
uncommon. A year later, budget cuts resulted in the first of a series of
sweeping layoffs of civil servants. Highway construction projects that had
employed some 15,000 workers in 1928 were suspended, creating immediate hardships in thousands of households. Salaries fell hopelessly in ar-
rears. By 1932, the pay of the vast majority of civil servants had fallen six
months behind. Thousands of government employees, traditionally secure
in civil service and public administration, were among the newest arrivals to
augment the swelling ranks of the unemployed.[8]

Opposition increased. Through the late 1920s and early 1930s, the conflict deepened and confrontations intensified. Mass demonstrations increased. Labor organized; union membership expanded; and the frequency
of strikes increased. Between 1929 and 1930, strikes halted production in a
number of industries, including cigar manufacturing, metallurgy, construction, and textiles. In March 1930, the outlawed National Confederation of
Cuban Workers (CNOC) organized a stunning general strike involving some
200,000 workers. The strike paralyzed the island, and ended only after a

wave of government repression. Several weeks later, railroad workers struck again and paralyzed national rail transportation. Strike organizers were arrested, and the trains resumed operation under army direction.

A kind of desultory warfare broke out in the countryside. The torching of canefields became commonplace, and millions of *arrobas* of cane went up in smoke. Armed bands operated throughout the interior—ambushing trains, cutting telephone and telegraph wires, destroying rail bridges and tunnels, and attacking isolated Rural Guard posts. Military escorts became a permanent and necessary feature of railroad traffic between Havana and Santiago. In November 1930, the government lifted constitutional guarantees throughout the island and proclaimed a state of siege. Army units in full combat dress assumed police functions throughout provincial cities and towns. Military supervisors displaced civilian governors in Pinar del Río, Matanzas, Las Villas, Camagüey, and Oriente. Army tribunals superseded civilian courts. Military censors supervised editorial boards of newspapers and magazines. Constitutional guarantees were restored on December 1, but suspended again ten days later—portents of the protracted struggle in the offing.

Repression on such a scale summoned into existence an extensive police apparatus penetrating every aspect of Cuban social life—not only to arrest, torture, and execute, but to maintain surveillance over the Cubans who were not in prison and the countless thousands who were. A secret police was organized: the *Sección de Expertos,* who were specialists—or, as they were known, "experts"—in the methods of torture. The *Partida de la Porra* served as a government death squad. Cuba assumed the appearance of an armed camp, and terror became the principal means of government. The government physically eliminated opposition, real and suspected. This was a regime that eliminated critics in anticipation of opposition and that constantly struck at people willing to conform, on the suspicion that they might eventually cease to be willing. Neutrality was suspect; criticism was subversive.

The organized opposition responded in kind, and several groups emerged to challenge Machado with arms. The ABC Revolutionary Society consisted of intellectuals, professionals, and students, who were organized around clandestine cells committed to creating conditions of revolution through systematic use of violence against the government. The *Organización Celular Radical Revolucionaria* (OCRR) also adopted a cellular structure and adapted armed struggle and sabotage as the means to overthrow Machado. Other new antigovernment groups, university professors, and normal school teachers became part of a vast underground network arrayed against Machado. At the same time, labor through the CNOC, the Cuban Communist Party (PCC), and university students (DEU) were also active in revolutionary activity.[9] By the early 1930s, open warfare had broken out in Cuba. The crisis was moving beyond a political settlement. As economic conditions deteriorated and social unrest spread, the struggle against Machado was changing daily into a movement that was more interested in overturning a system than in overthrowing a president.

By early 1933, the United States had come to recognize the gravity of conditions in Cuba. The new Roosevelt administration understood the sources of the crisis, and recognized that in Cuba, it faced nothing less than a crisis of hegemony. The U.S. grip over Cuba was slipping. The Customs–Tariff Law of 1927 had taken its toll on U.S. imports. In the decade between 1923 and 1933, Cuban imports from the United States had declined from $191 million to $22 million, while Cuban exports to the United States decreased from $362 million to $57 million. U.S. participation in Cuban import trade diminished from 74.3 percent during World War I to 66.7 in 1922, 61.7 percent in 1927, and 57.4 percent in 1931. Cuba dropped from the sixth to the sixteenth place as customer of U.S. exports. The Department of Agriculture estimated that the loss of Cuban markets for foodstuffs alone meant the withdrawal of some 817, 267 acres from agricultural production in the United States. Exports to Cuba of raw materials and manufactured products other than foodstuffs dropped from $133 million in 1924 to $18 million in 1933.[10]

The new ambassador Sumner Welles arrived in Havana in May 1933, on an assignment for which he had vacated his position as assistant secretary of state and interrupted his preparations for the December Pan American meetings in Montevideo. The State Department anticipated that Welles could complete his mission within three months, whereupon he would return to Washington to resume preparations for Montevideo. Welles had previously played a minor part in the formulation of Latin American policy, during the Woodrow Wilson administration. It had been a brief experience, but one with lasting effects. The 1910s had been difficult times for the State Department. A decade of armed intervention in Central America and the Caribbean had produced suspicion and enmity almost everywhere in the hemisphere. Anti-U.S. sentiment was flourishing, and rising. Washington derived little satisfaction from the accomplishments of military intervention. They had been meager. Indeed, the resort to armed intervention had created more problems than it had solved.

The lessons of these years were not lost on Welles. The fruits of armed intervention were everywhere in evidence; and it was a bitter harvest, indeed. The preservation of North American hegemony in the region, Welles recognized, could not rely principally on the use of armed force. On the contrary, the frequent resort to military intervention had actually contributed to creating conditions that threatened U.S. interests in the region. Armed intervention was no longer either an adequate means or an advisable option of U.S. policy. It offered too little, too late. It was too much a visible expression of North American hegemony and, as such, served to invite attack on the U.S. presence.

Welles's search for alternative policy approaches led him inevitably and logically to a shift of emphasis. Instead of continued reliance on military intervention to end disorders, Welles urged politico-diplomatic intervention to prevent disorders. This approach placed emphasis on an expanded role of North American diplomatic personnel, who would now actively participate in shaping both the content of policy in the United States and the course of politics in the host country. If Washington were to repudiate armed intervention to restore stability, it would have to seek, in advance, to exercise greater political intervention to prevent instability. Writing of Cuba (over which the United States had formal right of intervention under the Platt Amendment), Welles suggested:

Such actual intervention in or occupation of Cuba as the United States has been obliged to undertake is, of course, at best an artificial method of restoring outward tranquility so that constitutional government may once more be established. Of far greater value is the friendly advice which may be offered to the Cuban Government and to the Cuban people through our representatives.[11]

"The value of a policy of preventing the rise of conditions which lead to political disturbances, revolution, and civil war, in the Caribbean republics," Welles counseled Franklin Roosevelt four years later, "is, to my mind, far greater than the value of a policy which lets matters drift until civil war breaks out and then adopts measures of coercion."[12]

Hence, what Welles proposed was not so much a change of objectives as a change of means. Armed intervention could not guarantee more than temporary stability. In exchange for that short-lived political peace, the United States jeopardized long-term access to Latin American resources and markets. In the spring of 1933, Welles received the opportunity to test his approach.

Welles's instructions bore the distinctive imprimatur of the new policy. "You will point out to President Machado in the most forceful terms," the instructions stipulated, "that in the opinion of your Government, there can be expected no general amelioration of conditions in Cuba until there is a definite cessation of that state of terrorism which has existed for so long." The United States wished to prevent the conditions "which would tend to render more likely the need of the Government of the United States to resort to that right of formal intervention." In view of the possibility of "open rebellion against a Cuban Government," it was necessary to take "measures intended to prevent the necessity of intervention." To this end, Welles was instructed to offer "the friendly mediation" of the U.S. government to Machado and the political opposition for the purpose of obtaining "a definite, detailed, and binding understanding between the present Cuban Government and the responsible leaders of the factions opposed to it."[13]

These instructions involved two interrelated objectives. "First," Welles later recalled, "to assist the Cuban people themselves to solve the political crisis which had developed, and, second, to provide, by cooperation between our two Governments, a means for the rehabilitation of Cuba's national economy, and thereby likewise to reestablish, to the advantage of American agriculture and industry, the market which our own exports had previously enjoyed." The latter was as important as the former. "At a time when national economic recovery was the salient objective of the Government in Washington," Welles wrote, "it was clear that the immense market for American agriculture and industrial exports should be restored to us." [14] After only days in Havana, Welles wrote:

The negotiation at this time of a reciprocal trade agreement with Cuba . . . will not only revivify Cuba but will give us practical control of a market we have been steadily losing for the past ten years not only for our manufactured products but for our agricultural exports. [15]

Initially, Welles hoped that Machado could complete his term through May 1935, and thereby preserve constitutional legitimacy and political continuity. However, the success of this strategy depended upon the willingness of the president and the opposition to compromise. The president would finish his term, during which time the opposition could prepare for elections in November 1934—and the United States and Cuba could negotiate a new commercial treaty. In his first formal meeting with Machado on May 13, Welles spoke of U.S. responsibilities under the Platt Amendment. He urged Machado to open up the political system by implementing a "program of conciliation" that would lead toward honest elections in 1934—and, presumably, toward the triumph of Machado's foes. The United States was disposed to negotiate a new commercial treaty that would not only relieve economic conditions in Cuba but, Welles was confident, also turn the "attention of the general public from political agitation to economic interest [and] . . . have a marked beneficial psychological effect." But political reforms were necessary, Welles stressed; he reminded Machado that this Cuban government could not long survive, were U.S. support to be withdrawn. The U.S. government promised to offer economic concessions—if, in turn, the Cuban government pledged to offer political compromise to the opposition. [16]

Welles was not certain about the willingness of opposition groups to negotiate with the regime. Their participation in the mediations could be obtained only by the promise of Machado's removal. As early as May 13—after only five days in Cuba—Welles already envisioned the necessity of having to pressure the unsuspecting Machado into early retirement, as the central condition to a political settlement. "If the present acute bitterness of feeling against the President and the members of his Government persists or becomes intensified during the coming year," Welles reported, "it would in all probability be highly desirable that the present chief executive be replaced at least during the electoral period by some impartial citizen in whom all factions have confidence." [17]

Welles's worst fears were soon confirmed. On May 18, he described deteriorating conditions in Cuba to Secretary of State Cordell Hull. "Frankly, I am worried," he cabled. "I think the situation is very precarious, much more so than I anticipated." [18] Welles was now more explicit about the fate of Machado: "The feeling is so bitter and the state of agitation so general that I feel it may be necessary to suggest a change in the Presidency, through constitutional procedure, some time before the electoral period commences. But I am confident that in any event General Machado should be replaced, at least during the electoral period, by some individual in whom all parties have confidence." [19]

The mediations offered the means through which to obtain the desired political settlement. It was essential to end the threat of social revolution in Cuba, principally by eliminating its political source. Machado had outlived his usefulness. The order and stability that he had so deftly provided during his first term (the basis upon which he had received U.S. support for reelection) had disintegrated in his second term. Neither the application of repression nor attempts at reconciliation seemed capable of diminishing the intransigence of the opposition. After five years of sustained political strife and unrelieved economic stress, it had become apparent that Machado could not restore order. His continued presence was now the central issue for the political opposition, and was easily the greatest single obstacle to the restoration of political order. The impossibility of attaining political reform increased the improbability of averting social revolution.

The mediations also provided a forum through which the "responsible leaders" of the opposition groups could return from the fringes of illegality to the fold of legality. This signified nothing less than their repudiation of revolution; it was a way to relieve the mounting revolutionary pressure, by diverting the opposition from a conspiratorial solution to a constitutional settlement. The mediations provided the means through which opposition groups achieved their objectives and joined the political process in an orderly institutional fashion. Just as important as easing Machado out was the necessity of easing new power contenders in. The mediations conferred a measure of political legitimacy on sectors of the outlawed opposition—providing them with a vested interest in a settlement sanctioned and supported by the United States. This served as a recruitment process—a method by which Welles selected the participants of the mediations—determining, in the process, which groups were "legitimate," and which were not; determining, too, which groups were compatible with U.S. interests, and who would participate in the subsequent government. North American influence over Cuban government would be preserved, and the place of the United States as a powerbroker among political contenders would be maintained. This was nothing less than the renewal of hegemony built into the planned changing of the guard in

Havana, a method by which the United States established a political lien on a new group of powerholders. Further, this was precisely the type of U.S.-inspired settlement that Welles believed to be necessary in order to avoid military intervention.

The mediations began on July 1. The opposition was represented by the Unión Nacionalista, the ABC, the OCRR, university professors, women's opposition groups, and normal school teachers. Government representatives included leaders of the Liberal, Conservative, and Popular parties, with Secretary of War General Alberto Herrera representing the administration.

Methodically, Welles edged Machado closer to his expulsion. The president acquiesced to pressure for reforms. He restored the vice-presidency, conceded freedom of the press, released political prisoners, and revised the electoral code. In mid-July, Welles prepared to deliver the final blow. "At some time within the next two or three weeks," he wrote to Roosevelt, "the suggestion will be made that after a Vice President satisfactory to all parties has been selected and has taken office, the President resign and make it thus possible for the Vice President to remain in entire control of the Government until a new Constitutional Government has been elected in November 1934." Opposition groups would not participate in new elections, Welles explained, "if President Machado remains in control of the Government. They are confident that fair elections cannot be held so long as he remains in the Presidency."[20] Two weeks later, Welles informed Machado that a satisfactory solution to the crisis required him to shorten his term by one year.[21]

Machado responded first with incredulity, and then rage. He convened a special session of Congress to repudiate the proposed settlement, and vowed to remain in power through his full term of office. On August 5, he protested to Welles that the mediations had undermined his authority. Machado reiterated his commitment to "any fair solution proposed" but, he added, he would not be "thrown into the street."[22] In Washington, Cuban ambassador Oscar Cintas warned that the "improper course" pursued by Welles would lead to certain disaster: "One or two alternatives would result—either President Machado would be shot or American marines would be landed."[23]

In late July, Welles and Machado faced a new problem. Bus drivers in Havana had organized a strike to protest a new government tax. Under the direction of the PCC and the CNOC, the strike quickly spread to other sectors; within days, all movement of people and goods came to a halt. The strike had become general. Havana was paralyzed.[24] By the end of the first week of August, the strike had acquired the full proportions of a revolutionary offensive.

The strike changed everything. Welles increased pressure on Machado. The request for Machado's early retirement was unabashedly transformed into an ultimatum. The source of the new urgency was self-evident. If Machado could not be persuaded to retire, the general strike would sweep aside the whole government—an eventuality, Welles grimly predicted, with catastrophic consequences, inevitability requiring U.S. armed intervention. The strike announced the imminence of revolution. Only the most "forceful and positive action" by the United States, he insisted—and, specifically, the direct threat of armed intervention—could dislodge Machado. But in order to obtain authorization to threaten Machado with armed intervention as a means to force his retirement, Welles was obliged to also threaten Washington: Armed intervention would be inevitable, if he were denied the use of its threat. Welles now grimly predicted the necessity of armed intervention, if Machado did not resign. "If President Machado remains in power," he warned the State Department in calculated terms, "he can only continue through the exercise of the most brutal methods of repression. . . . If the present condition is permitted to continue much longer, I am positive that a state of complete anarchy will result which might force the Government of the United States, against its will, to intervene in compliance with its obligation under the Permanent Treaty." This, Welles reminded Washington, was a responsibility that the United States could not evade. He recommended that, "if at the end of a reasonable period" Machado continued in power, the United States formally withdraw recognition of his government; whereupon, Welles would meet with the government parties and opposition groups to prepare for the installation of a new government. The threat of intervention was not directed so much to Machado as it was to his supporters—including the traditional political parties, the congress, the cabinet, and the armed forces. The proposal to withdraw recognition, Welles assured the State Department, would not "in all probability force us to intervene." [25]

However, to the horror of the State Department, Machado challenged the United States to intervene. "Inform the President of the United States," Machado taunted Welles, "that [I] would prefer armed intervention to the acceptance of any such proposal." [26] Worse still for Washington, Machado seized the threat of intervention to appeal for national support for his government. He denounced U.S. intermeddling in Cuban internal affairs and vowed to defend national sovereignty—exhorting his fellow Cubans to defend the homeland against North American aggression. [27] He privately informed Welles that he would repel with arms the landing of U.S. troops on national territory. [28]

Welles's strategy was not without effect. The first defections occurred among the *machadista* parties. Progovernment party leaders viewed Machado's defiance with foreboding, sensing uneasily that this was a contest the president could not win. And what, then, would become of them? If the Machado government fell solely through U.S. pressure, the traditional parties faced the prospect of drastic reorganization—under the best of circumstances—or complete dissolution—as many opposition factions demanded. On the other hand, endorsement of the U.S. proposal and a timely defection from the president, who was facing an uncertain future, had the virtue of aligning the old parties with the new politics, thereby assuring their survival in post-Machado Cuba. If the new opposition factions could obtain legitimacy by participating in the mediations, the old political parties would guarantee longevity by supporting the mediator. In early August, leaders of the Liberal, Conservative, and Popular parties endorsed the proposed early retirement of Machado and began to prepare the legislation necessary to expedite his departure. But still, Machado clung to power.

Tensions mounted. The general strike deepened the crisis and raised for many, including Welles, the specter of social upheaval. A New York *Times* correspondent described conditions as "a race between mediation by the United States Ambassador and open revolution."[29] The moment was critical, and Welles was desperate. "The ominous signs provided by a paralyzing general strike," he later wrote, "wholly political in character, made it doubly clear that only some radical solution could forestall the cataclysm which otherwise was inevitable."[30]

Almost two weeks after Welles had submitted his original proposal, he devised a "new solution"—what he later called the "radical solution." On August 11, he reported holding a "confidential talk" with General Alberto Herrera, in which Herrera pledged to support a new proposal whereby Machado was to request a leave of absence and accept the resignation of all cabinet members except Herrera, who would thereupon become acting president.[31]

By offering Herrera the presidency, Welles deliberately invited the Cuban armed forces to intervene. He recognized that Herrera's only contribution to the "new solution"—certainly a contribution of sufficient magnitude to warrant his succession to the presidency—lay entirely in leading the army against Machado. Herrera's participation in the plan, Welles confidently predicted, insured "the loyal support of the Cuban Army," which was unanimously devoted to the general.[32]

The army was predisposed to act; and, on August 12, it moved against the president. As the balance of power tipped against the beleaguered government, the armed forces found their vulnerability increasing in the changing political conditions. The mediations had conferred legitimacy on the formerly outlawed opposition groups; the very sectors that the armed forces had been persecuting in the preceding years were now guaranteed positions of political authority in post-Machado Cuba. But it was the growing fear of U.S. intervention that finally moved the army to act. Welles had calculated correctly. Army leaders shrank in horror at the spectacle of Machado defying U.S. authorities. The "sole purpose" of the military coup, one army representative later explained, "was the avoidance of American intervention."[33] Like the old political parties, the army feared displacement by an armed intervention. U.S. intervention would have certainly resulted in a sweeping reorganization of the armed forces, and would have ultimately led to drastic reductions.[34]

Welles used the threat of armed intervention purposefully, and with effect.

Political and military leaders were prepared to go to great lengths to avert the calamity of intervention. If the price was only the removal of Machado, too many people had too much to lose not to acquiesce. When Welles demanded that Machado resign a year early—and invoked the specter of armed intervention—he effectively stripped Machado of his support. Welles possessed sufficient insight into the subtleties of Cuban politics to anticipate the consequences of publicly demanding Machado's retirement. In June 1933, Welles the mediator, committed to personal diplomacy as a means to persuade Machado into early retirement, had guarded his proposal carefully—fearing that a premature disclosure would "weaken" the president's control over congress and the armed forces.[35] Subsequently frustrated by his inability to convince Machado to resign, Welles publicly revealed the withdrawal of U.S. support and precipitated a realignment of the political balance of power—thereby releasing Machado's supporters to seek new arrangements to guarantee their survival in post-Machado Cuba.

Welles was the man of the hour. To the relief of his anxious superiors in Washington, he had delivered the coup de grace to the stricken Machado regime—and, yet, it appeared to be a wholly Cuban settlement. The crisis had passed without need for armed intervention. For his part, Welles—his mission to Havana accomplished—was now anxious to return to Washington, so as to resume his post as assistant secretary of state and begin anew his preparations for Montevideo. He had completed his mission—two weeks ahead of schedule.

All was not well in Havana, however. Herrera had encountered opposition, and Welles was forced to recommend Carlos Manuel de Céspedes for the presidency. The two men were longtime personal friends. But in Cuba, Céspedes was a political nonentity. Apart from his prestigious family name, his principal virtue consisted in a lack of affiliation with any political party or political tendency. He lacked a public personality; and, as such, he represented an inoffensive compromise candidate to the embattled extremes of the Cuban polity. He was without popularity, without a party, and without a program; and all at once he inherited a cabinet, a constituency, and a country in collapse. His was a government without a mandate. It was largely formed to facilitate Machado's succession and pay off debts incurred to the groups participating in the mediations. The government was made up of discredited political parties that had functioned under the pall of unconstitutionality and dissident clandestine factions that had operated on the fringes of illegality. It neither possessed popularity nor promised a program. This was a government summoned into existence largely in response to U.S. needs. And very early, it was in trouble.

Cuba remained in the throes of depression. The economic stagnation and social unrest that had plunged the *machadato* into crisis persisted unrelieved. Strikes continued. The labor militancy that precipitated the fall of Machado continued unabated.

There were other problems. Beset by contradictions from within and besieged by opposition from without, the authority of the new government deteriorated. Reports that machadista officials continued to hold their old jobs served to weaken the moral authority of the Céspedes government.[36] That the government had permitted the flight of large numbers of officials who had been responsible for atrocities offended public sensibilities. Legislators could not meet, for fear of precipitating a mob attack against congress. Many provincial governors, municipal mayors, and their staffs had gone into hiding—leaving local government unattended. Public order had collapsed. The rioting produced by Machado's flight continued intermittently through August. Angry mobs stalked Havana streets and outlying suburbs—bent on dispensing revolutionary justice to suspected machadista officials. Government offices were gutted, stores looted, and homes sacked.[37]

The end of the Céspedes government came from the most improbable and wholly unexpected sources. On the evening of September 3, sergeants, corporals, and enlisted men of Camp Columbia in Havana, who were meeting to discuss a backlog of army grievances, seized control of army headquarters. Under the leadership of Sergeant Fulgencio Batista, army protesters exhorted the troops to hold the post until the officers would agree to negotiate their demands. Antigovernment groups, principally the university students, immediately rallied around the mutinous troops. The intervention of civilians radically changed the nature of the army protest; it transformed the mutiny into a putsch and a governing junta. On September 5, a manifesto announced the installation of a new Provisional Revolutionary Government and proclaimed the establishment of a modern democracy and the "march toward the creation of a new Cuba."[38] Within a week, the junta dissolved, in favor of an executive form of government under Ramón Grau San Martín.

For 100 days, the new government devoted itself with exalted purposefulness to the task of transforming Cuba. This was the first government of the republic formed without the sanction and support of the United States. Under the injunction of "Cuba for Cubans," the new government proceeded to enact reform laws at a dizzying pace—committing itself to economic reconstruction, social reform, and political reorganization. On the day of his inauguration as president, Grau nullified the Platt Amendment. Traditional political parties were dissolved. Reform decrees followed in rapid succession.

The rhetoric of revolution notwithstanding, this was preeminently a reformist regime. It chose regulation over expropriation, the distribution of public lands over the redistribution of private property, the defense of trade union objectives over workers' party objectives. This was not a government without opposition, however. The forces of old Cuba responded to the September coup with unrestrained indignation. This was the ouster of the old political groups, and it came at a singularly inopportune moment. The government parties that had deserted Machado (as a means to survive the discredited regime) faced persecution and extinction, once again. So, too, did the ousted army officers who, for all their efforts to secure immunity from post-Machado reprisals, now found themselves vulnerable to prosecution and imprisonment. Foreign capital recoiled in horror at the new laws that regulated and restricted the freedom that it had traditionally enjoyed under previous governments.[39] Nor was it only old Cuba that opposed the provisional government. New political groups, including the ABC, the OCRR, and the Unión Nacionalista—organizations that, earlier, had paid dearly to acquire political legitimacy in post-Machado Cuba—were not reconciled to this abrupt and inglorious end to their debut in national politics.

Welles orchestrated the opposition. The fall of Céspedes had been a blow to his new prestige; and, as he immediately recognized, it required him to delay his departure from Havana. Only two weeks before the fall of Céspedes, Welles had reissued his request to return to Washington. By September 12, Welles recognized that the new developments would require him to remain in Havana indefinitely.[40]

But Welles's opposition to the new government responded to more than personal pique. The pro-U.S. government that he had labored so diligently to create collapsed ignominiously a mere three weeks after its organization. The old players had been displaced; the old rules had been discarded. Welles correctly sensed that both his authority in Cuba and no less than U.S. authority over Cuba were being challenged. Indeed, the very premises of the hegemonial system were in danger of passing into desuetude. The overthrow of the Céspedes government, the suppression of the traditional political parties, and the removal of the old officer corps represented nothing less than the dismantling of the internal structures upon which U.S. hegemony rested. The implications of the policies of the new government were not lost on Welles. "It is . . . within the bounds of possibility," Welles wrote with alarm two weeks after the coup, "that the social revolution which is under way cannot be checked. American properties and interests are being gravely prejudiced and the material damage to such properties will in all probability be very great."[41] Many of the government decrees, he protested, were outright "confiscatory" in nature and enormously prejudicial to U.S. property interests.[42] "Our own commercial and export interests in Cuba," Welles asserted flatly, "cannot be revived under this government."[43] In October, when the government announced an agreement with Mexico to train Cuban army officers, Welles drew immediate conclusions: "In view of the existing situation here and particularly in view of the fact that since the independence of the Republic of Cuba the training of Cuban officers had been undertaken solely in the United States or under the direction of American officers this step can only be construed as a deliberate effort by the present Government to show its intention of minimizing any form of American influence in Cuba."[44]

Welles was neither slow to respond nor unequivocal in his response. For the remainder of his stay in Havana, Welles pursued a policy calculated to isolate the government diplomatically abroad and weaken the government politically at home. In early September, Welles abandoned all adherence to nonintervention. Initially, his policy approach had rested on the central premise that the United States possessed influence over the inner councils of government—leverage that was lost after September 4. With the traditional political parties divested of power in government councils and the old officers deprived of command over the armed forces, the United States was deprived of direct access to and influence over the Cuban government. The choice was simple: The United States could accept these turn of events or use force to recover its former influence over government. On the day of the formation of the junta, Welles urged Washington to land "a certain number of troops"—ostensibly, to guard the U.S. Embassy and protect foreign lives and property. In fact, he acknowledged, Céspedes could not be restored without the "aid of an American guard." [45] Two days later, he proposed his most ambitious intervention proposal: He recommended a "strictly limited intervention," entailing "the landing of a considerable force at Habana and lesser forces in certain of the most important ports of the Republic." This "strictly limited intervention" would provide the "police force to the legitimate Government of Cuba for a comparatively brief period,"—thereby enabling the Céspedes government to function as it had, prior to its fall. [46]

But requests for intervention received no support in Washington. On the contrary, Roosevelt immediately moved to prohibit intervention for the purpose of protecting property alone. [47] Secretary of State Hull also shrank from intervention. "Despite the legal right we possessed," Hull later recalled, "such an act would further embitter our relations with all Latin America." Armed intervention in Cuba, Hull feared, would have undone "all our protestations of nonintervention and noninterference." [48]

Welles pursued alternate forms of opposition. If he could not overthrow the government from without, he would seek to undermine it from within. Nothing was so central to his objective as promoting conditions of continued instability and disorder. Three decades of policy imperatives were reversed: Stability and order were now inimical to U.S. interests in Cuba.

First and foremost, destabilization required denial of U.S. recognition. Earlier, Welles had threatened to withdraw recognition, in order to force Machado out of office. The denial of recognition of the Grau government had similar ends. Optimally, nonrecognition would produce the collapse of the government. But failing that, it would force the government into moderation, a way of exacting concessions from Grau in exchange for normalization of relations. "If our Government recognized the existing Cuban government before it has undergone radical modification," Welles argued, "such action would imply our lending official support to a regime which is opposed by all business and financial interests in Cuba; by all the powerful groups and in general . . . all the elements that hold out any promise of being able to govern Cuba. . . . Such action on our part would undoubtedly help to keep the present government in power." [49] Nonrecognition was also indispensable to encouraging continued instability and uncertainty. This was a deliberate orchestration of chaos, designed to maintain pressure on both the government and the opposition. Nonrecognition obstructed government efforts to reach reconciliation with its opponents, precisely because it offered the opposition incentive to resist the government. Those who otherwise might have supported the government demurred; those who opposed the government were encouraged to conspire and resist.

With the government thus thrown on the defensive, Welles was free to pursue internal subversion. To the deposed political groups, Welles urged continued resistance. To the displaced officers, he counseled a continued boycott of the army. Nonrecognition exercised a powerful restraint on government opponents; it encouraged them to believe that the regime could not long survive without U.S. support. On September 9, Welles reported that the officers had entered into a "definite compact" not to support "any government except a legitimate government." [50] As long as the new government remained unrecognized and as long as the United States claimed to uphold the authority of the "legitimate government" of Céspedes, the officers also could righteously claim to defend legitimacy. The officers who, only three weeks earlier, had led the army against Machado to prevent intervention now refused to lead the army under Grau to provoke intervention.

Within weeks, the opposition abandoned all hopes of reconciliation with the officers. Grau ordered the officers to return to their commands. When they refused, they were proclaimed deserters and arrested. A second blow to the antigovernment forces was not long in coming. In early November, a combined force of the ABC and Unión Nacionalista joined a rebellion of dissident army elements. After several days of fighting in Havana, government forces overcame the resistance and ended the revolt.

The arrest of the officers and defeat of the ABC and Unión Nacionalista had several immediate effects. Both reversals signalled the end of organized internal opposition to the Grau government. The principal opposition groups that originated from the previous government—and around which Welles had hoped to reconstitute the "legitimate government"—had been dispersed. The displacement of the former officer corps paved the way for a sweeping reorganization of the armed forces. Some 400 sergeants, corporals, and enlisted men received commissions and filled the newly created vacancies in the army command. Batista was formally promoted to the rank of colonel and appointed chief of the army.

The arrest of the old officers—to be sure—strengthened the position of the provisional government. It also set in relief the growing estrangement between the civilians and the soldiers. The civilians had carried Cuba deep into the uncertain realm of experimental government. As the civilians contin-

ued to advance on their "march to create a new Cuba," the army became
an increasingly reluctant escort. Military support of the provisional government was always more practical than political, more a form of self-interest
than a function of solidarity. This was the government that had sanctioned
the sedition and validated 400 new commissions. In short, this was the government from which the new army command derived legitimacy and to
which it was inexorably linked. But it was also true that the military leaders
were anxious for a political settlement, if for no other reason than to legiti-
mize their recent promotions. Indeed, many commanders feared that government policies would inevitably result in visiting grief on the new officers
corps. From the start, it had been only a coalition of convenience; and nothing had changed except that, by mid-autumn, the soldiers found themselves
increasingly inconvenienced by civilian policies.

These were the fateful flaws, the stress points perceptively discerned by
Welles. By mid-fall, his efforts shifted away from promoting unity among
government opponents to encouraging disunity among its supporters. He
perceived the inherent cross-purposes that separated the civilian reformers
from the army officers, and devoted himself to exploiting these contradictions. The army mutiny, he reminded Washington only days after the arrest
of the old officers, did "not take place in order to place Grau San Martín in
power." He noted—correctly—that the "divergence between the Army and
civilian elements in the government is fast becoming daily more marked,"
as Batista's authority and influence increased. The arrest of the former officers did not "indicate consolidation of the position of the government but
solely a decidedly increased prestige for the Army as distinguished from the
government."[51] Two weeks later, Welles reiterated his contention: "The
mutiny was not directed against Céspedes or his cabinet; it was not political
in its origin and it was not . . . in any sense responsive to a social movement."[52]

For the second time in two months, Welles appealed directly to the army
to overturn a government opposed by the United States. Throughout the
autumn months, Welles maintained a close—and increasingly cordial—contact with Batista. "The situation as regards my relations with Batista is,"
Welles conceded in early October, "of course, anomalous. I feel it necessary
to make plain, however, that there does not exist at the present time in
Cuba any authority whatever except himself and that in the event of further
disturbances which may endanger the lives and properties of Americans or
foreigners in the Republic it seems to be essential that this relationship be
maintained."[53] On October 4, only days after the arrest of the former officers, Welles reported having held a "protracted and very frank discussion"
with Batista. Welles informed the army chief that he was the "only individual in Cuba today who represented authority." Welles explained that leadership of the army had earned Batista the support of "the very great majority of the commercial and financial interests in Cuba who are looking for

protection and who could only find such protection in himself." Political factions that—only weeks earlier—had openly opposed him, Welles disclosed, were now "in accord that his control of the Army as Chief of Staff should be continued as the only possible solution and were willing to support him in that capacity." However, the only obstacle to an equitable political settlement—and, presumably, recognition and a return to conditions of normality—the ambassador suggested, "was the unpatriotic and futile obstinacy of a small group of young men who should be studying in the university instead of playing politics and of a few individuals who had joined with them for selfish motives." In a thinly veiled warning, Welles reminded Batista of the tenuous position in which his continued affiliation with the Grau government placed him. "Should the present government go down in disaster," Welles warned, "that disaster would necessarily inextricably involve not only himself but the safety of the Republic, which he has publicly pledged himself to maintain." [54]

They met again several days later, this time at Batista's request. In the days since their last conversation, Batista indicated to Welles, he was "deeply impressed by the fact that delegates of all the important business and financial groups in Cuba" had visited him to insist upon the creation of a government "in which the public could have confidence." Batista was now persuaded that the provisional government was a "complete failure" and that a new coalition government—one in which moderate political groups and commercial interests of the country could have confidence—was "an absolute necessity." Batista had also come to appreciate the necessity of U.S. recognition "before any improvement in conditions" on the island could be expected. [55]

Welles's comments could not have been interpreted by Batista in any other fashion than as an invitation to create a new government. Welles had forged a coalition—consisting of the new political groups, the old political parties, foreign capital, and the State Department—to which Batista could defect, and the ambassador would ratify the new army command and organize a government approved by Washington. By the end of October, Batista had arrived at the conclusion that "a change in government is imperative." [56] Some weeks later, Welles reported that Batista was "actively seeking a change in government—owing to apprehension of army intrigue against him, the constant and "inevitable" attempts at revolution, and fear of U.S. military intervention. [57]

Welles did not remain in Havana long enough to witness the fruits of his labor. In early December, the Grau government proclaimed him persona non grata. He was replaced in Havana by Jefferson Caffery. Several weeks later, Batista bluntly asked Caffery what the United States "wanted done for recognition." Reiterating Washington's determination to withhold recognition, Caffery urged the creation of a new government capable of inspiring confidence at home and abroad. [58] In mid-January, Batista transferred army support from Grau to Unión Nacionalista leader Carlos Mendieta. Within five days, the United States recognized the new government.

By the time of his departure, Welles had played a part in toppling two Cuban presidents and installing two others. Shortly thereafter, the United States and Cuba negotiated a new reciprocity treaty, which restored North American primacy in the Cuban economy. Welles's maneuvers during these six months proved successful in containing the contradictions of Cuban society. Economic depression and social turmoil had not produced revolution, but reform—and, ultimately, reaction. Of course, all these developments cannot be attributed to Welles's machinations. Instead, they were more the products of prevailing social forces, economic conditions, and political processes in Cuba. However, at the same time, this was a national system that was itself shaped by and functioned within a larger hegemonial framework. As a result, Cubans easily acquiesced to and accommodated themselves to the presence of the United States. In fact, this North American ambassador in Cuba functioned as an active powerbroker—one with access to the vast resources with which to deal (including armed forces), the power to concede or withhold economic aid, and the authority to confer or withdraw diplomatic recognition.

Welles played this part deftly, and with effect. He knew Cuba well, and he used this knowledge against Cubans. He clearly understood the conflicts and contradictions of the Cuban polity, and how to play power contenders against one another. He also operated out of a defined ideological framework, a world view that allowed him to recognize social forces as potential friend or likely foe to U.S. interests. He had sufficient perspicacity to recognize that Machado had been transformed from asset to liability and, later, that Batista could be converted from adversary to ally. Indeed, perhaps Welles's lasting impact was to move Batista from the shadows of the political arena into center stage. Of course, it is entirely plausible that Batista would have emerged triumphant in any case. He was not without political talent. However, the power struggle within the provisional government was intense, and very complicated. Batista's ascendency was by no means inevitable. Welles provided a vital margin of support, a difference that contributed to the emergence of Batista as the new strong man of Cuba. The stage was thereby set for the second act of this drama, two decades later.

NOTES

1. Gerardo Machado, *Por la patria libre* (Havana, 1926), pp. 14–16. See also Gerardo Machado, *Memorias: ocho años de lucha* (Miami, 1982), p. 11.

2. Division of Latin American Affairs, "Excerpts Regarding Government Finances and Kindred Matters from the Annual Report of the Consul General at Habana," April 12, 1929, 837.51/1342, General Records of the State Department, Record Group 59, National Archives, Washington, D.C. (hereinafter cited as DS/RG

59); José R. Alvarez Díaz et al., *A Study on Cuba* (Coral Gables, 1965), pp. 222–74; Luis E. Aguilar, *Cuba 1933: Prologue to Revolution* (Ithaca, 1972), pp. 56–58.

3. See Robert F. Smith, *The United States and Cuba: Business and Diplomacy, 1917–1961* (New Haven, 1960), p. 70.

4. Sergio Aguirre, *Eco de caminos* (Havana, 1974), p. 398.

5. "General Survey of Wages in Cuba, 1931 and 1932," *Monthly Labor Review* 35 (December 1932):1403–04.

6. José Antonio Taboadela, *Cuestiones económicas cubanas de actualidad* (Havana, 1929), p. 54.

7. For a discussion of the depression in Cuba, see Gustavo Gutiérrez y Sánchez, *El problema económico de Cuba. Sus causas, sus posibles soluciones*, 2 vols. (Havana, 1931); Raymond Leslie Buell et al., *Problems of the New Cuba* (New York, 1935), pp. 52–54.

8. Tomás Montero, *Grandezas y miserias* (Havana, 1944), p. 188; Edward L. Reed to Francis White, October 3, 1931, Francis White Papers, National Archives, Washington, D.C.; Francis White, "Memorandum," April 20, 1932, 837.51/1506, DS/RG 59; Fabio Grobart, "The Cuban Working Class Movement from 1925 to 1933," *Science and Society* 39 (Spring 1975):91.

9. Francisco López Segrara, *Raíces históricas de la revolución cubana (1868–1959)* (Havana, 1978), pp. 79–80.

10. See Charles William Taussig, "Cuba—and Reciprocal Trade Agreements," in National Foreign Trade Council, *Official Report of the Twenty-First National Foreign Trade Convention* (New York, 1934), p. 554; Harry F. Guggenheim, "Changes in the Reciprocity Treaty Which Would Probably Benefit the United States Export Trade with Cuba," March 30, 1933, 611.3731/390, DS/RG 59; Sumner Wells, *Relations between the United States and Cuba* (Washington, D.C., 1934), pp. 14–15.

11. Sumner Welles, "Is America Imperialistic?" *Atlantic Monthly* 84 (September 1924), p. 414.

12. Sumner Welles to Franklin D. Roosevelt, January 20, 1928, Franklin D. Roosevelt Papers, Franklin D. Roosevelt Library, Hyde Park, N.Y. (hereinafter cited as Roosevelt Papers).

13. Cordell Hull and Sumner Welles, May 1, 1933, 711.37/178a, DS/RG 59.

14. Sumner Welles, *Two Years of the "Good Neighbor" Policy* (Washington, D.C., 1935), pp. 5–7.

15. Sumner Welles to Cordell Hull, May 13, 1933, 837.00/3512, DS/RG 59.

16. Ibid.

17. Ibid.

18. "Long Distance Telephone Conversation between Secretary Hull and Ambassador Welles in Cuba," May 18, 1933, 611.3731/416½, DS/RG 59.

19. Sumner Welles to Franklin D. Roosevelt, May 18, 1933, Roosevelt Papers.

20. Sumner Welles to Franklin D. Roosevelt, July 17, 1933, 837.00/3579½, DS/RG 59.

21. Machado, *Memorias,* pp. 99–110.

22. Sumner Welles to Cordell Hull, August 5, 1933, 837.00/3603, DS/RG 59.

23. William Phillips, "Memorandum," August 8, 1933, 837.00/3629, DS/RG 59.

24. Grobart, "Cuban Working Class Movement," pp. 98–100.

25. Sumner Welles to Cordell Hull, August 8, 1933, 837.00/3616, DS/RG 59.

26. Ibid.

27. New York *Herald Tribune,* August 8, 1933, p. 2.

28. Machado, *Memorias,* p. 125.

29. New York *Times,* August 7, 1933.

30. Welles, *Two Years,* pp. 8–9.

31. Sumner Welles to Cordell Hull, August 11, 1933, 837.00/3633, DS/RG 59.

32. Ibid.

33. New York *Times,* August 12, 1933.

34. Charles A. Thomson, "The Cuban Revolution: Fall of Machado," *Foreign Policy Reports* 11 (December 18, 1935):257; Alberto Lamar Schweyer, *Como cayó el presidente Machado* (Madrid, 1941), p. 180.

35. Sumner Welles to William Phillips, June 6, 1933, 837.00/3537, DS/RG 59.

36. R. Hart Phillips, *Cuba: Island of Paradox* (New York, 1959), p. 55.

37. Carlos G. Peraza, *Machado, crímenes y horrores de un régimen* (Havana, 1933), pp. 320–21.

38. A copy of the proclamation was enclosed in Sumner Welles to Cordell Hull, September 5, 1933, 837.00/3753, DS/RG 59.

39. See Phillips, *Cuba,* pp. 69 and 72.

40. *Papers Relating to the Foreign Relations of the United States, 1933,* 5 vols. (Washington, D.C., 1952), V, p. 286 (Sumner Welles to Cordell Hull, August 19, 1933) and p. 428 (Sumner Welles to Cordell Hull, September 12, 1933) (hereinafter cited as *FRUS:V*).

41. Sumner Welles to Cordell Hull, September 18, 1933, 837.00/3934, DS/RG 59.

42. Sumner Welles to William Phillips, December 7, 1933, 837.00/4480, DS/RG 59.

43. Sumner Welles to Cordell Hull, October 16, 1933, *FRUS: V,* p. 487.

44. Sumner Welles to Cordell Hull, October 13, 1933, 837.00/4193, DS/RG 59.

45. "Memorandum of Telephone Conversation between Secretary of State Hull and Welles," September 5, 1933, 837.00/3757, DS/RG 59.

46. Sumner Welles to Cordell Hull, September 7, 1933, 837.00/3778, DS/RG 59.

47. Harold L. Ickes, *The Secret Diaries of Harold L. Ickes,* 3 vols. (New York, 1953–54), I, p. 87.

48. Cordell Hull, *The Memoirs of Cordell Hull,* 2 vols. (New York, 1948), I, p. 313.

49. Sumner Welles to Cordell Hull, October 5, 1933, 837.00/4136, DS/RG 59.

50. "Memorandum of Conversation between Secretary Hull at Washington and Ambassador Welles at Habana, by Telephone," September 9, 1933, 837.00/3939, DS/RG 59.

51. Sumner Welles to Cordell Hull, October 5, 1933, 837.00/4131, DS/RG 59.

52. Sumner Welles to Cordell Hull, October 16, 1933, 837.00/4206, DS/RG 59.

53. Sumner Welles to Cordell Hull, October 4, 1933, 837.00/4131, DS/RG 59.

54. Ibid.

55. Sumner Welles to Cordell Hull, October 7, 1933, 837.00/4146, DS/RG 59.

56. Sumner Welles to Cordell Hull, October 29, 1933, 837.00/4301, DS/RG 59.

57. Sumner Welles to Cordell Hull, December 5, 1933, 837.00/4475, DS/RG 59.

58. Jefferson Caffery to William Phillips, January 13, 1934, 837.00/4605, DS/RG 59.

3

Elected by Providence: Spruille Braden in Argentina in 1945

Albert P. Vannucci

A startling reference to Juan Perón as "the son of an American ambassador" was heard at a recent conference.[1] There is indeed a fairly widespread perception that the beginning of the extraordinary career of this most important of modern Argentine political figures was vitally nurtured, if not actually sired, by the U.S. diplomat Spruille Braden. The view is that, but for Braden's machinations against him, Perón might not have been able to capture the imagination and admiration of his fellow Argentines with such tenacity and longevity.

Braden served as U.S. ambassador to Argentina for only three months. He was then called to Washington to be assistant secretary of state for inter-American affairs. He was an influential actor in this capacity for about a year, before he and the policy he advocated fell into disfavor. He remained an additional ten months, before being publicly repudiated and retired. Despite the relative brevity of Braden's involvement in U.S. policy toward Argentina, his actions have passed into political folklore. As the British ambassador to Argentina at that time wrote, Braden arrived in Buenos Aires with "the fixed idea that he had been elected by Providence to overthrow the Farrell–Perón regime."[2]

The purpose of this chapter is twofold: to attempt to illuminate the reasons why Spruille Braden played such an active role in the internal developments of the country of his posting; and to elicit any lessons of current applicability for those entrusted with the care and advancement of U.S. relations with its sister American republics.

THE SETTING IN ARGENTINA

Spruille Braden had such an impact during his short stay partly because of the tumultuous state of political activity in the country at the time.

To understand Juan Perón's rise to power and Spruille Braden's contribution, it should be remembered that Argentina was then (as it remains
today) a country of enormous potential and ambition; it had experienced
extraordinary economic and social growth, unaccompanied by a commen-
surate level of political development.[3] Economic historians still marvel at the
"Argentine Miracle." For example, from 1860 to 1930, the population increased from 1.75 million to 11.6 million; productivity rose at an average
between 4.5 and 5.0 percent; and total capital increased at about 5 percent
a year.[4] However, even as late as 1943, politics remained dominated by a
few hundred Buenos Aires families.[5] Occupation of the presidency by Hi-
pólito Yrigoyen and his middle-class *Unión Cívica Radical* party from 1916
to 1930 did not represent either effective government or sustained political
development.

The watershed year was 1930, when the full impact of the world depression was realized. The middle-class government was discredited on all fronts.
It had taken no measures to meet the impact of the depression on the cities.
Graft and intervention flourished. The Conservatives conspired openly with
elements of the army.[6] On September 6, 1930, the military entered politics
overtly for the first time and removed the aged Yrigoyen. By means of a
"fraudulent" election,[7] it installed a Conservative government. Between 1932
and 1943, Argentina was "once again run almost exclusively for the benefit
of the landowning aristocracy."[8] This period came to be known as the "Era
of Infamy,"[9] because the military–conservative coalition members ensured
themselves victory at every election by "fraud, intimidation, or whatever
other means were necessary."[10]

The reversal to the pre-1916 political status quo occurred simultaneously
with the dramatic cessation of economic growth (largely due to the depression) and an end to population growth (due to "the elimination of overseas
immigration and the drastic reduction in the urban littoral birth rate."[11]) It
seems that, in every dimension—political, economic, and social—the great
growth of the preceding years was stopped in its tracks.[12] Rather, dynamism
became internalized, as the country attempted to accommodate the great
changes that had taken place. In every respect, the process of accommodation produced conflict.

Two of the most influential responses to the dislocations of the Great
Depression were a new industrialization and massive migration from the interior to the cities.[13] Each response posed problems that the Conservative
government was unable and unwilling to resolve.

To begin with, new industrialists emerged; they catered to the consumer-
goods market created by the upsurge in population and the rise of a middle
class. For them, economic survival entailed a radical departure from the
free-trade policies that had enriched the traditional industrialists who were
linked to food-processing industries. For the new industrialists, as Argentine
sociologist Torcuato di Tella observed,

it was a question of *Protección o Muerte.* The existing system was not prepared to give them the strong tariff protection they needed.[14]

The second response to the world depression—the migration to urban centers from the interior—was at least as disruptive to the ruling Conservatives.

The rural workers who flocked to the cities found themselves "transplanted in short order . . . transformed suddenly from rural peones, artisans, or persons with hardships into industrial workers . . . without at the same time finding the institutional channels necessary for integrating themselves into [their new environment]."[15] Once in the cities, they joined the officially unrecognized immigrant workers. For both, "politics [under the Conservatives] became increasingly divorced from economic and social reality."[16]

More significant than the cold shoulder that the urban worker got from the ruling oligarchy was the lack of any political alternatives. Gino Germani notes

the lack of a specific working-class party. . . . The predominant foreign origin of the workers and the high fluidity of the Argentine society had prevented the formation of a specific proletarian political tradition. Secondly, the attempt to demobilize the population and to return to limited democracy [that] occurred in the Thirties . . . contributed to crystallize the party system, preventing its readjustment to the new situation.[17]

World War II proved to be the catalyst for these explosive elements. At its outbreak, the Argentine economy was intimately connected with that of Great Britain, as it had been since independence. As di Tella has written, Argentina was "firmly controlled by an alliance between landed interests, exporting firms and British [interests]."[18]

For the early years of the war, the common basis of that alliance—trade with Britain—was seriously threatened by the succession of defeats suffered by the Allies. Perhaps more crucial in the long run was the succession of defeats that the troubled domestic politics delivered to the ambitious aspirations of the nation: As Arthur Whitaker, the dean of North American Argentinists, wrote of the period:

The nearest approach to a consensus that remained seems to have been in the widespread belief that the times were out of joint and that, sooner or later, and whether one wanted it or not, a drastic change was bound to come in an effort to set things right.[19]

On June 4, 1943, a group of army officers overthrew the government of Ramón Castillo. Colonel Juan D. Perón was a junior member of the 19-man *Grupo de Oficales Unidas* (GOU), which executed the coup. Occurring as it did in the midst of World War II, the true nature of this event was easily obscured. With benefit of hindsight, it is possible to say that, in the United States, consideration was never given to the crucial fact that "From top to bottom, Argentina in 1943 was indeed a fractured society."[20]

The coup provided the opportunity to address the country's great economic and social dislocations, and real progress was made in the areas of housing, tax reform, minimum wages, and medical assistance.[21] Unfortunately, progress in these areas was overshadowed by the failure to restructure the bankrupt political system. On the contrary, this coup ushered in a period of "tortuous political maneuvers,"[22] a "period rarely equaled . . . for civil–military intrigue and political confusion."[23]

Since before the 1943 coup and lasting long after all the Axis powers had surrendered, U.S. foreign policy was predicated on two assumptions: that the governments of Argentina were collaborating with the Axis, and that the governments of Argentina were emulating the continental fascists. Although widespread, these axioms were held most fervently by Secretary of State Cordell Hull and his protégé Spruille Braden. It is beyond the scope of this study to examine the many elements that both supported and refuted these two charges, but the most important can be summarized here.

Argentina was indeed the last country in the hemisphere to break relations with the Axis; it delayed almost two years after most of the other countries had done so.[24] As a result, Argentina was the last country from which Axis diplomats could send communications; the last base from which Axis espionage could be conducted under cover of diplomatic immunity; and the last country that allowed pro-Axis publications, individuals, and companies to function overtly. In these respects, Argentina's extended neutrality was an undeniable aid to the Axis.

However, to conclude that the governments in Buenos Aires were Axis collaborators required that a mountain of conflicting evidence be denied— including the following: Argentina—exclusively—supplied the Allies with such critical materials as tungsten, fats, leather, and oils, for the duration of the war; Argentina provided crucial wheat, corn, and meat to the United Kingdom; Argentina had a long history of following an independent foreign policy, adhering to neutrality in great power disputes, and resisting U.S. leadership of the hemisphere; Argentina was the only Latin state to be excluded from Lend-Lease—one basis for a massive buildup by its rival Brazil—and, while the Argentines may have explored arms procurements from Germany to balance the U.S. effort in Brazil, they actually received not a single item of armament from the Axis, from the beginning to the end of the war; and, finally, Argentine measures against Axis influence and interests were not much weaker than those of a score of other Latin governments—including that of the close U.S. ally, Getúlio Vargas in Brazil.

So, too, the charge that Argentina was emulating the political systems of the Axis countries was a combination of undeniable facts, avoidable misperceptions, and a tendency to view developments in Latin America in terms of what was happening in Europe. Certainly, the continuous state of siege; the actions against political parties, state governments, critics, and the press; and the increased military spending were ominous, when viewed from the perspective of the previous decade in Europe. But mitigating evidence was formidable, including: periodic suspensions of press restrictions, during which the governments were severely criticized; a highly independent judiciary, which often frustrated the governments' actions; and obvious confusion on the part of the inexperienced military officers who were attempting to govern a country in the midst of a long-overdue social revolution. As for most of those actions taken by Perón that were so offensive to Spruille Braden, they seem to have come from a ransacking of Argentine history. In Whitaker's assessment:

he found in Rosas his slogan of discipline and order, and the strong-arm squads of the Majorca to support it; in Rosas and Irigoyen a fervent nationalism spiced with anti-imperialism; in Irigoyen the popularity of attacks on the oligarchy; in Uriburu the Army's mission of national regeneration; and in the Conservative Restoration the demoralization of the chief political parties and the abandonment of laissez-faire in favor of economic controls.[25]

None of these observations is meant to justify all that occurred in Argentina after 1943 or to deny the unsavory aspects of Juan Perón's rule. However, they do suggest that the attempt to explain away all that occurred as part of a plan to copy a fascist model was simplistic.

Finally, every count in the indictment against Argentina was equally applicable to many other Latin governments of that era. At a time when the Argentine press was enjoying relative freedom to hurl broadsides at the government, the press in Paraguay, Bolivia, Haiti, Honduras, El Salvador, the Dominican Republic, and Ecuador were "severely restricted,"[26] and Brazil's Department of Press and Propaganda was described as "a full-fledged Ministry of Propaganda, patterned . . . on Dr. Joseph Goebbel's well-known model."[27] For varying lengths of time during this period, states of siege were imposed by the governments of Chile, Colombia, and Brazil. The five-year state of siege in Argentina from 1941 to 1946 was reprehensible, but the eight-year state of siege in Brazil (1937–45) was certainly not less so.[28] Similarly, Argentina's meddling in the affairs of its weaker neighbors was an outrage, but what about Mexico's conduct in Central America?[29] Nor was Argentina's the only government to deal harshly with communists. Brazil, too, outlawed the Communist party. Its leader there, Luís Carlos Prestes, was elevated to the status of martyr by repeated imprisonments; and the mere hint of communist sympathy was sufficient for periodicals and organizations to be suppressed,[30] and for demonstrators to be run over by police.[31]

Quite clearly, the United States could have justified a very different policy than it pursued for most of the period under study. The search to understand why Spruille Braden was such an ardent champion of a negative interpretation of developments in Argentina points to several organizational and personality factors: his identification with—and then leadership of—one faction within the State Department; his closed belief system on the subject of Perón; and his inflexible image of Argentina.

ORGANIZATIONAL FACTORS

Spruille Braden arrived at his post in Buenos Aires at the end of May 1945. He brought with him 13 years of diplomatic service in Latin America in varied positions, including two ambassadorial postings—the most recent to Cuba. During these years, he had become closely identified with one faction within the State Department—a group centered on Secretary of State Cordell Hull. This factiousness was the cause of considerable friction within the U.S. government; and Braden's association was both ideological and personal. It seems that at times, Braden participated in the feuding with relish and that, at other times, he got caught up in it unintentionally.

The Roosevelt administration was an incredible collection of the most diverse interests in the country. It included not only old-line party leaders—such as Cordell Hull—and representatives of banking, big business, and Wall Street law firms—like Henry Morgenthau and Henry Stimson—but also socialists—such as Henry Wallace—and intellectuals and experimenters—like Sumner Welles. This menagerie was held together by personal loyalty to Roosevelt and by a sense of crusading mission—at first, to restore the country to economic health and, later, to save the world from the fascist menace. Over a government full of latent conflict, Roosevelt presided in a manner that only aggravated the situation. His penchant for playing one man or department against another is now well-known.

The government agency most responsible for the conduct of foreign policy was also the center of the greatest confusion. In the five-year period between the June 1943 coup in Argentina and Braden's repudiation and ouster at State, there were four secretaries of state, five assistant secretaries in charge of Latin American affairs, and four ambassadors to Argentina.[32] In every instance but one, each new appointee attempted to reverse his predecessor's Argentine policy or at least, to modify the previous position on Latin America.[33] Perhaps the State Department's greatest obstacle was the fact that it was not allowed to serve its function. Partly as a result of the wars (World War II and then the Cold War), partly because of the methods of government preferred by Roosevelt and Truman, and partly because of its own inertia, State had to share the conduct of foreign policy with a great many other offices and departments. Dean Acheson wrote that the State Department was not only unprepared for war but "it never did seem to find its place."[34] It is certainly true that the most aggressive men in the government—such as Morgenthau, Jones, and Wallace—sought to assume functions that were ordinarily performed by State, whenever the opportunity presented itself. In the words of one irate Foreign Service officer, "[it] became a fad in Washington for every agency to have a hand in cooking the stew, so to speak, of foreign policy."[35] Not without some justification, Secretary of War Stimson believed that all the other departments should defer to his.[36]

But it was the presence of Cordell Hull, who was at the helm of the State Department for 11 years, that accounted for much of the department's decline in influence. Hull was selected in 1933 and retained until 1944 because of his enormous influence with Congress, where he had become one of the two or three most powerful members. Hull was never either a confidant or close advisor to Roosevelt. He did not sit in on meetings about military matters; he did not attend the Casablanca, Cairo, or Teheran Conferences; he did not participate in military discussions with Churchill; and he was never told about the atomic bomb.[37] Acheson did not exaggerate when he said, "The senior Cabinet officer became one of the least influential members at the White House."[38] In July 1943, Hull confessed to Henry Morgenthau, "The President runs foreign affairs. I don't know what is going on."[39]

One of the few things that Hull did know about was U.S. policy in Latin America. Given the urgency and weight of the other pressing matters, it is understandable that Roosevelt gave his Latin American policy almost no consideration and that his closest advisors gave it only little more. Hull, on the other hand, had carved out this area and a few others—most notably the advancement of reciprocal trade agreements—as his special concern. And, as a profile at that time observed, "In his chosen fields . . . Hull has tenaciously followed his own bent."[40] In Latin America, his "bent" was to promote the Good Neighbor Policy, for the establishment of which he took credit. That policy contained three elements: a U.S. pledge of nonintervention; a U.S. promise not to interfere in the domestic politics of the Latin countries; and U.S. expectation of reciprocity in exchange for its abandonment of intervention and interference. After Pearl Harbor, "reciprocity" came to mean assistance to the United States in the war effort. Argentina was clearly the most unenthusiastic Allied collaborator in the hemisphere, and this violation of the Good Neighbor Policy (as Hull saw it) brought forth all of the considerable anger and resentment that he could muster. As a result, Hull was the single most persistent advocate of a policy of coercion against Argentina. Economic sanctions, the rebuff of an overture from the Argentine foreign minister, the suspension of diplomatic relations, an eviscerating statement issued by President Roosevelt in September 1944, and countless other public and private denunciations were all Hull's doing. Roosevelt gave Hull considerable freedom to do as he liked in Argentina. In the words of one middle-level Foreign Service officer who served in both Buenos Aires and Washington, "Mr. Roosevelt more or less gave Argentina to Mr. Hull to play with, to keep him out of his hair."[41]

Yet, even before Hull's resignation at the end of 1944, there were opposing voices in Washington and a brief period of reconciliation after Argentina broke relations with the Axis in January 1944. The reason was that, even in those few areas that Roosevelt left to Hull's discretion, the secretary of state was not sole master. Sumner Welles, assistant secretary of state from 1934 to September 1943, also considered himself an architect of the Good Neighbor Policy; and Latin America was also one of his principal areas of interest. Welles placed a different emphasis on the components of the Good Neighbor Policy. Partly as a result of a disastrous experience when—as ambassador to Cuba in 1933—he had recommended interference,[42] Welles's position was that noninterference was a first and absolute prerequisite— from which reciprocity would follow.[43] In the face of Argentine intransigence, Hull was much less meticulous about preserving noninterference; and the two clashed head-on. It is difficult to say whether policy or personal differences first caused the rift between the two men; but, by the time of the June 1943 coup in Argentina, they were irreconcilable. Unlike Hull, Welles was an old and trusted friend of the president; he usually bypassed Hull to deal directly with the White House.[44] Hull grew bitter over what he considered Welles's disloyalty.[45] The result was that

the Department became divided into Welles men, who looked to the Under Secretary, particularly in the Latin American field, and Hull men, who sought guidance from the chief. . . . It poisoned the Department.[46]

Spruille Braden entered diplomatic service in 1933, the same year that Cordell Hull became secretary of state. By the time of the June 1943 coup in Argentina, Braden was well-known as a "Hull man."[47] In addition to shared views on the proper course of U.S. policy, Braden may have felt a responsibility to carry on the Hull line when, in November 1944, the secretary resigned at the age of 72, in ill health and broken spirits. This may have been especially so because Under Secretary of State Edward Stettinius, Jr., was chosen to succeed Hull—because "the President likes to be his own Secretary of State, and what he wanted was merely a good clerk."[48] Stettinius, who had been the boy wonder of big business, proved to be less successful as secretary of state. He has been politely described as "a decent man of considerable innocence,"[49] and—more bluntly—as being "as near zero as I think you can come."[50]

Although he, too, shared Hull's view, Stettinius suffered from indecision and from a large and powerful opposition. He went to both the Inter-American Conference on Problems of War and Peace in Mexico City (Chapultepec) and the UN San Francisco Conference determined to at least maintain

Argentina's isolation, if not increase it, and concluded each meeting having succumbed to the other Latin governments' demand for Argentina's inclusion. Among his problems, Stettinius had to contend with his assistant secretary of inter-American affairs, Nelson Rockefeller, with whom he was not on good terms. Rockefeller espoused Welles's position that even the hint of coercion was to be avoided at all cost, because it was counterproductive and a violation of the spirit of the Good Neighbor Policy.[51] The differences between the secretary and the assistant secretary came to a head during the San Francisco conference, producing a disagreement within the U.S. delegation that was described as "violent."[52]

U.S.–Argentine relations at the time of Braden's appointment were the most cordial that they had been since the June 1943 coup. Reflecting the differences in world views within the U.S. government, U.S. policy toward Argentina had changed no fewer than five times in the intervening two years. Periods of public praise and friendly gestures, invariably of short duration, were followed by virulent criticisms and hostile acts. In March 1945, U.S. policy was in its fifth phase. Succumbing to the united position of all the other countries in attendance at the conference in Chapultepec, Washington accepted precisely the kind of compromise that it had dismissed only weeks before. A unanimous resolution invited Argentina to sign the Act of Chapultepec and offered it full restoration to the inter-American community, if it declared war on the Axis and signed the Declaration of the United Nations.[53] Argentina immediately expressed its intention of complying with the recommendation and, in rapid succession, took all the suggested steps. In turn, the United States lifted its economic sanctions; sent a special mission to discuss joint prosecution of the war; concluded a collaboration agreement between the two navies; insisted that Argentina be seated at the United Nations Organization meeting in San Francisco—to the great annoyance of its Soviet war partner—and announced that it would name a new ambassador to fill the position left vacant, for almost a year, as a sign of displeasure.

The principal reason for this rapprochement was the collective pressure of the unified Latin governments and the desire of the United States to have a solid hemisphere front. Throughout this period, the Latin governments declined to share the U.S. view of Argentina as a hemisphere problem. Rather, they consistently defined it as a U.S.–Argentine feud and, more importantly, they chose to side with Argentina. At every opportunity, they sought to undermine U.S. sanctions and to champion Argentina's case. The reasons for this included the historical resentment of the United States, coupled with a newly perceived U.S. economic and political discrimination in favor of Europe. There was an ill-defined—but nonetheless strongly held—belief that the Latin countries were mere expendable pawns in a game in which all the important pieces were far away on the board. In addition, Latin governments suffered severe economic dislocation (with political ramifications) caused by the war and their contribution to it, and they found the United States unreceptive to even discussing their problems at inter-American meetings. Finally, they suspected a policy that singled out Argentina for ostracism—ostensibly because its government was oppressive and undemocratic—yet looked benevolently on the governments of Vargas in Brazil, Trujillo in the Dominican Republic, and Somoza in Nicaragua.[54]

The rapidly progressing reconciliation came to an end when Braden arrived in Argentina. Indeed, his three months there—plus the following months when he was assistant secretary—marked a new low point in relations. Braden was the most passionate architect of a new policy of coercion that exceeded any previous one in intensity.

Spruille Braden offered a sharp contrast both to the vacillating manner in which Stettinius pursued policy and to the direction of Rockefeller's policy. Braden brought with him a reputation as a blunt-speaking and ardent proponent of the Cordell Hull view of inter-American relations. Shortly before his selection, while ambassador to Cuba, he had sent a long memorandum calling for the United States to be "exacting and demand[ing]" in its dealings with "dictatorships and disreputable governments in the other American Republics."[55] In his memoirs, subtly titled *Diplomats and Demagogues,* Braden revealed the way in which he viewed the government in Argentina when he said that he was surprised to be offered the post because "they knew I was far from being an appeaser."[56] It has been speculated that Rockefeller may have sought to quiet his critics "by appointing a diplomat with a forceful reputation while retaining control of policy himself."[57] If so, Braden was a poor choice. From the moment of his arrival, he offered his own very different assessment of the situation. After only a few days in the country, he cabled that

So long as Perón and his military remain in control of this country we are faced with a fundamental policy issue, importance of which cannot be exaggerated. Appeasement will be fatal and we must rigidly stand on our principles.[58]

A few days later, he elaborated:

It is imperative for the security of [the] U.S.A. that other American Republics [be] in hands of friendly cooperative governments. . . . As Cordell Hull stated in memorandum [of] . . . October 2, 1944: the Nazi–Fascist movement "entrenched in Argentina is in a position to build up its strength and to prepare for future aggression. . . . Its poison will spread to other countries as we shall be confronted in not too far distant future with major threat to whole structure of post-war international security." . . . These . . . statements are as true today as when written. Perón as the one outstanding leader now on [the] Argentine scene is embodiment of present Fascist military control. . . . Elimination of Perón . . . would be a big step forward. . . . I feel that . . . our firm policy [should] specifically [be] a) no military cooperation or material be given Argentina; b) economic assistance be restricted . . . until such time as Nazi militaristic control of this country has been replaced by a constitutional and cooperating democracy. For us to fail to pursue this course would be to betray our guiding principles.[59]

To advance his objective, Braden embarked on a remarkable campaign that was targeted at audiences in the United States, as well as in Argentina. In his very first meeting with the press after arriving at his new post, Braden announced that his government had recognized the government of General Edelmiro Farrell "through necessity and not by choice" and that "we would like to see democratic Governments established everywhere."[60] In one of his first telegrams to Washington, Braden requested that the Foreign Economic Administration slow down the processing of export licenses for Argentina,[61] because "so long as Perón and military remain in control of this country . . . appeasement would be fatal."[62]

As the self-appointed leader of those who opposed Perón—"the real democrats," in Braden's assessment—the ambassador delivered a series of highly critical speeches "almost like a political candidate" himself.[63] He sought to enlist the cooperation of U.S. companies doing business in Argentina "to allow their Argentine employees free time to participate in Anti-Perónist demonstrations."[64] And most significantly, he sought to drive a wedge between Perón and his fellow army officers, by reversing the decision to relax the arms embargo. He also advanced this wedge by loudly—and successfully—calling for postponement of the scheduled inter-American defense meeting at Rio de Janeiro, because of the unacceptability of a Perón-dominated government as party to a mutual security treaty.[65] C. A. MacDonald has written that, clearly, Braden's objective was a military–civilian ouster of Perón; he cites the comment from Braden that "if some civilians could get the Navy and Air Force together they might get somewhere . . . if somebody started something we should recognize any revolutionary government and give them any help we can."[66] MacDonald also reports that his research in the British Foreign Office Archives uncovered evidence of suspicions in London that Braden went beyond mere rhetoric in urging the overthrow of Perón and that he was directly involved in the abortive military–naval conspiracy uncovered just after Braden left Buenos Aires.[67]

In all, Braden delivered an extraordinary volley during his three months in the country. Did his activity constitute an important determinant of the events at the time? Clearly, his term did see a dramatic deterioration in Perón's position. Before his arrival, the "tortuous political maneuvers" inside the country had quieted. Perón had risen to occupy the vice-presidency and head of the War Ministry. These positions were in addition to running the Labor Secretariat—the vehicle by which he had forged Argentina's first working-class mass movement, which would lead to a radical restructuring of political formations and the long-overdue social revolution. In both Buenos Aires and Washington, Perón was regarded as, in effect, the head of government. Yet, shortly after Braden's departure, Perón was ousted by a faction within the military. Sent into exile, he was retrieved by his "shirtless ones," who staged the famous *Plaza de Mayo* demonstrations.

Perón returned, and enjoyed an unassailable political position for a decade. Even after his second ouster in 1955, he continued to hold a grip on the affections of millions of his countrymen. For a decade and a half, his was the most viable of all the civilian groupings. He returned for a third term as president in 1973.

It seems beyond dispute that the U.S. ambassador's activities in the summer of 1945 emboldened those who opposed Perón and who had been unable to effectively organize before Braden's arrival. When those newly galvanized forces made their move to oust Perón, they discovered how badly they had miscalculated the redistribution of power that had occurred. In his excellent study *Juan Perón and the Reshaping of Argentina,* Frederick Turner writes, "Juan Perón was far more than the most important leader of Argentina in the twentieth century. In many ways, he was a prototypical figure of this century. His ideals were far grander than his lasting achievements. . . . One of the continuing appeals of Perónism was that it had a heart, not just a head, that it was concerned with people and their needs in the present. . . . Whatever the impact of rising expectations in other nations, Perón profoundly stimulated them in Argentina, and in doing so he lastingly reshaped his country."[68] Ironically, Ambassador Braden was recalled and promoted for his misperceptions of what Perón's emergence actually constituted. It was almost two years before his extraordinarily inaccurate assessments would catch up with him and result in his public repudiation and retirement.

It is interesting to speculate about what might have happened, had Braden not played the role that he did. U.S.–Argentine relations were clearly on the mend, when he took up his post. He led the United States into a very bitter and, ultimately, failed campaign of hostility. In the end, it was the U.S. government that repudiated his policies and ended them. Braden was dismissed, and Perón was courted. Within two months of Braden's departure, the much-postponed Inter-American Defense Conference was convened in Rio de Janeiro; an important mutual security defense pact was signed by all the Latin countries, including Argentina. The following month, the United States supported Argentina in its successful bid for a seat in the UN Security Council.[69] By November, rapprochement was complete. General Willis Crittenberger, chief of the U.S. Caribbean Defense Command, visited Argentina as a guest of the War Ministry and received a decoration from Perón.[70] That same month, the U.S. ambassador, James Bruce, referred to Perón as "a great leader of a great nation" and described U.S.–Argentine relations as "excellent."[71]

Braden may have acted as if elected by Providence, but Perón was actually elected by the Argentine people. The latter proved to be the more significant mandate.

PERSONALITY FACTORS

The search for explanations of Braden's behavior point to an examination of idiosyncratic variables in foreign policymaking: the personal animosities, closed belief systems, inflexible national images, and dysfunctional personality traits of leading foreign policymakers.

To a very wide extent, the image of Argentina held by Braden and other U.S. policymakers (and a large part of the U.S. public, as well) was that of "the bad boy of the Good Neighborhood." [72] Consistent with Boulding's observation that "the national image is essentially a historical image," [73] the negative U.S. image of Argentina certainly had solid historical bases. Opposition to U.S. leadership of the hemisphere was a consistent and major Argentine foreign policy objective, since the very beginning of U.S. hegemonic efforts.

This inflexible image not only prevented experimenting with policies that might have secured Argentine friendship and the desired cooperation, but actually encouraged Argentina to behave in the obstructionist manner that was consistent with its national image. It seems almost as if key policymakers purposely set about to ensure Argentine antagonism. As Under Secretary of State Stettinius proudly reported to President Roosevelt,

the exclusion of Argentina from the UNRRA [United Nations Relief and Rehabilitation Administration] meetings, from Bretton Woods, from the Aviation Conference, from the discussions of the Dumbarton Oaks conclusions, and the rumors that a Meeting of Foreign Ministers might soon be called without her participation, have hurt and hurt badly. . . . Our lend-lease policy and our refusal to permit exports for new Argentine development projects have resulted in a tremendous advantage for Brazil in the[ir] race for primacy. [74]

The chargé d'affaires in Buenos Aires wired that the government in Argentina was surprisingly "passive . . . in the face of the . . . buffeting it has received from the United States . . . the United States' affronts to its dignity, sovereignty, etc." [75] The result of acting as if Argentine intransigence were both inevitable and irreversible may well have been to encourage Argentina in behaving just that way.

The self-fulfilling quality of a strongly held negative national image was evident every time the United States pursued a coercive line. Shortly after the June 1943 coup, for instance, when the United States not only refused to discuss arms shipments but presented the new government with a list of demands, the result was to increase the already chaotic conditions within the junta, to dishearten the faction that favored closer ties to the United States, and to ensure that the new leaders would approach the Germans for arms. When President Ramírez sounded out German representatives, he told them that "the tone in which the North American ambassador had presented his demands had made his blood boil." [76] The result of Hull's scathing rebuff of Foreign Minister Storni's request for help was to create "the prevailing idea [that] . . . the United States refused our friendship so we must show them that we are strong enough to cause quite a lot of trouble." [77] When Ramírez's break of relations with the Axis received an indifferent response in the United States, Perón told the Chilean military attaché that

after the failure of Storni, Ramírez and other Argentines . . . to reach an accord with the United States and to have their proposals meet only cold reception[s], no Argentine from now on would dare make any future propositions since they would inevitably lead to the same negative results and would cause his own downfall. [78]

Similarly, the effect in Buenos Aires of the "Blue Book" prepared by Braden after his return to Washington was that the "Cabinet . . . discussed at length [an] immediate break in relations with the United States" and the formerly pro-U.S. foreign minister, Juan Cooke, became "utterly furious. . . . [He] supported [the proposed] break [with the United States] and . . . he is now going all out in a series of communiqués to refute our charges and to smear [the] United States *in return.*" [79] In his inimitable style, Juan Perón summarized the counterproductivity of this negative image of Argentina: "You may if you wish cut off the head of a hen and then eat it," Perón told a U.S. banker, "but you cannot compel a hen to lay an egg against its will." [80]

A second and related idiosyncratic variable that helps to explain the U.S. policy toward Argentina is the degree to which the belief systems of key policymakers were open or closed. Without replicating Olé Holsti's complicated study of John Foster Dulles's belief system and national image of the Soviet Union, [81] there appear to be many similarities with the belief systems and national image of Argentina that were held by Cordell Hull and Spruille Braden. In both cases, there are the same three assumed dichotomies: the good people versus their bad leaders; the good national interest versus the bad international movement; and the good state versus the bad party in control. For instance, in Cordell Hull's *Memoirs* (in a chapter titled "The Bad Neighbor") he wrote,

to me, the tragedy of this situation lay in the fact, as I saw it, that the overwhelming majority of the Argentine people were wholeheartedly democratic, opposed the Axis at least in thought, and wanted no part of their country utilized by Axis agents to bring harm to the United Nations. But over them was a Government determined to rule by any methods in dictatorial fashion. [82]

In a memo to FDR, Hull referred to that government as "the present military gang in control of Argentina." [83]

British Ambassador Kelly believed that Hull "became obsessed with the conviction that [Argentine military leaders] were Nazi agents aiming at the

Nazification of the whole of South America."[84] The effects of such beliefs upon U.S. policy were strong.

On the subject of Argentina, Hull's belief system was as negative and closed as Dulles's on the Soviet Union; maybe they both tended to interpret the very information that might have led them to change the model in such a way as to preserve it intact.[85] A similar conclusion could be made about Spruille Braden. As quoted above, only days after his arrival in Buenos Aires, Braden manifested the preconceived notions with which he assumed his new post.

Like Hull, Braden was confident that he knew both the real sentiments of the Argentine people and the true character of their political leaders. With no apparent trepidation, Braden reported that, "so long as Perón dominates [the] Army it is difficult to see what [the] Argentine public (majority of which I am convinced hate this regime) can do."[86] Of Perón, Braden made the detached assessment that "in his insane ambition he will fight like a cornered wild animal and is capable of anything (repeat anything)"[87] and also that

He has bit in teeth [and] is determined to go his way. . . . He has no conception of democratic system and his Fascist mentality is further evidenced by [the] fact, as he reiterated several times in our last interview, he genuinely feels he "has reason" on his side.[88]

Finally, Braden repeatedly demonstrated the kind of inflexibility characteristic of a closed belief system. In the midst of the electoral campaign and at a time when Farrell and Perón were making a serious effort to create better relations with the United States, Braden reported that

It is the conviction, with which I entirely concur, of all . . . opposition groups that Perón and clique are fundamentally Fascist. . . . Presently we have a clear case against the Argentine Government which may be measurably weakened with the passage of time if Perón is permitted to carry out his plan of ostensible but spurious compliance with [the] Mexico City and San Francisco obligations. It is therefore urgent to thwart Perón's plan and give the opposition . . . a chance.[89]

As if uncertain that his message had gotten across, three days later he repeated

It is my conviction . . . that the fundamental point to remember is that Perón, with his clique, is Fascist-minded dictator who will not change his spots even though he may shift tactics.[90]

A related factor, which may partially explain Braden's thinking, involves a longstanding issue within the Foreign Service. As C. A. MacDonald has observed,

The one possibility which Braden never accepted was that Perón might win a free election. This reflected received opinion amongst the ambassador's Argentine friends, the old political elite with whom he associated exclusively. He overlooked the significance of Perón's social programme and his links with organized labour.[91]

Braden came to government service fully credentialed to meet the description of the U.S. diplomatic corps as composed of "members of the upper classes . . . with degrees from Ivy League colleges."[92]

Other personality characteristics also played a role. Cordell Hull has been described as "a man of moral fervor,"[93] "a Southern Puritan, who believed in citing the Old Testament and the War of the Secession as means of solving contemporary problems,"[94] and

a doctrinaire liberal who believed it his duty to act according to the Wilsonian principle that Latin America communities should be taught to elect good governments and should, additionally, be conscripted into the American crusade against fascism.[95]

In May 1944, when the only certainty about the Argentine political scene was its confusion, Hull sent this cable to most of the U.S. Latin envoys:

Every informed person must agree that the present regime in Argentina by word and deed has demonstrated that it is inclined toward the Axis. . . . I cannot conceive how any supporter of the Allied cause can consider for a moment extending recognition or material encouragement to that regime.[96]

Four months later, when the situation was no less uncertain, Hull described

his bitter disappointment that the Argentine Government had been seized by force by Fascists and other dangerous elements at such a critical moment for the hemisphere. He said that . . . if we who have kept pure the ideals of fair play and cooperation do not continue to refuse to recognize those who have not, it will be the end of Pan Americanism.[97]

In their study of Woodrow Wilson, the Georges found the key to their subject's exercise of power in his compelling need to counter feelings of inadequacy.[98] They found that, when Wilson's self-esteem was at stake, he became emotionally involved and completely preoccupied with the chosen struggle that he had personalized.[99] There is evidence that Hull may have acted similarly. As noted, U.S. Latin policy was one of the very few areas that he had reserved for his special attention and that was also of relatively minor interest to the president. Hull's belief system included the tenet that Argentina was "a deserter who had not requested forgiveness";[100] but his conduct of a coercive policy was repeatedly frustrated by the lack of cooperation from the British, the reluctance of the other Latin countries, the opposition of Sumner Welles and those who agreed with him, and Hull's own lack of influence in the White House. There was ample reason for Hull to see Argentina's independent foreign policy as a rejection of "his" Good Neighbor Policy;[101] and there was more than a hint of emotional involvement when he told British Ambassador Halifax, "If my Government . . . should hesitate or falter . . . in carrying forward its known program of penalties against the Argentine . . . the United States would be discredited in the eyes of all countries."[102] There is repeated evidence that the entire issue of U.S.–Argentine relations may have been as emotional for Hull as the League of Nations was for Wilson. With amazing overstatement, Hull described the recognition of the Farrell government and its admission to the UN conference at San Francisco (which occurred shortly after his resignation as Secretary of State):

There was . . . an incipient, quietly conducted movement on the part of a few business interests, politicians, and marplots in this and other countries of the hemisphere to restore Argentina to full fellowship and diplomatic relations with the other American Republics. . . . From my hospital bed I talked frequently over the telephone with [Secretary of State] Stettinius at San Francisco and kept alive my original contention that Argentina had not yet made herself worthy of being a member of the Organization. . . . My position was that Argentina, before being admitted to the United Nations . . . should make full apology. . . . Early in 1945, the leaders of the opposition to [my] ideas were riding a high horse, and they succeeded by devious methods in securing admission of Argentina to the San Francisco Conference. . . . To me, the hasty recognition of the Farrell regime . . . and [its] admission to . . . the U.N. . . . was the most colossal injury done to the Pan American movement in all its history.[103]

One element in Hull's response to the trying developments in Argentina must have been his temperament. Dean Acheson described it this way:

Suspicious by nature, he brooded over what he thought were slights and grievances, which more forthright handling might have set straight. His brooding led, in accordance with Tennessee-mountain tradition, to feuds. His hatreds were implacable—not hot hatreds, but long cold ones. In no hurry to "get" his enemy, "get" him he usually did.[104]

Indeed, Hull opened his *Memoirs* by relating with admiration how his father pursued across the country—and finally murdered—the man who had wounded him years before in a Civil War battle.[105] The U.S. counsellor of embassy for economic affairs in Buenos Aires in 1943–44 later expressed the opinion that

Hull's . . . policy towards Argentina . . . was a regular old Tennessee feud, and every time he could sneak around the tree and see an Argentine in the sights of his musket he'd let go at him. It really became a personal vendetta, nothing more and nothing less.[106]

Writing in 1946, Arthur Schlesinger, Jr., observed that, during Hull's last year in office,

[he] was increasing sick and querulous, a tired old man propelled by his consuming hatreds for the Argentines and for Sumner Welles. Latin American diplomats still recall his outbursts of invective when they tried to discuss Argentina with him.[107]

John Morton Blum, the editor of Henry Morgenthau's *Diaries,* believed that Hull had "developed an 'almost psychopathic' anti-Argentine bias."[108]

Like Hull, Spruille Braden believed that "the Argentine Government is Fascist 'in every particular,' and that the United States has to take the leadership in solving the Argentine problem."[109] Even while he was an influential policymaker, Braden divided opinion. After his resignation was forced, the assessment of his policy and personality was almost unanimously negative. Dean Acheson, for example, who supported Braden during his last, beleaguered months at State, later said that

disillusion with my colleague Spruille Braden, well advanced by the end of the battle over intelligence, was completed by participation in his frustrating feud with Colonel Perón. . . . Braden was a bull of a man physically and with the temperament and tactics of one, dealing with the objects of his prejudices by blind charges, preceded by pawing up a good deal of dust.[110]

Braden's own memoirs provide a clue to both his personality and politics. The very first line of its Introduction reveals quite a lot about Braden's personality. He wrote, "To paraphrase Schopenhauer: if we were not all vain and so excessively interested in ourselves, life would be so dull none of us would be able to endure it."[111] In response to critics who found his performance in Buenos Aires and Washington to be high-handed and abrasive, Braden said: "I am reminded of the editorials that called me 'a bull in a china shop' . . . because I got tough with Perón, State Department appeasement of dictators having already become the official fashion."[112] His defense of his conduct reveals an interesting logic:

Sometimes we are accused unjustly of intervening, as I was while serving as ambassador in Buenos Aires. I was charged with speaking against Perón. . . . If this be intervention, so is every diplomatic utterance. And it will be a sad day indeed when a U.S. ambassador cannot defend and speak out for free, constitutional, representative government. Also it is fitting to observe that other governments, including those of some very small countries, often intervene in the domestic affairs of the U.S.[113]

The effect of these psychological variables upon policymakers was of clear import. The widely held negative image of Argentina and the closed belief systems and personality characteristics of key policy makers helped to shape policy by creating predispositions toward some courses of action and by eliminating others from consideration. As Hull himself recalled in his memoirs, "Had we sought a settlement with the Argentine Government we doubtless could have reached out."[114]

During his tenure as ambassador, Spruille Braden did not seek a resolution of the differences between the two governments. On the contrary, he worked diligently to preclude a reconciliation. For a multitude of reasons, he viewed it as his duty to assist—indeed, lead—an effort to remove the government to which he was posted. He failed in this immediate objective. Eventually, his interpretation of his responsibilities led to the end of his diplomatic career. His conduct remains significant for the still highly relevant questions that it raises for his successors.

NOTES

1. The comment was made on May 22, 1986, by Professor Enrique Menocal of Trenton State College during the Lauder Conference on International Studies and Languages for Management conducted by the University of Pennsylvania's Lauder Institute and the University's National Resource Center in International Studies for Management. Quoted here with permission.

2. Sir David Kelly, *The Ruling Few—or—The Human Background to Diplomacy* (London: Hollis and Carter, 1952), p. 307.

3. As the Argentine writer (and president) Domingo Sarmiento prophesied in 1888, "We shall reach the level of the United States. We shall be America as the sea is the ocean. We shall be the United States." Quoted in Thomas F. McGann, *Argentina, the United States and the Inter-American System 1880–1914* (Cambridge, Mass.: Harvard University Press, 1957), p. 61.

4. H. S. Ferns, *Argentina* (New York: Praeger, 1969), p. 121.

5. For a masterful treatment of Argentine economic history, see Carlos F. Diaz Alejandro, *Essays on the Economic History of the Argentine Republic* (New Haven: Yale University Press, 1970). Among the best general histories of the country are the following: James R. Scobie, *Argentina—A City and a Nation* (New York: Oxford University Press, 1964); Arthur P. Whitaker, *Argentina* (Englewood Cliffs, N.J.: Prentice-Hall, 1964); Peter H. Smith, *Argentina and the Failure of Democracy: Conflict among Political Elites, 1904–1955* (Madison: University of Wisconsin Press, 1974); Peter G. Snow, *Political Forces in Argentina* (Boston: Allyn and Bacon, 1971); David Rock, ed., *Argentina in the Twentieth Century* (London: Duckworth, 1975); and a new book by David Rock, *Argentina: 1516–1982: From Spanish Colonization to the Falklands War* (Berkeley: University of California Press, 1986).

6. Scobie, *Argentina*, p. 206.

7. Snow, *Political Forces*, p. 14.

8. Ibid.

9. Joseph R. Barager, ed., *Why Perón Came to Power; The Background to Perónism in Argentina* (New York: Alfred A. Knopf, 1968), p. 21.

10. Ibid.

11. Gino Germani, "The Transition to a Mass Democracy in Argentina," in *Contemporary Cultures and Societies of Latin America,* eds., Dwight Heath and Richard Adams (New York: Random House, 1965), p. 124.

12. It may be better to refer to the middle-class experiment in politics as a "great promise."

13. Ibid., p. 137.

14. Torcuato S. di Tella, "An Introduction to the Argentine System," in *Political Power in Latin America: Seven Confrontations,* eds. Richard R. Fagen and Wayne A. Cornelius, Jr. (Englewood Cliffs, N.J.: Prentice-Hall, 1970), pp. 110–11.

15. Germani, "Transition," p. 138.

16. Scobie, *Argentina,* p. 207.

17. Gino Germani, *Social Modernization and Economic Development in Argentina,* Report No. 70.6 (Geneva: UN Research Institute for Social Development, 1970), p. 69.

18. Di Tella, "Argentine System," p. 109.

19. Arthur P. Whitaker, "An Overview of the Period," in *Prologue to Perón: Argentina in Depression and War, 1930–1943,* eds. Mark Falcoff and Ronald H. Dolkart (Berkeley: University of California Press, 1975), p. 30.

20. Marvin Goldwert, *Democracy, Militarism, and Nationalism in Argentina, 1930–1966: An Interpretation* (Austin: University of Texas Press, 1972), p. 34.

21. Otis E. Milliken and Sarah E. Roberts, "Labor and Social Welfare," in *Inter-American Affairs, An Annual Survey,* ed. Arthur P. Whitaker No. 3: 1943, (New York: Columbia University Press, 1944), pp. 90 and 159–77.

22. Robert A. Potash, *The Army and Politics in Argentina, 1928–1945* (Stanford, Calif.: Stanford University Press, 1969), p. 240.

23. Ibid., p. 141. Argentina had six presidents in six years, during this period. This pattern of instability, like the pattern of military intervention into politics, became endemic as time went on. For example, Argentina had ten presidents in the ten years between 1973 and 1983.

24. Most of the Latin countries severed relations shortly after the Meeting of Consultation at Rio de Janeiro in January 1942, where a resolution recommending such action was passed. Argentina did so on January 26, 1944. Chile, the other holdout at the Rio meeting, did not break until January 19, 1943.

25. Whitaker, *The United States and Argentina.* (Cambridge, Mass.: Harvard University Press, 1954), p. 120.

26. U.S. Congress, House, "Inter-American Military Cooperation," Extension of Remarks of the Honorable Ellis E. Patterson, June 28, 1946, *Congressional Record,* 79th Cong., 2nd sess., 92, p. A3827.

27. Karl Lowenstein, *Brazil under Vargas* (New York: Russell and Russell, 1942), p. 238.

28. In a meeting with the German ambassador in June 1940, Brazil's President Getúlio Vargas "emphasized . . . his personal sympathy for the authoritarian states, referring . . . to the speech he recently made. [In an address delivered June 11, President Vargas had attacked 'the sterile demagogy of political democracy' and asked that virile peoples should remove the debris of old ideas.] He openly expressed his aversion to England and the democratic system." Prufer to Foreign Min-

istry, No. 518, Top Secret, June 21, 1940, *Documents on German Foreign Policy,* Vol. 9, p. 659.

29. In a letter to President Roosevelt in which Nicaragua's President Somoza pleaded for additional arms, he justified the request on the grounds that "the disturbed history of Central America gives testimony to the constant purpose of Mexico to exercise a direct influence in the life of these countries and in the organization of their Governments." Luis Somoza Debayle to Franklin D. Roosevelt, December 23, 1944, White House Central Files, Confidential File, Franklin D. Roosevelt Library, Hyde Park, N.Y., p. 2.

30. Frank McCann, Jr., *The Brazilian–American Alliance 1937–1945* (Princeton, N.J.: Princeton University Press, 1973), pp. 334–35.

31. New York *Times,* May 20, 1946, p. 20.

32. Cordell Hull was secretary of state from 1933 to November 1944, the longest tenure in that office's history. Edward Stettinius, Jr., served from November 1944 to June 1945. James Byrnes was secretary of state from June 1945 until January 1947, when he was replaced by General George Marshall. The assistant secretaries were: Sumner Welles from 1934 to August 1943; Edward Stettinius, Jr., until December 1944; Nelson Rockefeller to August 1945; and Spruille Braden until June 1947, when he was succeeded by Norman Armour. The ambassadors to Argentina were Norman Armour, Spruille Braden, George Messersmith, and James Bruce. There was an 11-month period after General Edelmiro Farrell became president when the United States had no ambassador in Argentina.

33. The only continuity was Bruce's maintenance of friendly relations with Perón, when Bruce succeeded Messersmith. As Lawrence Duggan observed, "The ship of state zigzagged; no one could tell with certainty where it was headed. The Latin American governments could not be sure that the man and the policy would be there tomorrow." Lawrence Duggan, *The Americas: The Search for Hemisphere Security* (New York: Henry Holt and Co., 1949), p. 102.

34. Dean Acheson, *Present at the Creation: My Years in the State Department* (New York: W.W. Norton, 1963), p. 38.

35. Merwin L. Bohan, oral history interview, June 15, 1974 (Independence, Mo.: Harry S. Truman Library, 1977), p. 8.

36. Stimson said, "The existence of a state of war radically revises the functions of a Secretary of War. . . . Suddenly his branch of Government becomes central. . . . It is inevitable. . . . In wartime the demands of the Army enter into every aspect of national life." Henry L. Stimson and McGeorge Bundy, *On Active Service in Peace and War* (New York: Harper & Brothers, 1947), p. 408.

37. Cordell Hull, *The Memoirs of Cordell Hull,* 2 vols. (New York: Macmillan, 1948), II, pp. 1109–10.

38. Acheson, *Present at the Creation,* p. 11.

39. John Morton Blum, *From the Morgenthau Diaries; Years of War 1941–1945* (Boston: Houghton Mifflin Co., 1967), pp. 241–42.

40. Robert Bendiner, "Who is the State Department? Cordell Hull, the Great Anachronism," *Nation* 155 (July 25, 1942):67.

41. Bohan, oral history interview, pp. 9–10. From 1942 to 1944, Merwin Bohan was counsellor of embassy for economic affairs in Buenos Aires. From 1945 to 1949, he held the same position in Mexico City.

42. Robert Bendiner, "Who is the State Department? The Old Welles and the New," *Nation* 155 (August 1, 1942):90.

43. Ironically, in 1933, it was Welles who repeatedly urged U.S. intervention in Cuba, and Hull who displayed reluctance. See Chapter 2.

44. Acheson, *Present at the Creation,* p. 12. Apparently, Roosevelt was not the only person who preferred to deal with Welles rather than Hull: "Diplomats, valuing his acute and precise comments, prefer discussions with him to those with his vaguer and somewhat rambling superior." Bendiner, "The Old Welles and the New," p. 88.

45. Hull, *Memoirs* II, p. 1230.

46. Acheson, *Present at the Creation,* p. 12. The forced resignation of Welles on August 26, 1943, and Hull's retirement 15 months later did not end the feud. Both continued to offer public assessments and generous advice to their followers left behind. For a full discussion of the divisions at State, see Randall Bennett Woods, *The Roosevelt Foreign Policy Establishment and the "Good Neighbors"* (Kansas City: Regents Press of Kansas, 1979).

47. In Hull's estimation, Braden was one of "the most expert persons in our service in Latin America." Hull, *Memoirs* I, p. 410.

48. Blum, *Morgenthau Diaries,* p. 392.

49. Charles E. Bohlen, *Witness to History 1929–1969* (New York: W.W. Norton, 1973), p. 166.

50. Bohan, oral history interview, p. 15.

51. Rockefeller was later told that Roosevelt had insisted on his appointment, over Stettinius's objection. Joe Alex Morris, *Nelson Rockefeller: A Biography* (New York: Harper & Brothers, 1960), p. 184. Henry Wallace reported that "Cordell Hull . . . was very disdainful of the way in which 'Little Rockefeller' had handled the Argentine situation. He indicated that Rockefeller from the very time he got in as Assistant Secretary had gone out of his way to appease Argentina. He referred to [him] . . . with . . . disgust." John Morton Blum, ed., *The Price of Vision: The Diary of Henry A. Wallace 1942–1946* (Boston: Houghton Mifflin Co., 1973), p. 456.

52. Beatrice Bishop Berle and Travis Beal Jacobs, ed., *Navigating the Rapids 1918–1971; From the Papers of Adolf A. Berle* (New York: Harcourt, Brace, Jovanovich, 1973), p. 532.

53. New York *Times,* March 6, 1945, p. 1.

54. For details of the Latin pressure on the United States during this time, see Albert P. Vannucci, "The Influence of Latin Governments on United States Foreign Policy: The Case of U.S.–Argentine Relations, 1943–1948," *Journal of Latin American Studies* 18 (November 1986): 355–82.

55. U.S. Department of State, Records of the Office of the American Republic Affairs, October 1945, quoted in Roger R. Trask, "Spruille Braden versus George Messersmith: World War II, the Cold War, and Argentine Policy, 1945–1947," *Journal of Interamerican Studies and World Affairs* 26 (February 1984):74.

56. Spruille Braden, *Diplomats and Demagogues—The Memoirs of Spruille Braden* (New Rochelle, N.Y.: Arlington House, 1971), p. 319.

57. C. A. MacDonald, "The Politics of Intervention: The United States and Argentina, 1941–1946" *Journal of Latin American Studies* 12 (1980):386.

58. Spruille Braden to James Byrnes, No. 1441, July 5, 1945, 711.35/7-545, *Foreign Relations of the United States, 1945,* Vol. 9, p. 389.

59. Spruille Braden to James Byrnes, No. 1498, July 11, 1945, 711.35/7-1145, *Foreign Relations of the United States, 1945,* Vol. 9, pp. 391–92.

60. New York *Times,* May 23, 1945, p. 9.

61. Spruille Braden to Edward Stettinius, Jr., No. 1111, May 31, 1945, 835.24/5-3145, *Foreign Relations of the United States, 1945,* Vol. 9, p. 537.

62. Braden to Byrnes, No. 1441.

63. MacDonald, "The Politics of Intervention," p. 386. His analysis refers to documents in the Messersmith Papers at the University of Delaware Library and the Berle Papers in the Roosevelt Library.

64. Ibid.

65. Ibid.

66. Ibid.

67. Ibid.

68. Frederick C. Turner and Jose Enrique Miguens, eds., *Juan Perón and the Reshaping of Argentina* (Pittsburgh: University of Pittsburgh Press, 1983), pp. 3, 6, and 243.

69. Memorandum by Ambassador William Dawson, IO Files: US/A/489, Secret, September 26, 1947, *Foreign Relations of the United States, 1947,* Vol. 1 (printed as Department of State Publication No. 8674, Washington, D.C.: Government Printing Office, 1973), p. 143.

70. New York *Times,* November 26, 1947, p. 8, and December 7, 1947, p. 27.

71. Ibid., November 5, 1947, p. 14.

72. Norman Armour to Sumner Welles, Strictly Confidential, December 24, 1942, 711.35/165, Record Group 59, State Decimal File, 1940–44, Box No. 1982, National Archives, p. 1. Even Dean Acheson, arguably one of the most able and sophisticated diplomats of recent U.S. history, was of the opinion that "Perón was a fascist and a dictator detested by all good men—except Argentineans." Acheson, *Present at the Creation,* p. 187.

73. Kenneth E. Boulding, "National Images and International Systems," *Journal of Conflict Resolution* III (June 1959):122.

74. Edward Stettinius, Jr., to Franklin D. Roosevelt, Secret, n.d., PSF Diplomatic Argentina, Box No. 32, President's Secretary's File, 1943–45, Roosevelt Library, p. 2.

75. Edward L. Reed to Cordell Hull, Confidential, October 7, 1944, No. 16317, Record Group 226, Box No. 739, National Archives, p. 4.

76. Potash, *Army and Politics in Argentina,* p. 220.

77. A. J. Drexel Biddle, Jr., to Cordell Hull, Strictly Confidential, No. 423, October 1, 1943, 835.00/1935-2011, Record Group 59, State Decimal File 1940–44, Box No. 4052, National Archives, p. 1. Biddle was the U.S. ambassador to Great Britain. He received this report from the chief of Polish political intelligence in Buenos Aires, via the Polish government in London.

78. Military Attaché (Johnson) Report from Chile, Secret, July 10, 1944, Military Intelligence Division, W.D.G.S., OSS, No. 84258, Record Group 226, Box No. 628, National Archives, p. 3.

79. Thomas D. Cabot to James Byrnes, Secret, No. 520, February 18, 1946, 835.00/2-1846, *Foreign Relations* 1946, Vol. XI, p. 218. Emphasis added.

80. Norman Armour to Cordell Hull, Confidential, No. 694, March 10, 1944,

711.35/221, Record Group 59, State Decimal File, 1940–1944, Box No. 1886, National Archives, p. 4.

81. Olé R. Holsti, "The Belief System and National Images: A Case Study," pp. 22–33 in William D. Coplin and Charles W. Kegley, Jr. (eds.), *Analyzing International Relations* (New York: Praeger, 1975).

82. Hull, *Memoirs* II, p. 1377.

83. Ibid., p. 1390.

84. Kelly, *The Ruling Few,* p. 297.

85. Holsti, "Belief System and National Images," p. 31.

86. Spruille Braden to James Byrnes, No. 1388, June 30, 1945, 711.35/6-3045, *Foreign Relations of the United States, 1945,* Vol. 9, p. 511.

87. Spruille Braden to James Byrnes, No. 1399, July 2, 1945, 711.35/7-245, *Foreign Relations of the United States, 1945,* Vol. 9, p. 513.

88. Spruille Braden to James Byrnes, No. 1445, July 5, 1945, 711.35/7-545, *Foreign Relations of the United States, 1945,* Vol. 9, p. 517.

89. Spruille Braden to James Byrnes, No. 2066, September 4, 1945, 835.00/9-445, *Foreign Relations of the United States, 1945,* Vol. 9, pp. 406–07.

90. Spruille Braden to James Byrnes, No. 2097, September 7, 1945, *Foreign Relations of the United States, 1945,* Vol. 9, p. 410.

91. MacDonald, "The Politics of Intervention," p. 387.

92. Charles K. Kegley, Jr., and Eugene R. Wittkopf, *American Foreign Policy: Pattern and Process,* 2nd ed (New York: St. Martin's Press, 1982), p. 357. After Braden's graduation from Yale, for example, he worked in his family's copper company in Chile.

93. Arthur M. Schlesinger, Jr., "Good Fences Make Good Neighbors," *Fortune Magazine* (August, 1946): p. 131.

94. Alberto Conil Paz and Gustavo Ferrari, *Argentina's Foreign Policy, 1930–1962.* Translated by John F. Kennedy (Notre Dame: University of Notre Dame Press, 1966), p. 33.

95. H. S. Ferns, *Argentina* (New York: Praeger, 1969), p. 183.

96. Cordell Hull to the Diplomatic Representatives in the American Republics except Argentina, Chile, Paraguay and Bolivia, May 23, 1944, 835.01/439a, *Foreign Relations of the United States, 1944,* Vol. 7, p. 310.

97. Memorandum of Conversation by the Chief of the Division of Caribbean and Central American Affairs (Cabot), September 16, 1944, 500.cc/9-1644, *Foreign Relations of the United States, 1944,* Vol. 1 (printed as Department of State Publication No. 8138; Washington, D.C.: Government Printing Office, 1966), pp. 929–30.

98. Alexander L. George and Juliette L. George, *Woodrow Wilson and Colonel House: A Personality Study* (New York: Dover Publications, 1964), p. 114.

99. Ibid., p. 115.

100. Hull, *Memoirs* II, p. 1409.

101. Harold Peterson believes that Hull's anger was due to the fact that he "had fathered the principle of unanimity since 1933." Harold F. Peterson, *Argentina and the United States, 1810–1960* (New York: State University of New York Press, 1964), p. 419. Hull's sense of possessiveness was highly exclusive. Arthur Schlesinger, Jr., reported that "State Department 'histories' like *Peace and War,* put together by Hull disciples, excise the name of Welles [with reference to the Good Neighbor Policy]

as implacably as ever stalinist historians cut Trotsky out of the Russian Revolution." Schlesinger, "Good Fences Make Good Neighbors," p. 132.

102. Hull, *Memoirs* II, p. 1413.

103. Ibid., pp. 1405–08.

104. Acheson, *Present at the Creation,* p. 9.

105. Hull, *Memoirs* I, p. 4.

106. Bohan, oral history interview, p. 9.

107. Schlesinger, "Good Fences Make Good Neighbors," p. 161.

108. Blum, *Morgenthau Diaries,* p. 195.

109. Frank McNaughton to Bermingham, "Spruille Braden," November 25, 1945, Papers of Frank McNaughton, Truman Library, p. 8. This is a confidential report of Braden's testimony during the closed Senate Foreign Relations Committee hearings on his nomination to be assistant secretary of state. Frank McNaughton was Washington correspondent for *Time* magazine from 1941 to 1949.

110. Acheson, *Present at the Creation,* p. 160.

111. Braden, *Diplomats and Demagogues,* p. i.

112. Ibid., p. 260.

113. Ibid., p. 428.

114. Hull, *Memoirs* II, p. 1421.

4

Adolf Berle in Brazil: 1945–46

C. Neale Ronning

Both Brazil and Adolf Berle were undergoing an important and difficult transition when the latter arrived in Rio de Janeiro as U.S. ambassador on January 24, 1945. Lawyer, economist, law professor, diplomat, and liberal political activist, Berle was one of the original and prominent members of Franklin D. Roosevelt's "Brain Trust." He was close to the president and served in a number of important domestic and international posts, in his long career in public service. "A short, intense, small-boned man with the energy of a dynamo, Mr. Berle had a brilliant mind and, according to some New Dealers whom he rubbed the wrong way, he knew it." [1]

The author of many studies on the corporate system, he was deeply concerned about corporate power and influence in the United States. He was equally concerned about the even cruder extension of that power and influence in Latin America. Late in his career, he summed up a dilemma that had long troubled him: "When Latin Americans insist that private investment costs them more in foreign exchange through remittance of profit than it brings in through inflowing investment of capital, they are frequently right." [2] Berle had long witnessed the modus operandi of the oil companies. At one point, this led him to remark that "the life of any ambassador is incomplete without a scrimmage with the international oil people." [3]

But if Berle could be critical of the corporate system in general and the oil companies in particular, he was also suspicious about the enemies of liberal capitalism. One of the reasons for his opposition to the policies of the oil companies was that "this sort of monkey-business was forcing the whole situation towards socialism about as fast as could be done." [4] A fear of communism and communist influence runs through his public documents of the post–World War II period.

From 1938 to 1944, Berle served as assistant secretary of state but, when—in late 1944—Secretary of State Cordell Hull resigned for health reasons, Berle and three other assistant secretaries tendered their resignations. The new secretary, Edward R. Stettinius, surprised the department by accepting all the resignations—except that of Dean Acheson.[5] One account notes that "Berle was supposed to keep his rank as Assistant Secretary but with such trifling assignments that there could be no doubt about the meaning of the whole thing: Berle had been resigned."[6] About a year after the event, Berle reminisced about that time when "the United States Government made it as clear as possible that they did not need me to run their affairs . . . *when they fired me as Assistant Secretary of State.*"[7] Like other early New Dealers, he was probably becoming aware of "a steadily ripening distaste for the large, noisy and enthusiastic 'dandruff-and-dirty nails' crew of New Deal reformers and pragmatists whom Roosevelt brought or attracted to federal service in and after 1933."[8]

To make matters even worse for Berle, changes meant the promotion and increasing influence of Dean Acheson, with whom he shared a strong mutual dislike—on personal as well as policy grounds. Acheson himself has recorded that "The fact that we disliked one another is too well known to attempt to disguise. . . . At any rate, for four years, until he became Ambassador to Brazil, we maintained a wary coexistence on the second floor of Old State."[9]

Five months into Berle's mission to Brazil, James Byrnes became secretary of state, and Acheson became Byrnes's chief deputy. With Byrnes frequently on extended trips to Moscow, London, Paris, and other capitals, Acheson often assumed the post of acting secretary of state. Berle also had doubts about the promotion of Spruille Braden, who became assistant secretary of state in charge of Latin American affairs only months after Berle took up his post in Brazil.[10]

President Roosevelt was aware of Berle's humiliation. With the help of the latter's longtime friend, Stephen Early (who was press secretary at the White House), the president sought to patch things up. He asked Berle to take over the important embassy in Brazil: "The Roosevelt charm was turned on, together with expressions of gratitude for the eminent services Berle had rendered at the Department."[11] Berle, of course, accepted the post.

Hopefully, this all-too-brief sketch has rendered an approximation of the intellectual and professional baggage with which Adolf Berle arrived in Brazil to take up this important post at a time that was so very crucial for Brazil—and no less so for the United States. The influence of that "baggage" will be the subject of a commentary on two key episodes in Berle's mission, which lasted from early 1945 until early 1946. However, we must first attempt an equally brief sketch of what was happening in Brazil.

The year 1945 was a crucial one in the history of Brazil. During the previous 15 years, Getúlio Vargas had led what is widely referred to as the

"Brazilian National Revolution." Immediately following the Revolution of 1930 (which Vargas had led), he served as head of the provisional government until 1934. Then he served as constitutional president, elected by Congress (1934–37)—and, finally, as dictator (1937–45).

It was especially in the years from 1937 to 1945 that the Nationalist Revolution took shape, although elements of it dated from 1930. The revolution was inspired as much by pragmatism as by ideologies, and its content is still a matter of considerable controversy.

Stated in oversimplified terms, the revolution had proceeded on three legs: industrialization, nationalism, and state intervention in the development process. Under the aegis of the *Estado Novo* (the "New State"), Brazilian enterprise was promoted and protected against imported products and even products manufactured in Brazil by foreign enterprises. Only through the development of Brazilian national industries, it was held, could Brazil move out of its semicolonial status. This was the beginning of the process by which the old rural, export-oriented class that had dominated Brazil since independence would be replaced by an emerging industrial bourgeoisie. Executive power, economic planning and nationalism, trade union organization (under state direction), improved urban labor conditions, and censorship of the media were all intended to enlarge and ratify the importance of the state and the industrial bourgeoisie.[12]

Members of the traditional, rural oligarchy had tolerated—but never accepted—Vargas and his objectives. As Octavio Ianni has observed, they had been the beneficiaries of the pre-1930 model of development, which was based on the hegemony of the agricultural sector with its "traditional relations of production and techniques of accumulation. . . . They suffered a serious defeat with the victory of the Revolution of 1930; but it wasn't a total defeat."[13] Their position was also strengthened by tensions within the industrial bourgeoisie itself—tensions between the more nationalist elements advocating state intervention to maintain and accelerate the process of industrialization and others more friendly to demands for the involvement of foreign finance and technology.

In addition to the industrial bourgeoise, the state sought increasing support from another emerging class: the state–organized and controlled labor sector. But the new industrial interests—whose members were still mentally and emotionally a part of traditional Brazil—were always uncomfortable in and suspicious of this state-directed alliance with labor. As Vargas became increasingly popular with the lower class and showed increasing interest in organizing it, the tension only mounted.

Although the new entrepreneurs were the beneficiary of many of the policies of the Estado Novo, they objected to its restrictions and regulations— especially in the final years of its existence. Because wartime profits had been so high, Vargas imposed an excess profits tax and—arguing that workers should share in the profits—increases in salaries. In June 1945, he decreed an antitrust law similar to the U.S. Sherman Antitrust Law of 1891.[14] Brazilian capitalists were not ready for even so moderate a measure. More importantly, it was seen as yet another step in Vargas's populist campaign to mobilize mass support. "The result was violent reaction, as much among liberals (the Fraternity of Lawyers), spreading to producer groups and associations (Manifesto of the Producer Classes) and even to political parties (Manifesto of the Democratic National Union)."[15]

There were also international tensions arising out of the nationalist revolution: U.S. investors and exporters were unhappy with Brazilian restrictions on what they regarded as their right to a free market. These tensions and their consequences will be discussed later in this chapter.

In early 1945, Vargas promised to hold elections later in the year; but, by September, a campaign with mass demonstrations was mounted by the Left and other Vargas supporters to call a constitutional convention while Vargas remained at the head of government. This helped to feed rumors within the military and elsewhere that Vargas was now conspiring with Luís Carlos Prestes (head of the Communist party and recently freed from years of prison under Vargas) to organize the slum dwellers for another coup d'etat.[16] One of Vargas's close associates has recorded that "the city was filled with panic . . . and everyone expected that at any moment the red flag of the Communist Party would be draped from public buildings, in barracks and in factories."[17]

On October 29, 1945, the military (under the leadership of General Góes Monteiro[18]) demanded and received Vargas's resignation. In some ways, Vargas had indeed helped to create the very conditions that led to his removal. Even while promising elections, he had added ambiguous statements that fired the imagination of many already suspicious minds. His last-minute appointment of his brother as chief of police in Rio de Janeiro confirmed the suspicion that he was planning a campaign of mass demonstrations demanding he remain in power.

But concern over Vargas's maneuvers should not be construed, as it often has been, as any deep commitment to the democratic process on the part of the core of the opposition. Rather, as Peter Flynn has observed, it was a reflection of "a generally shared fear of the organized working class and the threat, as they perceived it, in *trabalhismo* [the powerful political system linked to the trade unions]."[19] The core of this opposition was in the military and the UDN—a recently formed right-wing political group.

A Brazilian historian gives a similar account—one that is widely accepted among contemporary Brazilian historians:

The military *coup* of 1945, though ostensibly aimed at doing away with fascism and establishing democracy, was in fact an instinctive defensive reaction by the more conservative elements of Brazilian society against a process of change, exemplified by the recent transformation of the *Estado Novo*.[20]

At this crucial moment, Ambassador Berle decided to jump into the Brazilian political conflict, even though he fully realized that the prestige of the embassy and the United States would be involved. Only a few days after his arrival, he sensed the inevitability of the situation. The only question was how to make his move discreetly. On January 30, 1945, he noted:

I must say that the more I get into this, the tougher the assignment looks. For the young intellectuals who are all for democracy are against the Government and want the United States to do something about that; the entrenched Government group know that they have cooperated with the United States during the war up to the limit; and I am afraid neither side will be particularly happy at a merely "neutral" or "hands off" attitude. The problem is to find and hold a moral position capable of comprehending all elements.[21]

His first task in Rio, as he put it, would be "to find out who knows anything about Rio other than the Granfinos (high society)." The embassy staff was of little help: "The detachment of the Embassy from the life of what must be 98% of the population is surprising." Berle set about to inform himself as best he could. He also found it necessary to inform Secretary of State Stettinius (who served from the time of Hull's resignation in November 1944 until June 1945) and Assistant Secretary Rockefeller that, in sending personnel, it should be kept in mind that "the language of Brazil is Portuguese."[22]

Berle watched closely as the political contest unfolded. He was frequently sought out by the opposition and (as we shall later see) made contacts on his own or through intermediaries. Eight months after he arrived, he had decided that it was time for decisive action. That action came in the form of a speech "at a small and dull luncheon of Government-controlled *Sindicato dos Jornalistas* [Union of Journalists]" on September 29, 1945.[23] But according to General Góes, the luncheon was offered by members of the UDN and other members of the opposition.Góes also maintained that the speech was "probably suggested by elements of the opposition."[24]

Although the crucial portion of Berle's speech was cast in the form of a statement of good faith, it was clearly intended to make certain that the promised elections would indeed be held:

Brazilian affairs interest the entire world; but they are most clearly watched by the millions of American friends of Brazil who make up public opinion of the United States. . . .

The pledge of free Brazilian elections, set for a definite date, by a Government whose word the United States has found inviolable, has been hailed with as much satisfaction in the United States as in Brazil itself. Americans have not agreed with some who tried to misrepresent straightforward pledges and declarations as insincere or, as verbal trickery.[25]

The last sentence of the excerpt quoted above is perplexing—to say the least—since Berle himself had doubts and was presenting the speech as an obstacle to possible insincerity or verbal trickery. The speech also offered Brazilians a lesson in proper procedures for constitution making. Berle even informed them that, during the French Revolution, a constituent assembly had met but—because the election of a chief executive had been delayed— the procedure led directly to a reign of terror against which the assembly could offer no protection.[26] A clearer reference to the Brazilian situation would be difficult to find.

Berle told President Truman that he had showed the speech to Vargas beforehand and that the latter had offered no objection.[27] Vargas's daughter has given a different account; she says that the president did not see the speech in advance. Furthermore, when he was informed that the speech had indeed been delivered, his reaction was: "He dared?!"[28] The general who later led the coup against Vargas has also emphasized the president's irritation; he gives yet another version of the "prior approval" case. According to this version, Vargas told General Góes that he was very tired when Berle came to see him and that he asked Berle to read the speech—which he did, in "badly mumbled Portuguese." Góes then suggested that he might want to have the ambassador recalled.[29] The reason Vargas did not do so is remembered by his secretary:

Vargas was enraged by this inopportune and audacious attitude on the part of Berle. He called Oswaldo Aranha and told him that the Ambassador was going too far. He was no longer *persona-grata* and should return home. Oswaldo, who was becoming a sort of guardian of our relations with the United States, tried to smooth things over. He thought that such a move would provoke disagreeable repercussions and was also unnecessary, since Berle was planning to leave shortly and was already packing his bags.[30]

Immediately after the speech, the Brazilian foreign minister asked his ambassador in Washington to ascertain if the speech had been authorized by the State Department. He also informed his ambassador that Berle admitted he had spoken after having exchanged ideas about the matter with Spruille Braden, but without instructions from President Truman or the Department of State. From Washington, Brazilian Ambassador Martins confirmed that the speech had not been authorized by the department.[31]

Berle's own papers also suggest that Washington learned about the speech only after the fact. Since at least August, Berle had been telling the State Department and even President Truman that the United States should not interfere. On September 3, he told the secretary of state that representatives of the United States "on occasion may be compelled to express their views as Ambassador Braden is doing now in Argentina and as Sumner Welles did in Cuba in 1933." But such measures, he emphasized, should be only a last resort when "the government attacked has threatened the peace of the hemisphere, or has violated the standard of civilized nations."[32] And only two weeks prior to the speech, Truman—responding to one such communication from Berle—confided:

I think it would be disastrous to interfere in the internal affairs of Brazil at the present time.

It seems to me things are going along as well as anyone would wish. Vargas has certainly been our friend.[33]

Finally, it was only *after* the speech had been delivered that Berle sent a copy of the text to the department.[34]

The matter of whether or not Vargas had approved the speech was, of course, not the critical point. The strategy of showing the speech to him beforehand (assuming that to be the case) was a questionable one, to say the least, and would have put Vargas in an extremely difficult position. In the first place, it was tantamount to asking him if his promise to hold elections had been made in good faith. Second, Vargas certainly knew that, had he objected, the news would have been all over Rio in a matter of hours. Surely Vargas knew of Berle's contacts with the opposition; his objections to the speech would have been made known to them and given the most sinister interpretation. Showing the speech to Vargas beforehand was hardly a diplomatic gesture.

It scarcely needs to be pointed out that Berle knew he was intervening despite his promise to Brazilians of a U.S. policy of nonintervention: "The nonintervention policy of the United States was well-established and would be scrupulously adhered to."[35] And after his momentous speech Berle said that "It is going to cause a good deal of political comment and in a sense takes the Embassy off the pedestal and puts it into the firing line."[36] A few days later,he noted that in Brazil his speech was being referred to as "the atomic bomb that ended *Queremismo*" (from "queremos Vargas"—"we want Vargas"). He was happy for the support he was receiving in the press, which he saw as a sign that "diplomacy has changed."[37]

Why this intervention in Brazilian affairs by an ambassador who saw himself as a special friend of the country? There are a number of concepts that appear to have been central in Berle's thinking. Which one, if any, was uppermost would be difficult to establish. They are all part of a single complex explanation and are best seen in that way.

There was Berle's paternalistic attitude toward Brazil—something that was greatly encouraged by the colonial mentality of Brazilian middle and upper classes of that period. He saw a part of his mission as that of helping Brazil to find an economic and political model for development—and that model, with some reservations, was the United States. In March 1945, he was already concerned that the electoral campaign was focusing too much on personalities rather than issues. Thus, he said, "I am going to make a speech [not the one quoted above] on the history of industrialization in the United States, letting the Brazilians draw their own parallel. We ought to be able to get some real economic discussion out of the campaign—or the last state of the country will be worse than the first." [38] He was pleased to have a discussion with Mário Carneiro of the conservative Democratic Resistance, with whose members Berle had contacts, because he "had been trying to find young men to talk about handling obvious social and economic problems and this is a good place to begin." He was also working on "a campaign to try to work up a popular demand for elementary education." This, he noted, "is a very unambassadorial line of activity but with luck it might do some good." [39]

Another aspect of Berle's paternalistic mission was that of "saving Brazilians from themselves," or seeking out their best interest when they seemed headed in the wrong direction. At times, he saw his intervention as actually heading off an army revolt: "Perpetuation of a dictatorship means . . . a popular president with the support of the masses, and probably an army revolt." Sometimes, he believed that Vargas was sincere but that Berle himself was one of the few who understood it: "I still think he means what he says [to hold elections] and is not engaged in double talk. His enemies do not give him credit for this." [40] At other times, Berle emphasized that Vargas was in danger of being used by a communist–fascist conspiracy; Berle saw it as his mission to prevent this. Only a few days after his fateful speech, he seemed to think that he had headed off a pro-Vargas coup and prevented dire consequences for U.S.–Brazilian relations. Pro-Vargas demonstrations had been planned and were held on October 3. Many people, including Berle, thought that these demonstrations would be the signal for a pro-Vargas coup:

My own speech of September 29 was designed if possible to head off violent moves in either direction. . . .

Certainly if on October 3 those boys had pulled off their *coup d'etat* and the tide of public opinion in the United States had dealt with it as it had dealt with Perón, our situation would have been strikingly unpleasant. But this form of diplomacy means that the *easy* life of the diplomat is gone forever. [41]

Berle was probably influenced by his numerous contacts with the liberal–conservative opposition to Vargas. By his own account and that of Brazilians, these people were apparently a major source of his information about the political pulse of the country. One of his first contacts, only a few days after arriving in Rio, was Francisco Campos. Berle met him through the

Canadian ambassador "who had kindly offered to introduce [him] to intellectuals." Campos and others reported to him that "the soul of the country was dead . . . and that nobody could get anything done."[42] This, it should be noted, was the same Campos who had drafted the 1937 constitution for the Estado Novo and, in 1940, had proclaimed that "the *Estado Novo* is creating a new Brazil."[43] A "born-again liberal" when Berle met him, Campos later managed to become a staunch supporter of the post-1964 military government, and one of the authors of an even more authoritarian constitution of 1967.

According to Hélio Silva, Berle was influenced by an opposition group called the Democratic Resistance. Berle's wife, a compassionate medical doctor who took an active interest in Brazil's health problems, was acquainted with a Brazilian doctor who was active in the group. "Thus there was a bridge between these elements and Professor Berle. The Democratic Resistance began to influence the mind of the Ambassador."[44] This group was indeed a mixed bag; but, as Hélio Silva has pointed out, members came principally from two conservative intellectual centers—the *Centro Dom Vital* (Dom Vital Center) and the *Mosteiro de São Bento* (São Bento Monastery).[45] Prominent among the membership was Alceu Amoroso Lima, who had earlier written that "Brazil, as everyone can see, is suffering from a socialist invasion which long ago reached Argentina and Uruguay . . . but which we avoided until 1930. . . . The Revolution of 1930 opened the doors of Brazil to the doctrines and techniques of that new type of war . . . the real war of the twentieth century."[46]

All of this brings up the specter of "guilt by association"—a verdict usually reserved for members of the Left. Berle's keen intellect was not likely to buy just any explanation or opinion. Furthermore, he also expressed grave doubts about the opposition. But their rhetoric of political democracy undoubtedly found favor with the ambassador.

More verifiable and more important for our purpose was Berle's concept of those who supported Vargas's continuation in power. There seemed to be only two groups in favor of continuation: "The communists on the one hand, who are making great propaganda for a constituent assembly—with the implied continuance of the present government while it deliberates; and . . . the office-holding group or *'Queremistas'* on the other."[47]

This was a great oversimplification. A small group of communists did indeed offer support, but there was a much larger Left of which they formed only a small part. There is no evidence in Berle's account or in that of Brazilians that he ever sought a dialogue with the broader Left, which was certainly the most important part of the movement to keep Vargas in power legally. Indeed, he had little good to say about this important group: "The Left had been notoriously opportunistic, and while it damned Vargas as a dictator, it will damn, still more, any interference with its plans to make use of him while it can."[48]

And the Queremistas, as Berle saw it, were "men who were the backbone of the Fascist Party in 1937."[49] Again, this was certainly a gross oversimplification, if not an outright error. Former fascists there were, but there were also many of them within the opposition. Some supporters apparently believed now that Vargas's popularity with the masses made it possible for him to govern democratically and constitutionally. His secretary has recorded that, after a tumultuous acclamation in the Vasco da Gama stadium in late 1944, he urged President Vargas to consider measures that would move the country toward democracy.[50] Whatever the reasons, Vargas did—in fact—authorize the dismantling of most of the repressive measures of the Estado Novo. Both Berle and Vargas's Brazilian critics admit that most of this had been accomplished by the time he was removed from office.

Berle was also moved by his own legalistic and peculiarly North American concept of democracy. He conceded that, in many ways, Vargas had been perhaps the most democratic leader in Brazil, insofar as representation of the masses was concerned—even though this had been accomplished without elections. Now, he noted, "The working class . . . would like a chance to vote for him."[51] Berle also lamented that speaking out against dictatorship would probably satisfy a principle, but "it probably prevents any immediate progress towards much-needed economic reform."[52] Nevertheless, he concluded that "as my way of thinking runs we had best ask for democracy and get it." And three days later, after a long talk with Spruille Braden, who was on his way back from Argentina, he concluded that "the only way to have democracy is to have it; and that the United States was beginning to be expected to express a view."[53]

After the military coup and the removal of Vargas from office, Berle observed that "we are beginning a new phase and my concern is to see that it represents the masses of Brazil at least as well and if possible better than did Getúlio."[54] In the end, he defined democracy in terms of electoral politics—even though he conceded that the election itself would be largely a formality. The only thing that he could hope for, Berle said, "is the continuance of a free press, growing experience and working democratic machinery, and the evolution over a year or so of a real and representative movement based on labor and so far as possible peasants and small agriculturists."[55] Ironically, as Peter Flynn has observed, Getúlio Vargas was probably "the one man . . . who might have effected the smooth political transition required."[56]

Approximately two decades after the event, Berle still saw the move against Vargas as inspired by a "desire to protect democracy." When the army moved again—this time to overthrow João Goulart in 1964—"its real reason was a desire to protect democracy won when the army (with the backing of the country) compelled Getúlio Vargas to end his dictatorship in 1945."[57]

Growing U.S. irritation with Brazilian economic nationalism, of which Vargas was seen as the cornerstone, has also been suggested as one of the reasons behind Berle's intervention. There is, indeed, circumstantial evidence to support this, including an alleged acrimonious exchange on the subject between Berle and Vargas. This will be related in more detail later in this chapter, since it is more germane to another incident in Berle's diplomacy. As we shall see, however, there is also evidence to suggest that Vargas's economic nationalism alone is not an entirely convincing explanation. In any event, it must be seen as part of the whole context in which Berle decided to act.

Whatever Berle's reasons for the September 29 speech—and they seem to have been multiple and confused—this was calculated intervention in the politics of another country. Furthermore, it was only the most dramatic and publicized of a number of interventions "in the interest of Brazil." And it had been done on the initiative of the ambassador himself, without approval of the secretary of state or the president of the United States. Finally, it was not the sort of move that required quick action, when consultation and contemplation are impossible. Given his opinion of the State Department in general and some of his superiors in particular, Berle's independent course of action was probably to be expected.

After the October coup, the U.S. oil companies waited a "decent" 11 days before moving in to claim their share of the spoils. Vargas, the National Revolution, and the international situation had for some time interfered with their plans. Brief reference to some of the relevant factors in the international situation will provide us with useful background information.

After some initial hesitation the Vargas administration had become a loyal and valuable collaborator with the United States during World War II. This had made the United States willing to tolerate, for the time being, a number of annoying features of the National Revolution. Import restrictions, limitations on foreign investments (especially in petroleum and mining), preferences to Brazilian manufacturers, and, generally, state intervention and regulation were the most obvious. During the war, U.S. companies had not always been able to count on the strong arm of the State Department. But they could wait.

As late as March 14, 1945, President Roosevelt had praised Vargas and told Berle that he hoped that "Vargas would be reelected President but did not want to take any hand in it lest it do more harm than good."[58] With Roosevelt's death a month later and the war in its final phase, Vargas's collaboration became less important than it had been in the earlier priorities of the United States. Also of importance was the fact that U.S. industry would be shifting to civilian manufacturers, and foreign markets would be sought after. Brazil's foreign reserves, built up under wartime import restrictions, were an enticing prize. Investment opportunities, especially in petroleum and mining, would be aggressively sought after. The program of the National Revolution had been the main obstacle to all of this.

Brazilians, too, were becoming more and more aware of the need for a rapid development of their petroleum resources. In 1945, virtually all of their oil was imported and only a very small amount was refined in Brazil.[59] National efforts had not been very successful—the shortage of capital was an important factor—but there were strong pressures for avoiding foreign involvement.[60] Because it was seen as a national security issue, the problem had been turned over to the military since 1938.[61] The Constitution of 1937 and a decree law of 1938 were the fundamental laws prohibiting the participation of foreigners in this vital industry.

Throughout 1945, Berle was instructed to urge the Brazilians to change their petroleum law, import controls, and other restrictive measures. He carried out his instructions (but not with great enthusiasm), much to the chagrin of Vargas and other Brazilian officials. Six weeks before Vargas was removed from office, the president of Brazil's National Petroleum Council "was requested to outline the progress being made towards the realization of a plan which might permit and encourage the exploration of petroleum in Brazil." The reply was not encouraging: "Any change which might be made in the Constitution which would permit the entry into Brazil of foreign capital for participation in the petroleum industry would be most difficult."[62]

Vargas's reactions to the mounting pressures were confided to his secretary, Luís Vergara:

I know what our Yankee friends want. They want liberalization so they can stuff us with their wartime industrial surplus. They know that we have managed to save more than 600 million dollars in gold and they are voracious with the hunger of good business, but I am not disposed to give them these reserves because I want to use all of them to buy equipment for our industries, repair our ports and railroads and especially, in the installation of our planned hydroelectric power plants.[63]

A particularly unpleasant exchange between Vargas and Berle is also reported by Vergara. Berle had asked President Vargas if a Brazilian petroleum policy had been worked out. Vargas, obviously irritated, replied that this was a matter in which the Brazilian government did not consider itself obliged to satisfy the curiosity of foreigners. It would be resolved when Brazilians thought it appropriate to do so.

In the final days of the Vargas administration, bids had been opened for the building of privately owned refineries. However, under existing laws, bidding was restricted to Brazilians. Once Vargas was out of the way, the oil companies and the State Department were anxious to get down to business. As already noted, they waited just 11 days. A telegram from the State Department told Berle what the oil companies wanted and made it clear that the department expected them to have it. The message is so important and the language so unmistakable that it is worth quoting at length and in the original telegraphic form:

Harden, Standard Oil, New Jersey and Nave, Atlantic Refining, have called at Dept to express serious concern re project currently under consideration by Braz Govt whereby authorizations would be granted to Brazilian companies for construction and operation of two refineries. Under existing decree-legislation (Decree-Law 395 of April 29, 1938, and Decree 4071 of May 12, 1939) foreigners are excluded from direction, management or investment in refineries.

It appears that Braz Govt contemplates some arrangement between refineries and American and other foreign concerns now marketing petroleum products in Brazil, whereby latter would supply crude oil to refineries and then market refined products. Dept feels probable result of such arrangement would be to freeze foreign partici- pation in Marketing business at existing levels and among existing suppliers and distributors, and perhaps ultimately to squeeze it out entirely and bring about Brazil- ian monopoly of marketing as well as refining. . . .

Main emphasis should be directed toward elimination of basic cause of present difficulties, i.e., provisions of the decree legislation which restrict ownership and management. Meanwhile, however, Emb should seek postponement of action to give effect to recommendations of National Petroleum Council for establishment of two Brazilian refineries. Were these recommendations adopted, it would make more difficult elimination of nationalistic decrees. . . .

Emb might also note Brazil has received substantial public loans from US which have been made despite increased nationalism evidenced by numerous restrictions on foreigners. However, this Govt in the future will probably examine more closely commercial policies of borrowers, as witness current British talks. . . .

[I]t feels that this is an opportune time to press firmly present case.[64]

Here was unmistakable evidence that it wasn't simply Vargas's "statism"— the extension of the role of the state in Brazilian economic affairs—that con- cerned the State Department and the oil companies. They were even more fearful that an independent capitalist class might be developing in Brazil— one that would have its own set of interests, including the continuation of nationalistic decrees. Obviously, Brazilian refining interests might eventually want to see the exploitation of petroleum deposits in Brazilian hands, as well.

Berle's reply to the telegram was angry and blunt. He now saw himself in the role of defender of Brazilian sovereignty against the greed of oil com- panies supported by the State Department. First, he noted that Standard Oil had an airtight monopoly in Brazil (in conjunction with British Shell). A profit of 114 percent in 1944, he noted, had made this a valuable monopoly indeed. But refining was not the big prize: "They know that Brazil has oil reserves and will eventually find ways of drilling and producing oil here."[65] That was what the companies wanted and, in order to have it, it would be necessary to change the fundamental laws. Brazilian-owned refineries might well add to the already considerable nationalist sentiment.

The U.S. companies were going too far for Berle, and he bluntly told the department that "if representations are to be made along this line, I should prefer that they made in the Department, *leaving me out and noting my dissent.*"[66]

Four days later, Berle sent an insulting telegram to the department, in which he noted that the telegram quoted above "was substantially dictated by one of the oil companies and perhaps did not get full policy attention, with [the] result that it looked like diplomatic pressure in favor of [a] cartel group against [the] sovereignty of Brazil—and incidentally against another powerful American group."[67] The final reference—"against another powerful American group"—was to Gulf Oil. Berle notes that the National Petroleum Council of Brazil had required applicants for refinery permits to show that they had an available supply of crude oil. Gulf had agreed to supply the crude oil, which outraged Standard Oil of New Jersey. Prior to this, Berle notes, "local representatives of Standard–Shell–Texas–Atlantic group merely smiled. Crude oil was not available from anybody except through them and they weren't selling."[68]

A few days later, a representative of Standard Oil told Berle—quite frankly— that they did not want to see *any* oil refining in Brazil. However, since they thought that it would come about sooner or later, they wanted to be sure that they controlled it.[69] Meanwhile, as the State Department had told Berle, it would be necessary to employ "stopgap measures." That meant delaying for as long as possible, the granting of any refining concessions to Brazilians.

The department and the oil companies continued to press Berle to support them in their waiting game. A memorandum of a telephone conversation between Berle and members of the department notes that "Ambassador Berle made it clear that he was opposed to the Department's views in this matter, and while he would, of course, obey instructions given to him, he made it clear that he, as an individual, wished no part of it." As something of a modus operandi, it was agreed that instructions would be drafted with "the text of the precise language to be used," which Berle could then deliver without becoming personally involved.[70]

"Participation" had a very specific meaning for the department and the oil companies (although the companies were more flexible). The department left no doubt about this:

In pursuing this course, it is highly desirable that no impression be left with the Brazilian Government that this Government would view with favor the establishment of any fixed percentage of participation, minority *or otherwise.* As you no doubt realize, our acceptance of such a principle would inevitably encourage the adoption or furtherance in other countries of restrictive policies harmful to American commercial interests.[71]

The State Department continued to issue instructions to prevent the immediate building of Brazilian refineries, and Berle finally thought that he had worked out a compromise.

I think I see a chance to resolve this by not doing anything except getting the Brazilians to agree that the permissions to [build] refineries, when granted, will not constitute vested rights but will be subject to any changes in Brazilian laws later adopted. This will keep things fluid for a while, but will not prevent Brazilians from going ahead and getting their refining industry, which they badly need.[72]

Two days before this, Berle had informed the department that he and the embassy were "of course, encouraging the liberalization of laws and have made good progress along this line, already having received indications that if concessions are granted they will be subject to any changes in such laws."[73]

The department relentlessly pressed the case of the oil companies, while Berle continued to point out their monopolistic objectives. He bluntly told the department of the dangers he saw in the "changes in American diplomacy" and referred to their instructions as "highly dangerous and unsound." Shortly before returning to Washington for an extended stay, the exasperated ambassador warned that "If representation is successful, as it probably will not be, we should block the one real chance Brazil has had in many years to create [a] competitive refining industry in substantial partnership with American companies."[74]

In late December during his stay in the United States, Berle met with several officials of the State Department. The Memorandum of Conversation indicates that Berle's compromise was reluctantly accepted by the department:

Following further discussions of the varying points of view surrounding this general subject, Mr. Rayner stated that while he felt that a liberalization of laws could more readily be affected if such liberalization preceded rather than followed the granting of refinery permits he would bow to the Ambassador's view that such a course might be more prejudicial to the ultimate goal than were the granting of refinery permits [to] be allowed to pass without comment and steps taken thereafter to urge the desired liberalization.[75]

Berle had managed to stop the department's campaign against the Brazilian oil refineries. On the larger issue—the liberalization of Brazilian petroleum laws, in order to permit foreign participation—he managed only to deflect as much as possible the department's clumsy and insensitive attacks. There are three probable explanations for this.

First, Berle himself was plagued with doubts and ambiguities on the larger issue. His willingness to convey "the hope of the government of the United States . . . that Brazil would lend effect to its apparent intent to liberalize present laws so as to permit participation of foreign capital"—a mild and even ambiguous statement—reflected the ambassador's own lack of strong convictions on the matter. He believed that there was a need for foreign investment, given Brazil's lack of capital. "Brazilians are too nationalistic and merely keeping foreigners out is not a healthy way of going about it."[76] But he was rightfully distrustful of the oil companies and their designs on Brazil

and the rest of Latin America. In March 1945, months before the controversy over the refineries had developed, the petroleum attaché in the embassy had informed him that the Brazilians were thinking about liberalizing
their petroleum laws to allow foreign participation. In his diary, Berle noted
that "this is all very well, but I want to see if we can't work out a somewhat
better and safer method of oil concessions than has prevailed in Mexico,
Venezuela and Bolivia." A month later, he recorded the same sentiments:
"Of course, if Brazil wanted oil fast then they could simply open the country
to exploitation by the private companies. But that does something else besides get oil—and that something else is not too nice." [77] And when he
received the shocking telegram from the State Department, Berle confided
that he could understand why the Brazilians "don't want Brazilian oil in the
ground, or refined marketing, to fall into control of foreign cartels. I respect
this, and so does everybody else who has watched the results of oil policy
in Mexico, Colombia, and Bolivia." [78]

Second, the department's aggressive and uncompromising position on the
larger issue had been made very clear. Thus, as noted, Berle probably sought
only to deflect as much as possible the department's campaign. Although
Vargas had been replaced by an administration that reflected the more traditional, neocolonial attitudes still prevalent in the Brazil of 1945, strong
nationalist currents continued to grow, outside the government. Berle was
well aware of this and tried to convince the department that its high-handed
methods would only backfire. He constantly reminded his colleagues that
their tactics would not produce the desired results. There is evidence of this
in the previously quoted statement of a department member that "he would
bow to the Ambassador's view that such a course might be more prejudicial
to the ultimate goal than were the granting of refinery permits [to] be allowed to pass without comment and steps taken thereafter to urge the desired liberalization." [79] Did Berle believe this, or was he only playing devil's
advocate? Had the department's memorandum taken liberties with Berle's
expressed views? Possibly, it was a combination of all three.

Third, circumstances also explain why it was possible for Berle to avoid a
fuller confrontation of the larger issue. The State Department and the oil
companies were waiting with their full offensive on investment liberalization
until a new government would be in office and a constitutional convention
could lay the groundwork for a new petroleum law. Berle resigned only a
few days after those important events took place and, as we shall see, the
way was then open for a more serious offensive.

Berle submitted his resignation to President Truman on February 6, 1946;
five days later, he observed that "the Brazilian incident is almost over for
me." [80] What followed is beyond the scope of this discussion, but a brief
summary of some post-Berle diplomacy will show a distinct contrast with
what has been described here and will, thus, put Berle's efforts in a better
perspective.

For the State Department and the oil companies, there now appeared to be few obstacles in the way. First of all, the embassy under new direction seemed eager to serve the department and the oil companies without question or reservation. Second, members of the Dutra administration, which assumed power on January 31, 1946, actually asked the embassy to intervene on a number of occasions. And third, some members of the constitutional convention, which began its work in early February, were equally eager to enlist the embassy on their side. A few examples of this changed atmosphere follow:

In late March 1946, the chargé d'affaires asked for a statement of the State Department's policy on petroleum and advised that "if Embassy is to assert discreetly and tactfully any influence toward liberalization of the constitution to permit foreign capital to participate, it must be done now." As if to encourage the department, he noted that "it has been suggested by certain [of the] Brazilian Gov[ernment] that [the U.S.] Embassy's influence would be helpful." [81]

Both the embassy and the department were well aware that, although the Dutra administration was favorable to the objectives of the oil companies, there was strong and growing opposition outside the government. Members of the Dutra administration were also aware of the growing opposition and, thus, asked the chargé for "personal and confidential" communications outlining what the United States would regard as satisfactory provisions. Eventually, the chargé could report an intermediate victory:

All the oil company representatives in Rio are fairly well satisfied with the provisions of the new Constitution as they pertain to petroleum. They all feel that the door is now open to foreign capital under such conditions as may be established by a new petroleum law. [82]

A battle had been won, but the war continued. It was now essential to get the right kind of petroleum law. Ambassador Pawley, who had replaced Berle, proudly informed the State Department that "since arriving in Brazil [I] have endeavored through conversations with [the] President, Cabinet members, principal Senators, Representatives, to obtain preparation groundwork for [a] petroleum law which would be acceptable to American companies." The ambassador even told President Dutra that the Peruvian government had employed the law firm of Herbert Hoover, in writing their new petroleum law; Pawley kindly gave Dutra a Portuguese translation of the Peruvian law. [83]

When Dutra told the ambassador that "Communists and Vargas [now a senator] were mainly responsible" for the delays, Pawley asked him "not to overlook small groups of selfish national interests [obviously, Brazilian investors!] who would strongly pressure Government and if successful retard Brazil's progress for many years." Pawley finally asked the State Department if it would be advisable to suggest outright to the Brazilian government that they employ a U.S. firm to help in the drafting of a new and satisfactory petroleum law.[84] The department responded that official sponsorship of draft legislation or the minimum position of U.S. companies might be open to charges of interference in Brazilian internal affairs. It was suggested that, instead, the Brazilian government be advised to

employ as advisor to drafting committee person or firm experienced in oil legislation such as Max Thornburg author [of] Guatemalan law, Hoover Curtice and Ruby whose Curtice wrote Peruvian law, Schuster Feuille authors [of] Dominican Republic law or possibly DeGolyer and McNaughton whose Garner [is] now technical advisor to committee. In addition Harmon [the petroleum attaché] could be available [for] consultation.[85]

The details of what followed cannot be related here. It must suffice to say that, unfortunately for the oil companies and the State Department, they had not anticipated the ground swell of Brazilian pubic opinion against the wholesale liquidation of valuable national resources in favor of a few foreign companies. If the U.S. interests believed that the cause against them was championed only by Vargas, a few communists, and "selfish" Brazilian interests, they had a rude awakening. In the words of a Brazilian historian, this was when "from all sectors of Brazilian life, from every corner of the country, from all classes and social strata, the campaign erupted" against the proposed new petroleum law; and it was that popular movement that succeeded in preventing the proposal from becoming law.[86] Above all, the United States had not counted on opposition within the military, and its cooperation with the nationalist movement. The military that had overthrown Vargas was not the only military in Brazil! Brazil soon developed its own state-owned petroleum industry.

Notes

1. Albin Krebs, "Adolf A. Berle, Jr. Dies at Age of 76," New York *Times* Biographical Edition, February 25, 1971, p. 453.
2. Adolf Berle, *Latin America: Diplomacy and Reality* (New York: Harper & Row, 1962), p. 45.
3. Beatrice Bishop Berle and Travis Beal Jacobs, eds., *Navigating the Rapids, 1918–1971; From The Papers of Adolf A. Berle* (New York: Harcourt, Brace, Jovanovich, 1973), p. 559.
4. Berle and Jacobs, *Navigating,* p. 562.
5. Robert H. Ferrell, ed., *The American Secretaries of State,* Vol. 14 (New York: Cooper Square, 1965), p. 19.
6. Max Ascoli, "Introduction" to Berle and Jacobs, *Navigating,* p. xxx.
7. Berle and Jacobs, *Navigating,* p. 570. Emphasis added.
8. Lisle A. Rose, *The Coming of the American Age, 1945–1946* (Kent, Ohio: Kent State University Press, 1973), p. 253.

9. Dean Acheson, *Present at the Creation* (New York: Norton, 1963), pp. 14–15.

10. Berle and Jacobs, *Navigating,* p. 570.

11. Ascoli, "Introduction," Berle and Jacobs, *Navigating,* p. xxx.

12. L. C. Bresser Pereira, *Desenvolvimento e crise no Brasil, 1930–1967* (Rio de Janeiro: Zahar, 1968), pp. 100–13.

13. Octavio Ianni, *O colapso do populismo no Brasil* (Rio de Janeiro: Civilização Brasileira, 1958), p. 54.

14. Edgard Carone, *A terceira república (1937–1945)* (São Paulo: Difel, 1976), pp. 197–203. See also Ianni, *O colapso,* p. 56.

15. Carone, *A terceira república,* p. 196.

16. José Nilo Tavares, *Conciliação e radicalização política no Brasil* (Petrópolis: Vozes, 1982), p. 81.

17. Queiroz Junior, *Memórias sobre Getúlio* (Rio de Janeiro: Copac, 1957), p. 114.

18. In Brazilian writing, General Pedro Góes Monteiro is variously referred to as Góes Monteiro, General Góes, General Góes Monteiro, or simply Góes.

19. Peter Flynn, *Brazil: A Political Analysis* (Boulder: Westview Press, 1978), p. 110.

20. Hélio Jaquaribe, "The Dynamics of Brazilian Nationalism," in *Obstacles to Change in Latin America,* ed. Claudio Veliz (London: Oxford University Press, 1965), pp. 171–72.

21. Berle and Jacobs, *Navigating,* p. 520.

22. Ibid., pp. 518 and 526.

23. Ibid., p. 551.

24. Lourival Coutinho, *O General Góes depõe* (Rio de Janeiro: Coelho Branco, 1955), p. 431.

25. Adolph Berle to the Secretary of State, September 29, 1945, Berle Papers, Ambassador's Despatches, 1945, File 74, Roosevelt Library, Hyde Park, N.Y. Complete text of speech as enclosure.

26. Ibid.

27. Adolph Berle to President Truman, October 1, 1945, Berle Papers, Truman, File 77, Roosevelt Library.

28. Hélio Silva, *1945: Por que depuseram Vargas* (Rio de Janeiro: Civilização Brasileira, 1976), p. 219.

29. Coutinho, *O General Góes depõe,* p. 432.

30. Luis Vergara, *Fui secretário de Getúlio Vargas* (Rio de Janeiro: Globo, 1960), p. 245. In yet another version, Adyr Pontes Sette, *A verdade sobra a deposição de Getúlio Vargas* (Juis de fora: Gazeta Comercial, 1947), p. 84, maintains that Berle showed the speech to Vargas but the latter strongly disapproved of it.

31. Silva, *Por que depuseram Vargas,* pp. 221–22.

32. Adolph Berle to the Secretary of State, September 3, 1945, Berle Papers, Ambassador's Despatches, 1945, File 74, Roosevelt Library.

33. President Truman to Adolph Berle, September 13, 1945; Berle Papers, Truman, File 77, Roosevelt Library.

34. Berle to the Secretary of State, September 29, 1945 (Note 25 above).

35. Berle and Jacobs, *Navigating,* pp. 522–23.

36. Ibid., p. 551.

37. Ibid., p. 553.
38. Ibid., p. 523.
39. Ibid., pp. 524 and 531.
40. Ibid., pp. 548 and 553.
41. Ibid., p. 553.
42. Ibid., p. 521.
43. Jarbas Medeiros, *Ideologia autoritária no Brasil, 1930–1945* (Rio de Janeiro: Fundação Getúlio Vargas, 1978), p. 29.
44. Silva, *Por que depuseram Vargas,* p. 214.
45. Ibid., p. 213.
46. Medeiros, *Ideologia autoritária,* p. 261.
47. Berle and Jacobs, *Navigating,* p. 548.
48. Ibid., p. 549.
49. Ibid., p. 551.
50. Vergara, *Fui secretário de Getúlio Vargas,* p. 152.
51. Adolph Berle to the Secretary of State, August 22, 1945, Berle Papers, Ambassador's Despatches, 1945, File 74, Roosevelt Library.
52. Berle and Jacobs, *Navigating,* p. 548.
53. Ibid., p. 548–49.
54. Ibid., p. 557.
55. Ibid., p. 554.
56. Flynn, *Brazil,* p. 110.
57. Berle, *Latin America,* p. 17.
58. Berle and Jacobs, *Navigating,* p. 576.
59. George Philip, *Oil and Politics in Latin America* (London: Cambridge University Press, 1982), p. 231.
60. Getúlio Carvalho, *Petrobrás: do monopólio dos contratos de risco* (Rio de Janeiro: Forense-Universitária, 1976), pp. 17ff.
61. Gabriel Cohn, *Petróleo e nacionalismo* (São Paulo: Difusão Europeia do Livro, 1974), pp. 48–49.
62. Memorandum of Conversation, September 18, 1945, *Foreign Relations of the United States, 1945,* Vol. 9 (Washington, D.C.: Government Printing Office, 1968), pp. 686–87 (hereinafter cited as *FRUS*).
63. Vergara, *Fui secretário de Getúlio Vargas,* p. 244.
64. Secretary of State to Adolph Berle, November 10, 1945, *FRUS, 1946,* 11, pp. 523–24.
65. Adolph Berle to the Secretary of State, November 13, 1945, *FRUS, 1946,* 11, p. 525.
66. Ibid., p. 527. Emphasis added.
67. Adolph Berle to the Secretary of State, November 17, 1945, *FRUS, 1946,* 11, p. 529.
68. Berle and Jacobs, *Navigating,* p. 560.
69. Ibid., pp. 560–61.
70. Memorandum of Conversation, November 23, 1945, *FRUS, 1946,* 11, p. 532.
71. Secretary of State to Adolph Berle, November 30, 1945, *FRUS, 1946,* 11, pp. 533–34. Emphasis added.
72. Berle and Jacobs, *Navigating,* p. 563.

73. Secretary of State to Berle, November 30, 1945 (Note 71 above).

74. Adolph Berle to the Secretary of State, December 12, 1945, *FRUS, 1946,* 11, p. 537.

75. Memorandum of Conversation, December 21, 1945, *FRUS, 1946,* 11, p. 539.

76. Berle and Jacobs, *Navigating,* p. 559.

77. Ibid., pp. 524 and 531.

78. Ibid., p. 559.

79. Memorandum of Conversation, December 21, 1945 (Note 75 above).

80. Berle and Jacobs, *Navigating,* p. 565.

81. Chargé d'Affairs Daniels to the Secretary of State, March 29, 1946, *FRUS, 1946,* 11, p. 540.

82. Chargé d'Affairs Daniels to the Secretary of State, October 8, 1946, *FRUS, 1946,* 11, p. 551.

83. Ambassador Pawley to the Secretary of State, December 20, 1946, *FRUS, 1946,* 11, pp. 55, 557.

84. Ibid.

85. Secretary of State to Ambassador Pawley, December 27, 1946, *FRUS, 1946,* 11, p. 557.

86. Nelson Werneck Sodre, *História da burgesia brasileira* (Rio de Janeiro: Civilizacão Brasileira, 1946), p. 329.

5

Lincoln Gordon and Brazil's Military Counterrevolution

Jan Knippers Black

More than most U.S. governments, that of John F. Kennedy was launched with a measure of genuine idealism. But like all previous governments of the United States and of other great powers, the Kennedy administration cloaked its less edifying pursuits—for example, of political and material advantage—in the rhetoric of broadly shared values and moral ideals. And more than most, it confused the two.

There were doubtless many among the Kennedy coterie who considered the promotion of democracy and economic equity to be the most important goals of the Alliance for Progress. But the Alliance was multifaceted. The elaborate arguments of the season's economists notwithstanding, it cannot be assumed that the motives behind the promotion of more attractive incentives to U.S. investors were altogether altruistic.

Perhaps it was clear even to some of those strategists who were unencumbered by humanitarian concerns that it was no longer possible to promote economic development, even to the limited degree necessary to expand markets for U.S. overseas investors, without at the same time promoting urbanization, education, the spread of mass communication, and social organization—factors that inevitably give rise to demands for more nearly open and participatory politics. Thus, the Kennedy administration had declared itself prepared to welcome such democratizing trends, but within limits. A redesigned and revitalized program to strengthen Latin American military establishments and paramilitary and police organizations—more or less under U.S. control—was to ensure that those limits would be maintained.

Obviously, the most important test of the Alliance for Progress was in Brazil, Latin America's largest and most populous state. It was also a state where more-or-less democratic constitutional government appeared to be taking root and where the resources and markets crucial to economic development appeared to be infinite. To represent his administration in that key state, President Kennedy chose a Harvard professor who had distinguished himself as an economist and advisor to government agencies, and who had participated in the formulation of the Alliance for Progress: Lincoln Gordon. Gordon was retained in that role when President Lyndon Baines Johnson succeeded the assassinated Kennedy in late 1963.

Meanwhile, Brazil had entered into a period of crisis. Popular participation in politics was gradually expanding; and the newly participant sectors, such as organized labor, had to be courted and rewarded with economic benefits. A system of incremental redistribution could be maintained only so long as economic growth was such that favor to one pressure group was not necessarily at the expense of another. But by the early 1960s, inflation had become rampant and the economy had ceased to grow. The economic crisis, generated in part by production geared for the few and increasing demand by the many, deepened when a credit freeze was imposed by Western financial institutions.

In early 1964, Brazil's moderately reformist, civilian, constitutional president, João Goulart, was overthrown in a military coup d'etat and replaced by a military government—a new kind of military government characterized by leaders who were well-trained, self-confident, and determined to hold power indefinitely.

The first several thousand Brazilians to be arrested in the wake of the coup—and the many thousands more who were purged from their jobs or elected positions—came mainly from the ranks of supporters of the deposed regime or from among the leaders of labor, peasant, and student groups. But the military rulers gradually tightened the dictatorial noose; they silenced—by one means or another—politicians, journalists, intellectuals, clergymen, and others who sought to speak for the already silenced and dispossessed. By the late 1960s and early 1970s, torture of political prisoners had become systematic, and death squads operated with impunity. Meanwhile, the gap between rich and poor had become a yawning chasm: Multinational corporations and their Brazilian affiliates enjoyed an "economic miracle" with growth rates in the 10 percent range, while the earning power of most Brazilians dropped precipitously.

It was not until the late 1970s that Brazilians began to reclaim their freedoms of speech and assembly, and that elections—retained by the regime as a legitimizing ritual—began to be taken seriously by candidates and voters alike. The country's first civilian president in 20 years was elected in 1984.

That the United States gave considerable aid and comfort to the perpetrators of Brazil's counterrevolution is now a matter of record, and many Brazilians find Ambassador Lincoln Gordon to be the villain of the piece.[1] This chapter traces the activities and recommendations of the ambassador during those crucial years before and after the overthrow of Goulart, and looks at Gordon's relationships with the Brazilian government and its detractors. But the issue it addresses is not whether or not Gordon's role was a central one. Clearly, it was. The question, rather, is whether or not the outcome of Brazil's crisis of 1964 and the role of the United States in that outcome would have been significantly different had someone other than Gordon been the ambassador. In other words, how much of the credit or blame is owed to Gordon as an individual.

GORDON IN THE FAST TRACK

Lincoln Gordon had made a point of remaining aloof from partisan politics. Nevertheless, his credits and credentials made him a natural choice for the illustrious team that was being assembled by the incoming Kennedy administration to mark off the margins of the New Frontier. A child prodigy, he had enrolled at Harvard at the tender age of 16 and graduated in three years. Thereafter, he received a Rhodes Scholarship to study at Balliol College, Oxford; three years later, in 1936, he received his Ph.D. there. He became known in scholarly circles for his extraordinary memory for detail and his loquaciousness.

From Oxford, Gordon returned to Harvard and began to work his way up the academic career ladder. He was also initiated, early on, into the intoxicating business of advising government leaders and agencies. During the war years, he advised the National Resources Planning Board, engaged in economic analysis for the National Defense Advisory Commission, and served on the War Production Board and with the Civil Production Administration. After the war, he served in the Economic Cooperation Administration, where he helped to administer the Marshall Plan. He was also a delegate to the UN Atomic Energy Commission and a consultant to NATO and to the U.S. Department of State.[2]

Gordon returned to more-or-less full-time teaching in 1955, having become professor of international economics at Harvard's Graduate School of Business Administration. There, in 1957, he began a research project on economic development in Brazil, in collaboration with a number of Brazilian economists and political scientists. Consequently, he became a member of the Ford Foundation's first team to visit Brazil, in the summer of 1959, to look into the possibility of Foundation support for certain activities and institutions. During that time, he acquired a reading knowledge of Portuguese and Spanish and familiarity with Brazilian history, politics, economics, and culture. He also began to attend seminars and conferences on Latin America and to acquaint himself with a wide range of ideas concerning inter-American cooperation for development.

With the election of John F. Kennedy in 1960, a sizable contingent of the Harvard faculty began updating resumes and packing bags. The post of national security advisor went to McGeorge Bundy, who had worked under Gordon on the Marshall Plan task force. Gordon was first tapped by New Deal lawyer and veteran diplomat Adolf Berle to serve on a task force on policy toward Latin America. In that capacity, Gordon says, he drafted the economic chapters of the first formulation of the proposed Alliance for Progress.[3]

In early 1961, Secretary of State Designate Dean Rusk invited Gordon to become assistant secretary for economic affairs. Gordon rejected that offer, but his counteroffer to work half-time in the further development and negotiation of the Alliance for Progress was enthusiastically accepted. He became the administration's principal witness in congressional hearings for the $600 million appropriation to implement the Act of Bogotá and provide Chilean earthquake relief. He also served on a second Latin American policy task force chaired by Adolf Berle.

In April 1961, Gordon joined a delegation headed by Treasury Secretary Douglas Dillon to a meeting in Rio de Janeiro of the governors of the Inter-American Development Bank. On a return trip, Dillon raised a notion that had been touched upon the previous week by Richard Goodwin of the White House staff—that Gordon might be an appropriate choice for ambassador to Brazil.

The offer was formalized in the Oval Office in May; but the nomination was delayed until late August, as Gordon was scheduled to be a delegate to the inter-American conference at Punta del Este during that month. In the interim, while traveling in South America with Adlai Stevenson, Gordon received a call from President Kennedy urging him to accept the position of assistant secretary of state for American republics affairs. Gordon replied that he much preferred the earlier offer. Thus, the nomination for the ambassadorship came through on August 24, and Senate confirmation followed in short order.[4] Gordon arrived in Brazil to assume his new post in mid-October, which was less than two months after Brazilian President Jânio Quadros resigned, leaving the presidency to João Goulart, who was—in the eyes of conservative Brazilians and of the U.S. foreign affairs bureaucracy—a dangerous communist, or nationalist-populist, or pushover for communists and nationalist-populists.

THE UNITED STATES AND BRAZIL ON A COLLISION COURSE

In the Brazil of the early 1960s, the Kennedy administration and its envoy did not begin to write on an empty slate. On the part of the U.S. foreign policymaking elite, attitudes toward particular Brazilian leaders, parties, movements, institutions, and sectors were firmly established. The converse was also true.

Early in the twentieth century, U.S. influence in Brazil began to eclipse that of Brazil's first postindependence patron, Great Britain. Brazil's political and economic nucleus was shifting from the sugar-producing states of the Northeast to the coffee-producing South-Central states, and the United States was the best customer of the coffee producers. While most Latin American leaders were protesting the gunboat and dollar diplomacy practiced by an expansionist United States in Central America and the Caribbean in the first three decades of the century, Brazilian leaders were supportive. While some South American states vacillated or remained aloof, Brazil was fully cooperative with the United States in both world wars.

After World War II, however, the country experienced an influx of foreign (mainly U.S.) capital and a spurt of economic growth, accompanied by a blossoming of political parties and interest groups that were participating enthusiastically in the newly opened electoral system. For the first time, public opinion came to be a significant factor in the formulation of both domestic and foreign policy.

The policy thrust that came to be labeled "independent" made its first appearance during the last administration of Getúlio Vargas (1951–54). His government was openly unsympathetic with the U.S. approach to the Cold War and was concerned about the lack of restraint on foreign capital. Under his watch, restrictions were placed on foreign investment and on the repatriation of profits, and the government established a monopoly over the exploitation of petroleum.

U.S. officials were less than pleased with the election of Juscelino Kubitschek in 1955, and were particularly concerned about the election of João Goulart (who had served as Vargas's minister of labor) to the vice-presidency. To the distress of the U.S. Embassy, Kubitschek signed a trade agreement with the Soviet Union; but he dealt generously with U.S. investors.

Jânio Quadros, elected to succeed Kubitschek in the presidency, was a fiscal conservative. His policies were not viewed as threatening to business, domestic or foreign; but he was a maverick. He did not like to be pushed around, and that in itself made him a thorn in the side of U.S. officialdom. Quadros rejected a special offer of U.S. assistance that he saw as a bribe to induce support for the U.S. Bay of Pigs invasion of Cuba; and, for several months, he refused to see any U.S. official at all. U.S. Ambassador John Moors Cabot commented that Quadros should be kept on a "short leash."[5] But the nuisance of dealing with Quadros was of little consequence compared to the panic that spread through the U.S. foreign affairs bureaucracies when Quadros resigned, leaving the presidency to his vice-president, Goulart.[6]

Like Quadros, Goulart had little patience with U.S. Cold War hysteria, inclining instead toward anticolonialism and nonalignment. He even hedged his bets openly by adorning one wall of his oblong private office in the presidential palace in Brasília with a life-sized photograph of himself with

Kennedy—and another wall, with a similar photo of himself with Khrush-chev.[7] However, unlike Quadros, Goulart was serious about economic na-tionalism and had a considerable following on the labor-left.

The more conservative elements of the military, with encouragement from some Brazilian and U.S. business interests, sought to deny Goulart the pres-idency in 1961; but the Third Army, from Goulart's home state of Rio Grande do Sul, pledged to defend him. After consulting with congressional leaders, the military antagonists ultimately reached a compromise; they allowed Goulart to take office,but under a parliamentary rather than a presidential system. The U.S. government welcomed the restriction on Goulart's power.

In 1962, even under the constraints of the parliamentary system, Goulart was able to have enacted a law limiting annual profit remittance abroad to 10 percent of registered capital investment. A plebiscite in January 1963 restored to Goulart full presidential powers; and he began more vigorously to promote his program, which included modest land and tax reforms, the extension of voting rights to illiterates, and the legitimization of the Com-munist party. In the meantime, however, a myriad of projects were under way to block his legislative proposals and to cripple his support groups; and various conspiratorial movements, plotting his overthrow, were gathering momentum.

In general, U.S. businessmen, with more than a billion dollars invested in Brazil, were unhappy with the presidency of Goulart, and Brazilian busi-nessmen linked to the multinational corporate structure were like-minded. Some of these businessmen formed an organization called the Institute for Research and Social Studies (IPES) to agitate—and, later, to conspire—against the government of Goulart. Even before assuming his post in Brazil, Ambassador Lincoln Gordon had one close friend among the leaders of IPES; and, as time wore on, he became friendly with others among the group's leadership. He concedes that he did not disguise from IPES leaders the embassy's view that Goulart was mismanaging the economy and was planning a takeover.[8]

A more shadowy organization known as the Brazilian Institute for Demo-cratic Action (IBAD) pumped (by its own admission) the equivalent of some $12 million into the 1962 congressional and gubernatorial elections. IBAD was outlawed in 1963, after a Brazilian congressional investigating commis-sion uncovered circumstantial evidence that its funding came from foreign sources. A former CIA agent later confirmed that IBAD was a CIA "political-action" operation.[9] These organizations flooded the communications media with scare propaganda. At the same time, periodicals that took a pro-labor or nationalistic stance were denied advertising and driven out of business; a large proportion of the companies that could afford to advertise were U.S.-owned, and all of the major advertising agencies were.

Like many conservative Brazilians, U.S. officialdom was particularly pan-icked by peasant unrest in the Northeast and by the successes of Brazilian politicians who were sympathetic with the plight of the peasants. In 1962, the United States signed with the Brazilian government the Northeast Agreement, involving a commitment of $131 million. Several observers concluded that the program's two interrelated purposes were to defeat leftist candidates and to suppress or co-opt the peasant movement. AID was supposed to work through the Superintendency for the Northeast (SUDENE), a Brazilian federal government agency; but SUDENE objected to AID's strategy, so undermining SUDENE became one of the purposes of the program.

Meanwhile, with funds and direction provided by the CIA and other U.S. government agencies, parallel organizations were established or reinforced to compete with labor and student organizations supportive of the Goulart government. In the fall of 1963, the executive director of the American Institute for Free Labor Development (AIFLD) met with the governor of São Paulo and was briefed on plans for a coup. AIFLD then arranged a training session in Washington for a special all-Brazilian group.

By mid-1963, the U.S. effort to undermine Goulart had been formalized in an approach called "islands of administrative sanity," a phase originated by Lincoln Gordon. Under this policy, aid to the central government was suspended, while more than $100 million was committed to state governors who were pro-U.S. and anti-Goulart. Gordon maintains that the purpose of this policy was to keep Alliance for Progress projects going; but he notes that others—including Thomas Mann, who became President Johnson's chief advisor on Latin American affairs—apparently saw it primarily in political terms.[10] The public safety assistance program was geared at that time to the "islands of administrative sanity" policy; most of the policemen trained in 1963 were from the key states of Minas Gerais, Guanabara, and São Paulo. And the largest sum ever expended on the program in Brazil was expended in 1964.[11]

These and other conspiratorial efforts might have been of little consequence had the Brazilian armed forces been disposed to uphold and defend the constitutional government. Clearly, the civilian political structure was poorly equipped to cope with economic stress and class conflict. Nevertheless, Miguel Arraes was elected governor of Pernambuco despite the efforts of the United States to defeat him. Despite the propaganda and campaign funding provided by IBAD, IPES, and related organizations, Goulart's Brazilian Labor party (PTB) gained strength in the elections of 1962; and the congress restored full presidential powers to Goulart in 1963. AIFLD boasted of having drawn a number of labor leaders into the conspiracy against Goulart; but it is doubtful that AIFLD can take much credit for the ineffectiveness of the labor movement as a whole, at the time of the coup. AID and other U.S. agencies in the Northeast had succeeded in undermining SUDENE; but, despite all their efforts, the peasant movement had not been contained or deradicalized.

Thus, the disposition of the military was crucial. The United States had been cultivating Brazilian military leaders since World War II. Many of them had been trained at military institutions in the continental United States or in the Panama Canal Zone; and the United States had established and helped to operate Brazil's own Superior War College (ESG). Furthermore, in the early 1960s, the emphasis on training in counterinsurgency and civic action greatly expanded the number of officers who were exposed to U.S. military indoctrination. The Cold War world view to which they were exposed had made these officers contemptuous of politicians and suspicious of those who advocated social reform. And extensive training in systems analysis and managerial skills had convinced them that they were the only group capable of governing.

Gordon says that, shortly after he arrived in Brazil, Admiral Silvio Heck— one of the three military ministers who had signed the 1961 manifesto designed to prevent Goulart from assuming office—asked for an appointment with him. Heck told Gordon that Goulart was a communist and that there was a plan—supported by most of the military and many civilians, as well— to overthrow him. He said he hoped that, when the time came, the United States would not take a dim view of it. Gordon maintains that he was non-committal, but that he checked out the story and concluded that the plotters did not have nearly as much support as Heck had reported.

From time to time in 1962, the embassy was approached by groups plotting a coup. Gordon says that the standard response was that it was a Brazilian affair. But he did not conceal the embassy's distress about the tendencies of the Goulart government. And he did not pass on the embassy's information about conspiracies to friends of Goulart. At the ambassador's suggestion, President Kennedy (who, according to Gordon, was concerned in the fall of 1962 about growing instability) transferred Colonel Vernon Walters from Rome to Rio de Janeiro to serve as military attaché.[12] Walters had served as the U.S. liaison officer with the Brazilian Expeditionary Force in Italy during World War II and maintained a close friendship with several of the Brazilian officers involved—particularly, Brigadier General Humberto Castello Branco, who was to become army chief of staff. Later, during a 1976 interview, Walters said that, in Italy just before he was transferred, someone high in the Kennedy administration told him that Kennedy would not be averse to seeing the Goulart government overthrown if it could be replaced by an anticommunist one.[13]

GORDON AND GOULART: A PAS DE DEUX

Looking back from 1986 to the ambience of 1961, Gordon recalls that the Alliance for Progress was inspired by fears as well as hopes:

The fears were not overdrawn. The Soviet model of economic development has by now been so thoroughly discredited that one easily forgets how many Latin Americans, especially among intellectuals, were attracted to the notion of affiliation with the USSR. Marxist philosophy remains quite popular, but not, in most cases, as a guide to action. The danger of spreading demagogic nationalist populism was even greater. The Alliance helped to avert it for a time, but it takes on renewed strength in each period of North American neglect, up to and including the present.[14]

As to the country where Gordon was to serve, his fears were—from the very beginning—more vivid than his hopes. Apparently, he has not yet decided what he would like the record to show with regard to his assessment of Quadros. In a letter to the author, dated May 15, 1986, Gordon said that Quadros's resignation left him wondering whether his task was going to be anything like what he had hoped. "Based on his record as Mayor of São Paulo city and Governor of the State, we considered Quadros a natural partner in the Alliance for Progress—an opinion not contradicted by the three-hour session the Stevenson party had held with him in June." Yet, in a speech delivered just two months earlier in March 1986, Gordon had expressed frustration that, in Brazil, the "central purposes of two successive presidents—Quadros and Goulart—were not economic and social progress, but rather the pursuit of personalistic and illegitimate power."[15]

Gordon's attitude toward Goulart, however, has been subject to no such equivocation. From the beginning, Gordon's disdain for Goulart was personal as well as political; he saw the Brazilian president as overly extroverted and unpolished—a crude gaucho.[16] Goulart, who died in 1976, was more discreet. His general assessment of Gordon is not to be found in print.

Gordon would have us believe that he offered his opinions to the Brazilian government on matters of personnel and policy only when they were solicited—and, even then, reluctantly. Brazilians who served the Goulart government paint a different picture.

Wilson Fadul—who, in 1986, was president of the State Bank of Rio de Janeiro (Banco de Estado de Rio de Janeiro, or BANERJ)—served as minister of health during the presidency of Goulart. Then, as now, Brazil's pharmaceutical industry was 90 percent controlled by foreign investors. Foreign firms had established local affiliates; but most primary materials were imported, at prices up to 20 times those of the world market. In September 1963, the Brazilian government—on Fadul's initiative—decreed a prohibition against the importation of pharmaceutical raw materials at prices varying by 10 percent from world market prices. Shortly thereafter, Fadul was visited by Ambassador Gordon and the director of USAID in Brazil, Jack Kubisch.

Gordon made a presentation on behalf of U.S. pharmaceutical interests in São Paulo, who charged that the new decree unconstitutionally favored domestic businesses over foreign ones. Fadul responded that he could not receive such a complaint, as it had not been issued through the proper channels. Twenty-four hours later, Fadul received a message from Kubisch to the effect that Brazil would no longer receive free shipments of DDT to fight malaria, but might purchase the DDT at world market prices (an empty gesture, since Brazil had accepted the deadly substance, which was already banned in the United States, only reluctantly—but that's another story).[17]

Gordon's intercessions with regard to many other policy matters—for example, fiscal control measures; debt management; resource development; public employment; credit, wage, and tax policies; labor organization; land reform; profit remittance; and relations with so-called communist countries—are already on the public record. Nor did he shrink from expressing himself on questions of personnel. He complained to U.S. congressional committees and to Brazilian opposition leaders—as well as to Goulart himself—about the influence of communists on the Brazilian government and, when pressed for particulars, singled out cabinet ministers and other high-level officials of whom he disapproved.

Brazilian historian Luiz Alberto Moniz Bandeira says that Gordon acted as if he were running the country. On one occasion—Moniz says—Gordon announced, at an airport interview, the selection of a new minister of finance—information that had not yet been made public by the Brazilian government.[18]

When it suited his purposes, Gordon bypassed Goulart and his ministers entirely and dealt with those he chose to treat as representing Brazil. As noted, his dealings with the anti-Goulart governors were given formal expression in 1963 in the "islands of administrative sanity" policy. Apparently, he also cut his own deals, early on, with the Brazilian armed forces—as in the case of the military assistance accord signed in January 1964 between Brazilian General Araujo Castro and the U.S. ambassador's deputy, John Gordon Mein. Moniz Bandeira says that Goulart told him that the accord had not been cleared with him—that, in fact, he had not even been told about it.[19]

The confrontation between Goulart and his detractors—including U.S. officials—became more pronounced in March 1964. Gordon cabled to Washington a plea for additional assistance to the military; and the conspiracy against the constitutional government moved into high gear.

On Friday the 13th, Goulart staged a rally, at which time he announced plans for a modest land reform, for the expropriation of domestically owned oil refineries, for the imposition of rent controls and ceilings, and for other initiatives that Gordon and his associates saw as ominous. Colonel Walters visited General Castello Branco that evening and watched the rally on television with him.

Goulart's rally in Rio was followed, six days later, by an anti-Goulart rally in São Paulo—the "March of Family with God for Liberty," organized by IPES affiliates. Meanwhile, Gordon was in Washington, discussing with upper echelon policymakers his options for dealing with the situation in Brazil.

Returning to Brazil on March 22, Gordon and his embassy task force drew up plans to offer material assistance to the anti-Goulart conspirators, should such assistance become necessary. The plans called for supplying petroleum and for having a U.S. carrier task force standing by. Subsequently, it was decided that arms and ammunition should also be made available. Gordon passed the plans on to Washington on March 27, along with his conviction that Goulart was seeking dictatorial powers and that civil war might break out.[20]

The class conflict that was becoming manifest in the country at large had its effects within the military, as well. On March 25, 3,000 sailors and marines, who were calling for basic social reforms, had rebelled against their anti-Goulart officers. On March 30, Goulart's televised address in defense of the mutineers provided the conspirators the pretext and catalyst that they felt they needed.

On March 31, General Mourão Filho, commander of the Fourth Military Region, began moving his troops from Minas Gerais toward Rio. Other commanders fell into line, under the leadership of General Castello Branco; and, by April 1, it was all over. Goulart, unable to mobilize any important sector of the military in defense of the constitutional government and unwilling to spill civilian blood in vain, fled to Uruguay.

U.S. contingency plans were put into operation on March 31. Under "Project Brother Sam," commanded by Major General George S. Brown, the Air Force was ordered to send six C-135 transports to pick up 110 tons of small arms and ammunition assembled at McGuire Air Force Base in New Jersey for reshipment. The aircraft carrier Forrestal and its support vessels headed toward a position off the Brazilian coast to await orders from Gordon. Some aspects of the operation were canceled on April 2 and 3; but the arms at McGuire Air Force Base were to remain available, in case Gordon determined that Brazilian security forces needed them. The Carrier Task Force, having moved into its cover operation, was nevertheless to continue toward the South Atlantic, in case Gordon should see a need for a demonstration of U.S. naval power. In an April 2 dispatch, Gordon had indicated that the "democratic forces" might still need fuel.[21]

The new regime quickly consolidated its grip on power, and needed none of the material assistance assembled specifically for Project Brother Sam. However, a $50 million loan from AID's emergency contingency fund was extended, within hours of the military takeover; and, for a decade thereafter, U.S. economic and military aid to Brazil remained at unprecedented levels.[22] On April 2, Gordon had cabled Senator Carl Hayden, a member of the appropriations committee, recommending that "the greatest possible consideration be given to any request [by the new Brazilian government] for economic emergency assistance." He described the demise of the Goulart government as "a great victory for [the] free world," possibly preventing "a total loss to [the] West of all South American Republics." He also noted that the change in government should "create a greatly improved climate for private investments."[23]

CLAIMING CREDIT WITHOUT BLAME

Gordon still denies that, as U.S. ambassador to Brazil, he played any role—even a cheerleading one—in the overthrow of a constitutional government. He maintains, instead, that the coup d'etat of 1964 was a counter-coup.

Goulart had chosen to emulate Vargas and carry out a coup of his own. In that sense, the revolution was a countercoup. I tried to encourage the rapid restoration of constitutionalism, starting with my appeal to Kubitschek on the evening of March 31. But just as the revolution took place without our participation, so did the subsequent events of Institutional Acts and large-scale "cassations."[24]

However, for the U.S. role in Brazilian events (as he portrays them) during his ambassadorship, Gordon is willing to claim very considerable credit. He did receive the usual initial briefings from the Departments of State, Defense, Treasury, Commerce, and Labor and from the USIA and the CIA, on specific issues; and managing the second-largest U.S. diplomatic mission in the world involved a very active flow of communications with Washington. However, Gordon says that there were no formal instructions as to policy objectives, nor was he in need of any.

On a few occasions, such as that of the Cuban missile crisis, Gordon says that he received detailed instructions on when to inform the Brazilian president and what to ask of him. And Gordon cites an occasion in 1965 when he received instructions that he considered misguided—to press Brazil for some contribution to the Vietnam war effort; he was able to dissuade President Johnson from that course. On most matters, however, Gordon says that he was expected to take the initiative and recommend policy or act on his own. He notes that, after all, he had been a part of the Latin American policymaking group, in intimate contact with both the White House and the Department of State.

In addition to giving him greater latitude for individual initiative than some other ambassadors enjoyed, his intimacy with U.S. officials at the highest levels enhanced his influence on Capitol Hill, as well as in Brazil. Gordon says, "I was in regular contact with the President [speaking in this case of Kennedy] on each visit to Washington, and on close personal terms with Bundy and Rusk, both of whom I had known for years. I also knew McNamara quite well and saw him regularly."[25]

Ambassador Covey T. Oliver, who was a Fulbright Hays scholar in Brazil during Gordon's first years there and then served as ambassador to Colombia before replacing Gordon in 1967 as assistant secretary of state for Latin American affairs, says that Brazilians were very well aware of Gordon's access and influence in Washington, which—plus Gordon's assertive manner—gave great weight to his views on what was or should be happening in Brazil. Oliver remembers seeing, on a hill in Rio, a sign suggesting that Gordon was to be Brazil's next president.[26]

Given such levels of access and influence, Gordon bristles at the suggestion that there could have been any line of action undertaken by any U.S. agency beyond his purview. He says that the CIA station was instructed to do nothing without his approval and that the possibility of a "two-track" policy—such as later evolved under the Nixon administration with respect to Chile, in which the U.S. ambassador was less than fully informed—was "totally noncredible" with regard to his own tenure in Brazil.

In fact, it does appear that the level of consensus and continuity in U.S. policy toward Brazil in the 1960s was extraordinary. Gordon says that there were no substantial differences between the objectives and approaches of the Kennedy and Johnson administrations. "I do not believe," he says, "that our actions during the March–April crisis would have been different if Kennedy had survived. Nor do I believe that he would have withheld Alliance support for the post-revolution efforts to reduce inflation and rekindle economic growth."[27] Be that as it may, the general pattern of support for programs designed to undermine movements springing from or appealing to the aspirations of the lower classes and to strengthen the military and other groups favorably disposed toward U.S. economic and security policies was elaborated on Kennedy's watch, along with some measures designed more specifically to weaken Goulart and to embolden his enemies.

Furthermore—whereas, in some Latin American countries during those same years, U.S. departments and agencies were often found to be working at cross-purposes—efforts of the "country team" in Brazil appeared to be remarkably well-focused and coordinated, as well, with those of U.S. corporations having interests there. Gordon says that he knows of no significant interagency disagreements about the U.S. role in Brazil in 1964. Nor do other sources report significant dissidence, although there are indications that the Peace Corps resisted efforts by AIFLD to draw volunteers into projects seen as supportive of the military regime.

At least with reference to Brazil during the period under examination, the general thrust of U.S. policy from one administration to the next and from agency to agency was a seamless web. How, then, is one to filter out Gordon's own ideas and prescriptions from those of policymakers at other levels and in other departments. Gordon might be given credit for having been able to see and willing to admit—at least on some occasions—that the most formidable obstacle to the attainment of U.S. objectives in Latin America was not communism, but nationalist populism. The designations of allies and enemies, however, and the prescriptions for U.S. action flowing from such an assessment were no different from those inspired by fears of the "communist menace." Thus, while it is possible to credit Gordon with authorship of tactical initiatives—such as the positioning of the U.S. carrier task force offshore as the coup got underway—and with effective advocacy of high levels of U.S. aid after the "revolution," it would be extremely difficult to isolate his imprint on more fundamental aspects of policy. Even the economic goals of the Alliance for Progress, as he pursued them in Brazil, looked remarkably like the timeless business of protecting U.S. investments.

Ultimately, atrocities committed by Brazil's military government gave rise to serious friction within the U.S. country team. Ambassador John Tuthill, who replaced Gordon when the latter became assistant secretary of state for Latin American affairs in 1966, protested the dissolution of the Brazilian congress in December 1968 and the fierce repression that followed. Tuthill was replaced, six months later; but, in the interim, the U.S. military mission dealt directly with the Brazilian government and froze embassy civilians out of the communication process.[28]

Repression was less severe between the installation of military rule in 1964 and Gordon's retirement from government service in 1967. Nevertheless, the violations of civil liberties and human rights created an image problem, both for the "revolutionary" government and for its U.S. backers. Declassified documents at the LBJ Library in Austin include an April 6, 1964, telegram from Secretary of State Rusk to Ambassador Gordon, complaining that such "excesses" as the invasion of the New York *Times* offices gave the new government a poor image. Gordon's return telegram, dated April 7, spoke of exerting U.S. influence "to maintain the greatest possible color of legitimacy."[29]

The ever-expanding purges, the frequency of arbitrary arrests, and the less frequent but well-publicized cases of torture of political prisoners were no secret in Washington; and some U.S. officials felt obliged to express concern. In 1965, about a week after he assumed the position of assistant secretary of state for Latin American affairs, Jack Vaughn was invited to dinner at the home of presidential advisor Thomas Mann to meet the Brazilian ambassador. On that occasion, Vaughn called attention to the media reports of abuses of civil and human rights. Both Mann and the ambassador were indignant that the subject had been raised. They did not deny the allegations, but urged Vaughn to look at the larger picture. Vaughn believes that, partly as a consequence of that indiscretion, his office was sometimes circumvented when decisions affecting Brazil were being considered.[30]

Later in the year, Vaughn accompanied Attorney General Robert Kennedy on a visit to Brazil. In a dinner party conversation with Gordon and Roberto Campos (the Brazilian finance minister and a former student of Gordon), Kennedy was highly critical of the Brazilian regime for its use of repression. Campos's retort was to the effect that Kennedy had no business meddling in Brazilian affairs.

During the first three years after the coup, Gordon (often in league with Mann and Bundy and with the upper echelons at the CIA) was—in private as well as in public—a committed advocate of U.S. political and economic support for the Brazilian generals; and he brooked no opposition from others among U.S. policymaking circles.[31] Gordon says that he privately complained to President Castello Branco after the issuance of the second Institutional Act in October 1964, which asserted the president's power to suspend congress (among other things) and rule by decree.[32] In his public statements, however—both to Brazilian audiences and to U.S. ones, including the U.S. Congress—he expressed nothing other than unqualified praise for the military regime.

In a letter to the editor of *Commonweal* in 1970, Gordon said, "During the period before mid-1967, no cases of torture were brought to my attention."[33] In fact, in just the first six months after the coup, some two dozen fully documented cases of torture were placed on the public record. *Torturas e Torturados* ("Torturers and the Tortured") by congressman and journalist Márcio Moreira Alves was published in Brazil in 1966.[34] A Foreign Service officer who served in Brazil from 1964 to 1969 says that Gordon was interested only in whitewashing the military government. The officer says he did indeed report, during Gordon's tenure, that some political prisoners were being tortured; but his reports were ignored.[35] Jack Vaughn says he does not recall ever, as assistant secretary, having seen a report from Gordon that called attention to repression.[36]

Finally, in the spring of 1969, Gordon joined publicly with other academics in signing a telegram to then Brazilian President Artur da Costa e Silva, which protested arbitrary actions against professors, students, and others. Commenting on that initiative, Gordon told the author in 1975 that he wondered if the terrorism of the late 1960s could have been controlled without the adoption of the Fifth Institutional Act. He said he did not necessarily think that terrorists were entitled to civil rights as we know them; but he felt that, in that move against the universities, the Brazilian government had gone too far.[37]

THE LEGACY

In the 1980s, the United States remained Brazil's most important single trading partner—although it no longer accounted for nearly half of Brazil's trade, as had been the case in the early 1960s. The intimate ties and the patron–client relationship between U.S. and Brazilian military establishments, which had been so apparent and so destructive in the 1960s, dissolved in the 1970s. The dissolution came about partly because of discord on specific issues: territorial-water claims, Brazil's nuclear power accord with West Germany, and Carter's human rights policy. But, more importantly, it came about because, once in power, the military—like other sectors of Brazilian society—came to be resentful of occupying a subordinate position in an unequal relationship, of being expected to subordinate national interests to U.S. interests. And the United States, having already played the military card, was left with less leverage. Finally, it came about because Brazil's accelerated process of industrialization had set in relief the very real conflicts of economic interest between the two countries.

By 1986, Brazil's major concerns in its dealings with the United States were with tariffs and quotas—with what Brazil viewed as growing U.S. protectionism, along with U.S. charges of Brazilian protectionism—and with the high U.S. interest rates that had plunged Brazil into an abyss of debt. Meanwhile, the Reagan administration had failed miserably in its attempts to interest Brazilian leaders in its Central American exploits and its new Cold War agenda.

However, the consequences of the crises and the decisions of the 1960s continue to reverberate in the 1980s. In the heady years of the 1960s, perhaps without realizing it, U.S. policymakers came upon the limits of the country's facile ability to stage-manage Latin America's political dramas. The economic and technological modernization that the United States was so enthusiastically promoting gave rise to democratizing trends; these, in turn, fed upon and strengthened nationalism, which limited the ability of the United States to control Latin American choices of policies and policymakers. Thus, it became necessary for the United States either to loosen its grip and accommodate the new political forces or to repress them.

The Kennedy administration tried to have it both ways—by courting democratic elements, on the one hand, while maintaining the familiar limits by strengthening antidemocratic elements, on the other. Not surprisingly, political leaders of Latin America's era of burgeoning democracy chafed at the limits. Some rejected them and came to be seen by U.S. policymakers as dangerous subversives. Others grudgingly accepted the limits and, unable to cater to their domestic constituencies, lost their political bases to the "subversives." The consequent political fluidity was viewed with alarm in Washington, as well as in the corporate suites and country clubs of Latin America. Kennedy administration liberals, feeling betrayed, began to back away from their erstwhile democratic allies in Latin America. After Kennedy's assassination, the Johnson administration, seeking to pull the Latin American drama back to the U.S. script, turned to the area's armed forces—forces that had been carefully groomed for political leadership.

The militarization of Brazil in 1964 was not an aberration; it was a harbinger. In the years that followed, one constitutional government after another fell victim to military coups. Whereas in 1961 only three Latin American governments were generally considered dictatorial, by 1976 only three or four were generally considered democratic.

With the possible exception, in some countries, of the early Kennedy and early Carter years, all postwar U.S. administrations, when faced with a showdown over the limits of U.S. control, have opted for repression over accommodation—a line of action that flows logically from the theoretical underpinnings of the more general policy of "containment." But the politics of force also has its limits, as the high cost of thwarting change in Central America in the 1980s has been proving.

Lincoln Gordon came to the upper echelons of the U.S. government as a member of a generation of leaders that writer David Halberstam labeled "the best and the brightest." Even more than most previous generations of leaders, they were convinced that they knew better than Latin American and other Third World leaders and peoples what was best for them. In a speech prepared for the twenty-fifth anniversary of the launching of the Alliance for Progress, Gordon attributed the failure of the program to achieve its more far-reaching goals to the U.S. "neglect" of Latin America in the 1970s, rather than to any problem in the nature of U.S. attentions to the area.[38]

Gordon was certainly a prominent player in the pursuit of U.S. goals in Brazil in the 1960s. And as an architect of the economic aspects of the Alliance for Progress, an official extraordinarily well connected with higher level policymakers, and a man extraordinarily confident of the shrewdness of his own views, he is probably entitled to as much of the credit or the blame for the formulation of those goals as any other single U.S. official of the period. Yet, it seems unlikely that U.S. policies and actions would have differed in any significant way, had some other individual been serving at that time and place as ambassador. Ambassadors are rarely drawn from the ranks of those who question the basic premises of U.S. policy. The U.S. stance in Brazil in the 1960s flowed logically from those premises—a clear and consistent line of reasoning that continues to lead to the tarnishing of the U.S. image and the squandering of U.S. influence throughout the world.

NOTES:

The author would like to acknowledge the research assistance of Danice Picraux in the preparation of this chapter.

1. For comprehensive coverage of the U.S. role in Brazil's military counterrevolution, see Jan Knippers Black, *United States Penetration of Brazil* (Philadelphia: University of Pennsylvania Press, 1977); A.J. Langguth, *Hidden Terrors* (New York: Pantheon, 1978); Luiz Alberto Moniz Bandeira, *Presença dos Estados Unidos no Brasil* (Rio de Janeiro: Civilização Brasileira, 1973); Phyllis Parker, *Brazil and the Quiet Intervention* (Austin: University of Texas Press, 1979); and Rene Armand Dreifuss, *1964: A Conquista do Estado* (Petrópolis: Vozes, 1981).

2. Letter from Lincoln Gordon to the author, dated May 15, 1986. Also *Who's Who in American Politics*, 2nd ed. 1969–70 (New York: R.R. Bowker, 1969), p. 438; and Langguth, *Hidden Terrors*, pp. 59–60.

3. Gordon letter.

4. Ibid.

5. Peter D. Bell, "Brazilian–American Relations," in *Brazil in the Sixties*, Riordan Roett ed. (Nashville: Vanderbilt University Press, 1972).

6. In the Brazilian system at that time, president and vice-president were elected separately and did not necessarily represent the same parties or constituencies.

7. The author observed the photographs in the president's office in March 1964.

8. Lincoln Gordon, interviewed by the author, March 12, 1975.

9. Eloy Dutra, *IBAD, Sigla da Corrupção* (Rio de Janeiro: Editôra Civilização Brasileira, 1963); and Philip Agee, *Inside the Company: CIA Diary* (London: Penguin Books, 1975), pp. 599–624.

10. Gordon interview.

11. U.S. Congress, Senate, Committee on Foreign Relations, Subcommittee on Western Hemisphere Affairs, *United States Policies and Programs in Brazil: Hearings*, 92nd Cong., 1st sess., May 4, 5, and 11, 1971.

12. Gordon interview and letter.

13. Parker, *Brazil*, pp. 62–63.

14. Lincoln Gordon, "The Alliance for Progress at Birth: Hopes and Fears," speech delivered in Washington, D.C., March 13, 1986, commemorating the twenty-fifth anniversary of the launching of the Alliance for Progress.

15. Ibid.

16. Langguth, *Hidden Terrors*, p. 84.

17. Wilson Fadul, interview with the author, Rio de Janeiro, July 22, 1986.

18. Luiz Alberto Moniz Bandeira, professor of history, Universidade Estadual de Rio de Janeiro, interview with the author, Rio de Janeiro, July 15, 1986.

19. Ibid.

20. Parker, *Brazil*, pp. 64–70.

21. National Security Files, Country File: Brazil, Containers 1 and 2, Cables, Vol. 1–3, 11/63–4/64, Lyndon Baines Johnson Library, Austin, Tex.

22. U.S. Congress, Senate, Committee on Appropriations, *Foreign Assistance and Related Appropriations for 1965: Hearings on H.R. 11812*, 88th Cong., 2nd sess., 1964, pp. 26–27 and 379–96.

23. Parker, *Brazil*, pp. 82–83.

24. Gordon letter. "Cassation" refers to the purging of elected officials. In the 1975 interview with the author, Gordon said that he had visited Kubitschek to encourage him to prevail upon members of congress to assert themselves in the formation of a new government.

25. Gordon letter.

26. Covey T. Oliver, telephone interview with the author, May 4, 1986.

27. Gordon letter.

28. See Black, *United States Penetration*, pp. 216–30.

29. National Security Files, Country File: Brazil, Container 2, Cables, Vol. III, 4/64.

30. Jack Vaughn, telephone interview with the author, June 18, 1986.

31. Ibid.

32. Gordon interview.

33. *Commonweal* 92(August 7, 1970):378.

34. Márcio Moreira Alves, *Torturas e Torturados* (Rio de Janeiro: Editôra Idade Nova, 1966).

35. Interview with the author, Washington, D.C., April 14, 1986. The officer, fearing reprisals, requested that his name not be used.

36. Vaughn interview.

37. Gordon interview.

38. Gordon, "Alliance for Progress at Birth" speech.

6

In the Years of Salvador Allende

Nathaniel Davis

Oscar Levant once wisecracked: "I've given up reading books; I find it takes my mind off myself." The answer to Levant's dilemma appears to have fallen into my lap: I am to write a book chapter on my own service as U.S. ambassador to Chile. However, I am a bit surprised to discover how intractable the task turns out to be.

Besides the difficulty of writing about one's self without puffery or apology, there is the problem of the relationship between an ambassador's personal role and U.S. policy toward the country in question. The focus of the present volume is on the chief of mission's influence, not on the U.S. government's policies, which are largely determined in Washington. Policy positions are not entirely formulated there, however, as I shall argue shortly.

U.S. policy and an ambassador's actions cannot be disentangled for other reasons—including the fact that every diplomat is, by definition, an instrument of the president and U.S. governmental purposes. A good diplomat must be a loyal and reliable agent; and it is a continuing source of surprise to me how often high-ranking diplomats perceive their role as the articulation and pursuit of personal goals and views. No matter how altruistically motivated or deeply convinced, a diplomat who disagrees with his chief should not use his office to undermine or corrupt the president's policies.

There is only one great reservation, in this regard; and that is that an ambassador serves the president under law. The oath of office of any public servant is to the U.S. Constitution and the legal order, and only within that context is the officer committed to serve his constituted superiors. To cite an example where the issue came up, the Costa-Gavras film *Missing* suggested that my colleagues and I "fingered" an innocent young U.S. citizen at the time of the Chilean coup and had him killed. The film's dialogue and the glowering presence of Richard Nixon in photographs that dominated the scene of malfeasance conveyed the impression that we were furthering the president's purposes in disregard of oath and duty. If the film were true, it would have signaled the utter corruption of the rule of law in our public service.

However, short of committing unlawful acts, an ambassador must faithfully advance the policy goals set by the president. A Foreign Service officer is trained to do this; and, if one believes in professional diplomacy, it becomes necessary to accept this relationship and to be prepared to carry out policies with which one may not agree. In the process, the diplomat inevitably accepts responsibility for both personal actions and U.S. policies. If the Foreign Service officer's disagreement with policy is profound and all pervasive, then the appropriate recourse is to resign one's office. I found myself pushed to this extremity in another situation, when I resigned as assistant secretary of state for African affairs in disagreement with President Ford and Secretary of State Kissinger's decision to intervene covertly in the Angolan civil war in 1975; but I did not resign as U.S. ambassador to Chile. Consequently, I share responsibility for U.S. policy there during my incumbency, and must now address both U.S. policy and my personal actions. This question will become particularly important in connection with U.S. covert programs in Chile between 1971 and 1973.

Chile was a very particular place when my family and I went there in 1971. Salvador Allende had promised that he would lead his countrymen to socialism along a peaceful, constitutional "Chilean Way"—power having been gained in free elections and the country's transformation being achieved institutionally, without a dictatorship of the proletariat, and with minimum human cost. Richard Nixon saw the Allende experiment as a second bridgehead (along with Castro's Cuba) for the spread of communism throughout the hemisphere. Henry Kissinger felt the same way. U.S. policy became two in one: calling for a correct U.S. outer posture, on one level; and, on a second level, the application of unacknowledged pressure against the Chilean government—and support to opposition forces—in order to prevent Allende's consolidation of power, and limit his government's ability to carry out policies contrary to perceived U.S. interests. The execution and impact of these policies will be a recurring theme in this chapter, but it may be useful to present a brief overview at the start.

There are some who think that an ambassador's background, personal qualities, skills, language competency, contacts, and judgment do not really matter anymore—in Chile or elsewhere. They seem to believe that, in the current era of rapid communications and instant visits, the chief of a U.S. diplomatic mission has sunk into the role of hotelier, plane greeter, message deliverer, and coat holder. Having experienced the State Department process at both ends, I continue to believe that an ambassador's role is crucial—for better or for worse. After all, *somebody* has to try to understand what is going on in the country in question and make wise policy recommendations to the harassed principal officers of the U.S. government. A never-ceasing dialogue on policy goes between an embassy and Washington. Moreover, effective embassy reporting and analysis shape Washington's understanding of the reality with which the U.S. government is dealing. In fact, an ambassador and his embassy colleagues speak from a pivotal vantage point: They are on the spot, reporting and interpreting reality; and the ambassador's recommendations on a controversial issue strike an almost always divided—certainly not unified—policy community in Washington. The weight of his opinion may tip the balance. This somebody must also act in the foreign capital, between under secretaries' visits. Diplomacy—wherever its practitioners reside—is a profession of communication, empathy, and perception. It is rooted in contacts and personal relationships. Eloquence, depth of knowledge, and force of personality do matter—both in representing one's country abroad and in interpreting realities in Washington.

The actions of some strong ambassadors have been described earlier in this book. Their example illustrates that the ambassador does make a difference. True, embassy-to-Washington telegraphic links have gotten faster since Sumner Welles and Spruille Braden were operating in the field; but, even in their time, a telegram could have been sent fast enough to curb or redirect their activities—if speed of communication had been the issue. It was not. Today, too, strong-minded U.S. ambassadors in embassies on all five continents are cutting wide swaths, for good or ill.

Having acknowledged the inseparability of policy and ambassadorial action, I must still recommend that a diplomat be judged (partly at least) on the basis of his personal effectiveness in carrying out the president's policies. John Peurifoy was highly effective in Guatemala when Washington's objective was to topple Arbenz. U.S. policy may have been wrong, and destructive of long-term U.S. interests in the hemisphere; but Peurifoy was a well-chosen instrument of U.S. policy.

Then there is the question of ambassadorial attitude. Personally, I liked Salvador Allende and most of the key figures around him—a great deal more, in fact, than Richard Nixon or Henry Kissinger did. This was probably lucky. If one likes people or dislikes them, they generally know it. All too many diplomats—many of them professionals who should know better—think that they can denigrate and even detest the host country and its people, and still be effective. A president of the United States may be able to, but an ambassador generally cannot.

The kind of ambassador that I think the United States needed in Chile in 1971 was a person with a modicum of understanding, flexibility, and goodwill. Actually, I did also have some relevant substantive and technical qualifications. I had served in three Marxist-run countries—the USSR, Czechoslovakia, and Bulgaria—and had worked on U.S. relations with communist regimes during assignments to both the State Department and the National

Security Council staff at the White House. I had also worked in Latin America—with postings in Venezuela and Guatemala and, briefly, as interim Peace Corps director in Chile. I spoke Spanish. Santiago would be my third post as chief of mission.

When I presented my credentials to Salvador Allende in October 1971, the leftist Chilean newspaper *Clarín* fantasized in print, saying that my chiefs in Washington had instructed me as follows: "Smile whenever you can; be as ingratiating as possible; talk with the journalists. . . . The gringo followed instructions to the letter."[1] There had been no such instructions, of course; but *Clarín* put its finger on a central characteristic of my mission in Chile, as I conceived it. I did consciously try to maintain a modest presence and operate in a low key, relying more on private talks than resounding polemics. I sought to be a reasonably amiable presence on the Santiago scene, rather than a public rallying point for the opposition and a lightning rod for the left-extremists. Clearly, the United States needed to "cool it" in Chile; and that is what I tried to do.

Richard Fagen, then in Santiago as a professor with the Latin American Faculty of the Social Sciences, noticed the phenomenon. He described the change of leadership at the U.S. Embassy as follows:

Edward Korry . . . was very suspected because of his open hostility to the government in power. . . . Nathaniel Davis, his replacement, arrived at a difficult and delicate moment. For the first several months, his profile was extraordinarily low. . . . It was clear to all that the effective operative head of the Embassy was Harry Schlaudeman, the Deputy Chief, . . . [and] a hard liner.[2]

While Fagen got the lowered profile right, his idea that I was standing in my deputy's shadow would have considerably surprised my deputy, as well as the embassy staff. The State Department inspectors who visited the Santiago post in early 1973 commented in their report that "this is a tightly organized Embassy in which the Ambassador's policy and operational control over all U.S. agencies represented is about as complete as it ever can get."[3] In light of subsequent controversy and the accusations of coup plotting and other improper embassy activities, it was perhaps just as well that I asserted strong control over the activities of all elements of the mission, including the military attachés, MILGROUP officers, and the CIA station. I took vigorous measures to ensure that there was no spirit of adventurism emanating from the embassy and its staff. My objective was a circumspect U.S. mission.

What were the results of the "low profile" on the part of both the embassy staff and myself? I think that our style of embassy conduct contributed—along with other elements of U.S. policy and action—to avoidance of the symbolic confrontation that characterized U.S.–Argentine relations in 1945, when Perón and Braden became the standard-bearers in a kind of political war. Peurifoy became such a symbol in Guatemala in 1954; and Ambassador Earl Smith carried the banner for a point of view and set of values and attachments in Cuba in 1958–59. We escaped a repetition of this phenomenon in Chile.

There were substantial differences in outlook within the embassy. To the end, several officers believed that the political and economic slide in the country would not result in a generalized crisis, but would prove to be a surface phenomenon that the regime would overcome. Others, including myself, perceived a more fundamental deterioration—which, in all likelihood, would ultimately lead to a confrontation. I did not suppress dissenting views; I forwarded them to Washington with clear identification of their personal nature and of embassy differences.

The perception of the trend of events mattered in Washington. In a funny backward way, the advocates of more "decisive" interventionist steps tended to become more quiescent (and certainly more cautious) whenever the signs of a coming crisis and showdown multiplied—even without drastic action on our part. I did not tailor reporting to hush the madcaps on the Potomac; but I did make sure that the dynamic of Chilean events was clearly presented.

Before proceeding further, it may be useful to amplify the earlier description of Washington's two-level policy regarding Chile. The policy was delineated in National Security Decision Memorandum (NSDM) 93, promulgated secretly on November 9, 1970—almost a year before I went to Chile.[4] At the level of publicly articulated policy—our "outer" face—President Nixon made the following statement with respect to Chile in his annual foreign policy report to the Congress, issued in February 1971: "Our bilateral policy is to keep open the lines of communication between the U.S. and Chile. . . . In short, we are prepared to have the kind of relationship with the Chilean government that it is prepared to have with us."[5]

On the level that was secret, NSDM 93 mandated cessation of new U.S. credits to Chile; sharp reductions in economic assistance; the denial of new U.S. guarantees of private investment there; use of U.S. influence to constrict credits to Chile that might be extended by international financial institutions; and other reductions in economic ties.

It was soon evident that the difficulty with these inconsistent and somewhat contradictory secret and public U.S. policies was that they were hard to keep straight, hard to keep secret, and hard to make fully understood—even within the inner counsels of the U.S. government. For example, Admiral Elmo Zumwalt, the chief of naval operations, complained in his memoirs that "no one in Defense, not even Mel Laird to Tom Moorer I conjecture—I cannot be absolutely sure—knew precisely what administration policy toward Chile was [in late 1970 and early 1971] because Henry had made an elaborate point of not telling them."[6] Zumwalt himself burned his fingers, by encouraging Allende to invite the U.S. nuclear carrier Enterprise to visit Valparaiso in February 1971. Evidently, such a visit was more public embrace than the White House desired; and Nixon and Kissinger thereupon repudiated Zumwalt and rebuffed Allende.

To take another example, the U.S. Commodity Credit Corporation (CCC) extended a $4 million supplier line of credit to Chile in late 1972, to enable Chile to buy U.S. surplus agricultural products. This was an unvarnished mistake: The CCC had simply not gotten the word that such credits were against U.S. policy. So, the inherent dissembling in the secret and public U.S. policies toward Chile caused problems.

Despite the difficulties that NSDM 93 produced, it must be said for Henry Kissinger that he well understood the danger of the United States' becoming an exposed foreign adversary, against which Allende could rally his people and Chile's friends. In this sense, the two-level policy was a considerable success in terms of military policy, exchanges and information policy, assistance policy, economic policy, and policy with respect to nationalization disputes.

So far as military policy was concerned, it might be useful to contrast the Chilean experience with an earlier one—the history of U.S. military relations with Castro's Cuba. In 1959, Ambassador Smith was succeeded in Cuba by an able professional Philip Bonsal. Bonsal tried to assume a low, non-confrontational posture with respect to Castro; but matters had gone too far, and Washington was hurling thunderbolts. One of these was the severance of U.S.–Cuban military relationships. The Soviets, for their part, shipped more and more arms to Cuba, as part of an action–reaction cycle between the United States and the USSR. As Bonsal put it, "the reluctant and cautious Russians had been forced into the Revolution's own warmly welcoming arms by the drastic actions of the Americans." [7] It is in this context that the continuing cooperative military relationship between the United States and the Allende government may, perhaps, be judged. It should be emphasized that Salvador Allende and his governmental colleagues were full partners in the bilateral U.S.–Chilean military tie. Allende's civilian minister of defense countersigned every contract, every agreement, every arms purchase, and every training arrangement with the United States.

I supported the continuance of military cooperation between the two countries—while endeavoring to ensure, at the same time, that MILGROUP representatives stopped short of political involvement of any kind. Our MIL-GROUP and attaché personnel had to walk a narrow path in maintaining collaborative programs but avoiding coup plots. Unfortunately, it did become necessary to send a few U.S. military officers home, in order to ensure compliance with my directives and enforce our policy of strict political self-restraint. I am gratified that these measures appear to have been effective, and much appreciate the scrupulous adherence to the rules by U.S. officers who worked in Chile during the months preceding the 1973 coup. The decade since then has exposed no evidence of any U.S. officer's failure to steer clear of coup plotting.

Educational and cultural exchanges, leader visits, travel of students and scholars, religious and missionary activities, news reporting and visits by journalists, and other such contacts between the United States and Chile went forward essentially undisturbed throughout the Allende time. U.S. libraries, binational centers, and the teaching of English to Chileans continued. U. S. films were shown, and USIA film libraries flourished. Contacts with Chilean media were easy and extensive. Binational boards for selecting grant recipients operated without hindrance.

The Peace Corps continued operations during the Allende period—working in forestry science, animal husbandry, the study of Chilean animal species for both scientific and industrial purposes, oceanography, and other technical fields. The station NASA continued to track nonmilitary satellites and other vehicles, without interruption or harassment. The American Institute for Free Labor Development (AIFLD) carried on its Chilean program at a moderate level, with no destructive political blowups.

The Agency for International Development (AID) conducted a shrinking activity, but it did not close down. AID's most important continuing program, which was sustained throughout Allende's time, was the supply of nonfat dried milk to Chilean schoolchildren. The "half-liter" milk program was a major Allende campaign plank in 1970; and the United States maintained the program without interruption, in spite of its obvious political utility to the Allende government. In fact, AID provided all the milk and milk-substitute beverages served in Chilean elementary schools throughout Allende's three years as president.

Salvador Allende himself wanted to keep lines of communication and cooperation open, and harbored little ill will. Whatever his faults, he was essentially generous minded and broad spirited. Many of his colleagues were friendly and constructive in their attitudes. President Nixon and Dr. Kissinger understood the advantages of an outwardly correct posture and a nonconfrontational approach to programs like the Peace Corps and NASA, while State Department officers at all levels were laboring to keep avenues of modest cooperation open. So far as my own role was concerned, all these programs had my support and consistent advocacy with colleagues and superiors in Washington. I also acted vigorously to ensure that programs and personnel presented as few targets as possible for those activists in the Chilean government and left-extremist parties who were looking for opportunities to "roll up" U.S. activities and the U.S. presence in Chile.

What about the U.S. "invisible blockade," which Salvador Allende denounced in his celebrated speech to the UN General Assembly in December 1972? The Chilean president's eloquence and his perception of the secret U.S. strategy contained in NSDM 93 was such that one might almost think he had read the document. However, the strategy was not really an economic blockade; it could more accurately be described as a largely unsuccessful credit squeeze. Except for a less-then-effective "copper boycott" by the Kennecott Copper Corporation, there were no embargoes. By and large, Chile could buy everything it could pay for.

There was no question that the Nixon administration did not wish to extend new loans, nor acquiesce in international lending institutions' doing so. U.S. private banks reduced and later virtually discontinued the extension of new loans to Chile. However, one must bear in mind that Chile had declared a moratorium on the payment of interest and principal on most of its foreign debt in November 1971; the balance between official U.S. malevolence and Chile's bad credit rating is hard to measure, as one looks for the cause of Chile's difficulties. Moreover, Chile received a steady stream of credit from other Latin American countries, Western Europe, Eastern Europe, the USSR, and other sources. Chile's indebtedness increased by almost $2 billion during the three years that Allende's government was in power; and it received more economic help and promises of help than any previous Chilean government in an equivalent period. By September 1973, Chile had close to the highest per capita debt of any country in the world (exceeded only by Israel).

Because of a twist of fate, the U.S. government actually did give to Chile more than $100 million in debt relief, as a result of multilateral negotiations in Paris in April 1972. The debt-rollover agreement between Chile and her 11 principal governmental creditors stipulated that follow-up bilateral implementing understandings should be worked out with each creditor government; but the United States never did so—not as a result of kindness, but rather of the conviction in the White House and the U.S. Treasury Department that we should not negotiate such an understanding until our nationalization dispute with Chile was resolved. The paradoxical result was that Chile negotiated bilateral understandings with her other creditors and made installment payments on monies due to them, but paid nothing to the United States. In fact, the U.S. government gave the Chileans the largest sum— and percentage—of de facto relief of all Chile's creditors. So far as my own role was concerned, I urged my colleagues in Washington to proceed with the bilateral negotiation. This was also the position of my State Department colleagues, but our arguments fell on deaf ears.

Then there was Chilean nationalization policy. The Allende government assumed ownership of the holdings in Chile of the great U.S. copper companies, Kennecott and Anaconda. It then made a determination that it would pay no compensation for these mines. Just before its copper determination, the Chilean government also "intervened" in the case of the Chilean Telephone Company, a subsidiary of the International Telephone and Telegraph Corporation (ITT). This meant that Chile seized operational and financial control of the enterprise. A number of smaller U.S. firms were also bought out or seized.

By the time I got to Chile, there was not the slightest chance of a true resolution of these disputes. I very much doubt that there ever was, from the day Salvador Allende took office. In any case, the objective of U.S. action had to be damage limitation, if it were not to be revenge or stalemate. In a number of Latin American countries—in Peru during the International

Petroleum Company (IPC) crisis of the mid-1960s, for example—the nationalization dispute progressively devoured the relationship between the
United States and the country in question. Cooperative relationships were
distorted, and nationalization disputes became all absorbing. Fortunately,
this did not happen in Chile.

What was my own role? I was most anxious to prevent the U.S.–Chilean
nationalization dispute from propelling the relationship of the two countries
onto the rocks. At several crucial points, I think I had a considerable personal influence in this regard. Elsewhere I have described how, before I
went to Chile, it was touch and go whether the United States would even
continue to maintain an ambassador in Santiago.[8] I believe that I helped to
minimize the likelihood of such a break. In April 1972, I had a role in de-
fusing Allende's ill-timed announcement of plans to expropriate ITT's holdings in Chile; this reopened the door for U.S. adherence to the Paris debt-
rescheduling agreement discussed above.[9] In October 1972, I convinced the
Chilean foreign ministry to withdraw a note charging the U.S. government
with "economic aggression"; and both countries were subsequently able to
initiate more constructive bilateral talks on the nationalization issue.[10] I also
helped to prevent a rupture in the U.S.–Chilean copper nationalization talks
in March 1973.[11] I was not the only North American working to prevent
nationalization issues from destroying the U.S.–Chilean relationship; but I
do believe that an ambassador with punitive and intransigent convictions
might have produced a different result. As it was, the United States never
found itself forced to invoke the Hickenlooper and González amendments—
both of which would have mandated formal punitive retaliatory acts against
Chile, resulting in the termination of economic assistance and the blocking
of multilateral loans over which the United States had veto power. The United
States never pushed the nationalization dispute beyond the point of no return. As events ultimately unfolded, the postcoup Pinochet regime did compensate the great U.S. copper companies and ITT.

The question of covert U.S. action in Chile has become central to any
historical judgment of the ambassadorial role during the Allende time, and
even to the totality of U.S. policy and action there. CIA-conducted activities
can be divided into three phases: (1) programs in 1970; (2) actions just prior
to the September 11, 1973, coup; and (3) activities in between. I became
ambassador to Chile partway through the in-between phase; but I believe
some discussion of 1970 programs and the first year of Allende government
is necessary, in any evaluation of these issues. On September 15, 1970,
President Nixon instructed CIA Director Richard Helms to mount a clandestine coup attempt in Chile, which came to be known as "Track II." He
directed Helms to keep this effort secret from the secretary of state, the
secretary of defense, and the U.S. ambassador to Chile at the time, Edward
Korry. The CIA station in Santiago and the U.S. Army attaché there—working behind the ambassador's back—passed money and arms to Chilean

military plotters and attempted to engineer the abduction of the commander in chief of the Chilean Army, General René Schneider Chereau. Later—in an action related to the CIA-supported plan, but not part of it—another Chilean group of plotters tried to kidnap the general and mortally wounded him in the ensuing shoot-out.

In considering the ambassador's role at the time, it is a crucial fact that the CIA action was carried out under presidential order, but behind the ambassador's back. Earlier in this chapter, there was some discussion of an ambassador's obligation to serve the president faithfully. A reciprocal obligation exists: The president and his immediate staff must invest sufficient confidence in the ambassador to make the president's purposes and directives clear, and to support the ambassador in carrying them out. In the case of Track II, Nixon and Kissinger left Korry blind-sided and short-circuited in his responsibility to represent the president. Quite apart from the question of reciprocal obligation, it is foolish for a president to work behind the back of his own ambassador. In a sense, this relieves the ambassador of his duty to be the intelligent instrument of the White House, because an ambassador cannot be an effective agent for carrying out policies that he is not told about. The president can remove an ambassador, or any appointed officer of the executive branch, at any time; and such action is entirely proper. However, it is not legitimate to set members of the ambassador's mission to working against him; the ambassador should stand in the same relationship to senior U.S. agency representatives abroad as the president himself stands with respect to the Cabinet officers in his administration.

When the revelations about CIA activities in Chile came to public knowledge in 1974, a bill was introduced in the U.S. Congress designed to ensure that the ambassador's right and responsibility to lead his mission would be safeguarded in the future. The bill stated as follows:

1. The United States Ambassador to a foreign country shall have full responsibility for the direction, coordination and supervision of all United States Government officers and employees in that country. . . .

2. The Ambassador shall keep himself fully and currently informed with respect to all activities and operations. . . .

3. Any department or agency having officers or employees in a country shall keep the . . . ambassador . . . fully and currently informed.[12]

The leadership of the CIA in 1974 was not pleased with this new development; neither was Secretary of State Kissinger. In negotiations between CIA representatives and congressional drafters, a key phrase was introduced at the beginning of the text of the bill: "Under the Direction of the President." After passage, this phrase was interpreted by the CIA (with Dr. Kissinger's support) as meaning that the language of the new law would not become operative until the president issued an executive order or implementing instructions. This was not done for more than a year, thereby effectively blocking the applicability of the law. The CIA also took the position that the agency's statutory responsibility to protect intelligence sources and methods created a conflict of laws and limited the scope of the ambassador's authority under the new legislation. Implementing instructions were finally issued in 1976, under Senate prodding.[13] This legislation, which strengthens the ambassador's authority and responsibility for CIA operations—and operations of other U.S. agencies abroad, including military personnel attached to embassies and MILGROUPS—was a direct legacy of Chile.

Before laying this particular subject to rest, I might mention that, over the years, a number of ambassadors have told me that they had expressed the preference to their station chiefs not to be told of "dirty tricks" and the nitty-gritty details of CIA operations. This attitude has always struck me as a dereliction of duty—quite aside from the fact that the ambassador will be held accountable for CIA activities, regardless of any effort on his part to preserve "plausible deniability" of incriminating knowledge. Most ambassadors who have taken this position have been political appointees; the need for experience, determination, alertness, and follow-through in establishing and maintaining control over CIA operations is an additional argument in favor of appointing experienced professionals to sensitive ambassadorial posts. I should add, however, that my predecessor, Edward Korry, was a political appointee who was abundantly endowed with the force of personality, acumen, vigor, and determination required to assert leadership over his CIA station. It was not his fault that Richard Nixon's direct orders resulted in the CIA people and the army attaché operating behind his back. In fact, Korry was acute enough to suspect what was going on; he ordered his deputy, Harry Schlaudeman, to investigate the situation. Fortified by a direct presidential order, however, the embassy officers who were conducting Track II apparently stonewalled efforts of the top embassy leadership to get at the truth.

Besides Track II, there was also a Track I in 1970. This consisted of programs that were proposed to the regularly constituted covert action oversight committee in Washington—the so-called "Forty Committee"—and subjected to consultation with the State and Defense Departments and Ambassador Korry. The objective of these programs was to block Allende's runoff election in the Chilean congress on October 24, 1970—seven weeks after he had won a plurality, but not a majority, of the popular vote. The Forty Committee went so far as to authorize bribing Chilean congressmen to vote against Allende; but Ambassador Korry says he vetoed that idea, and I have no reason to doubt him. A propaganda scare campaign seems to have been mounted. The U.S. government also considered various elaborate strategies for circumventing the Chilean constitutional provision that prevented outgoing President Eduardo Frei from succeeding himself. All of these ideas came to naught, as did ITT's efforts to work out a cooperative program with the CIA to block Allende's confirmation.

The verdict on Track I and Track II is simple. The effort was a total failure. Besides, when these U.S. clandestine efforts ultimately leaked or were made public by the Church Committee in 1974–75, the result was damaging to the U.S. government, the Christian Democrats, and other democratic forces in Chile. With the possible exception of Richard Nixon and Henry Kissinger, Track I and Track II have virtually no defenders. Even David A. Phillips, whom the CIA put in charge of Track II, regards the effort as misguided and doomed from the start.

The foregoing is prologue to a discussion of the ambassador and covert operations during my own tenure. By the time I went to Chile on October 13, 1971, Track II—or CIA operations behind the ambassador's back—had faded into a few relatively inconsequential remnants.[14] By the way, I was not told of the existence of Track II until Church Committee investigators questioned me about it in July 1975, almost two years after I left Chile.

The first information of any kind given to me about CIA operations in Chile was during my consultations in the State Department in August 1971. This was eight months after Secretary of State William Rogers had first cabled me in Guatemala, requesting my assent to his nomination of me as ambassador to Chile. It was also six months after I had gone to Washington for consultations, which would have provided a face-to-face opportunity for briefing; it was four months after my appointment had leaked to the press; and it was some weeks after the nomination had been formally transmitted to the U.S. Senate for confirmation. This raises an interesting question. By the time I was told about U.S. covert operations—even the less sensitive, non–Track II ones—it was a bit late for me to back out of the appointment. I am not suggesting that I would have. No doubt, I would have gone anyhow—at least if the briefing had not included Track II. For a professional, going where ordered is part of the obligation, and accepting the down-side of an assignment is part of being in the career. After all, the majority of our ambassadors are obliged to work with somewhat unsavory regimes or with U.S. action necessities that they might not have freely chosen. But I wonder about the distinguished private citizens who are recruited for diplomatic service. Do we really let them know what they are taking on, before things go so far down the track as to make withdrawal an embarrassing public mess?

I share responsibility for these shortcomings. After Chile, I served for a year-and-a-half as director general of the U.S. Foreign Service, and tendered offers of ambassadorships to at least 100 people—both professionals and private citizens. In many cases, I myself did not know the full nature of U.S. covert operations in the country in question, let alone whether the candidate fully understood his exposure. It is also interesting that not one of these candidates—professional or otherwise—came back to me with the request to be fully briefed on covert programs, before deciding whether to accept the proffered nomination. I am not sure what this proves. Perhaps it only shows that an ambassadorship still carries luster, and that we fallible mortals do not always reach out to confront tomorrow's moral choices.

Before addressing the question of U.S. covert action during the "in-between" time, I shall jump ahead and address the accusations that the U.S. Embassy, under my direction, engaged in the plotting that led to the toppling of the Allende regime, in the end. To me, at least, the verdict is straightforward, even if less than universally believed. I instructed all members of the embassy staff to stay clear of coup plotting and, to the best of my knowledge, they did. The Forty Committee had never authorized CIA involvement in coup plotting. The Church Committee afterward examined the evidence and investigated the facts, with access granted to top-secret CIA, State Department, Pentagon, and White House documents. It concluded: "Was the United States *directly* involved, covertly, in the 1973 coup in Chile? The Committee has found no evidence that it was." [15]

The qualification "directly" is troublesome. The Church Committee report explains, however—and responsible Church Committee investigators have confirmed to me—that the qualification refers to three reservations the committee and its staff had. The first was a suspicion that the 1970 Track II may have had an afterlife in the memories of Chilean military officers, who were aware of CIA and U.S. attaché contacts with the plotters of 1970. Apparently, the idea is that knowledge of CIA support for plotting in 1970 would carry over to a confidence in U.S. government support in 1973. However, the CIA was quite successful in concealing its Track II contacts with Chilean military plotters in 1970—particularly its concrete acts, such as the handing over of weapons. I know of no evidence that the plotters of 1973 were aware of these CIA actions, or that they were influenced by the memory of Track II in counting on U.S. support. In point of fact, the leaders of the plot decided—in a considered and deliberate decision—not to consult U.S. representatives. [16]

The Church Committee's second reservation was that President Nixon, Henry Kissinger, and other key Washington figures nurtured an ill-disguised hostility to Salvador Allende, and that this attitude must have entered the consciousness of the plotters and left them with a sense that the U.S. government supported their cause. This may have been true, but animosity to Allende is not in itself complicity in the plot against him. There are many cases in which the political leaders of great states notoriously dislike each other, even when their governments are supposed to be close friends. This does not altogether invalidate the Church Committee's point. Nevertheless, if antipathy can be equated with guilt, culpability in international politics could be found almost everywhere.

The Church Committee's third reservation relates to the committee investigators' knowledge that the CIA had succeeded in penetrating the ultimately successful plot well enough to be able to report on its development with considerable accuracy. Therefore, some "signals" must have been given to the plotters. This line of reasoning was essentially speculative, and not based—so far as I know, and so far as the investigators have explained to me—on any evidence that the CIA's intelligence gathering actually did transmit signals of support. I have discussed these issues at greater length elsewhere,[17] but this may be worth noting here: The inference that successful intelligence gathering must, by its existence, send substantive messages in the opposite direction calls into question the whole rationale of worldwide intelligence collection. Moreover, it constitutes an assertion that there cannot be an effective distinction—or wall—between intelligence collection and covert action.

In any case, neither the Church Committee, with its access to the most secret and highly sensitive U.S. government records, nor any investigators in the period of more than a decade since 1975 have produced evidence of U.S. complicity in the plotting or execution of the Chilean coup. There have been many charges and many stories; and I have examined the significant allegations, insofar as I have become aware of them.[18] Whatever criticism the principal U.S. actors in the Chilean drama have received or deserved in connection with the 1973 coup, the fallout would actually have been much worse, had U.S. representatives jumped into the coup plotting in 1972–73 and subsequently been caught—as I am sure we would have been.

How about the "in-between" period, between 1970 and 1973? The facts about U.S. covert action during the almost three years of Allende's presidency are laid out in the Church Committee report,[19] and have not been added to significantly in the ensuing decade. In essence, the United States funded opposition parties and media in the magnitude of about $2 million a year, or a little more than $6 million in total. The Chilean parties that benefited importantly were the Christian Democrats, the National party, and smaller radical splinters. Santiago's dominant independent, conservative newspaper, *El Mercurio,* was the principal recipient in the media. Several private sector organizations received smaller amounts of money, mostly to support voter turnout campaigns; and an ultrarightist group known as *Patria y Libertad* received sums totaling something less than $50,000 in 1970 and 1971 (but nothing during my incumbency).[20]

While the facts about what was done are clear enough, the arguments about U.S. motivations and about the necessity and ethics of financing Allende's opposition reverberate to this day. Since I have addressed these questions elsewhere,[21] I hope it will suffice here to review the general conclusions. First, the purpose of financial aid to the opposition was to keep the democratic non-Marxist forces in Chile afloat, not to destabilize and sink the Allende government partway through its term. Official U.S. policy on this question was unvarying throughout my time in Chile, even in the most privileged and confidential policy documents. This is not to deny that some of the principal actors on the Washington scene, including both the president and his National Security advisor, contemplated more radical measures to rid the hemisphere of Allende. Whatever inclinations there may have been in this regard, however, they were never turned into policy.

Then there is the question of the redundancy, as some have claimed, of aiding the opposition in order for it to survive. I believe it is unlikely that the opposition would have stayed afloat without our help. The Allende government was systematically using the power of the state to drive the opposition financially and economically into the ground. There were times when it came very close to succeeding—not only with respect to the democratic parties of the opposition, but also in the case of the media, and its suppliers of newsprint and other essential goods and services. At the same time, the parties in the government were receiving subventions from the Soviet Union and other Marxist regimes, and were skimming off money from foreign trade and other governmental operations to finance their own political activities.[22]

None of the foregoing, taken by itself, makes U.S. covert support to the Chilean opposition ethical. I greatly respect those who have concluded that U.S. covert operations abroad are a mistake in any and all situations. There are powerful arguments to be made in support of this position, and they may be right. I suppose I have to add, though—somewhat ruefully—that I had no such choice when I became U.S. ambassador to Chile, since U.S. covert funding of political parties there had been going on for the better part of a decade. It is also true that the abrupt cessation of such an activity can be a political intervention of an opposite nature—with profound and possibly disastrous consequences—just as the initiation of such an activity can be. In fact, there are those who say that this is what happened when President Carter ended the covert funding of the mullahs in Iran, thereby helping to consolidate Khomeini's following and accelerate the fall of the shah. I shall not try to pass judgment on the validity of this view, but it may illustrate the point.[23] One could give other examples; the dynamic force of withdrawn support can be as real as an initial extension of support.

There is also the problem in U.S. foreign policy that arguments against covert action are not consistently applied. When William V. Shannon (later one of President Carter's ambassadors) was on the New York *Times* editorial board in 1975, he thundered:

If the United States . . . possessed competent leadership, . . . it would have provided Portuguese democrats with money and political support to help them offset the advantages of the Portuguese Communists in propaganda and organization. The Swedish and German Social Democrats have helped their counterparts in Lisbon but the flow of money from them has been trivial compared to the heavy subsidies to the Portuguese Communists by the Soviet Union.[24]

Shannon wrote these words shortly before it was revealed that the CIA was, in fact, taking the very action he advocated; he had also been one of those who joined in the condemnation of covert action in Chile. This represents situational ethics, and Shannon was far from alone in expressing them. More recently, U.S. liberals who opposed U.S. covert action in Chile have applauded concealed U.S. interventionist acts contributing to the ouster of Duvalier in Haiti and Marcos in the Philippines—grudgingly, perhaps, and with cries of "too late"; but not with consistent opposition, in principle, to U.S. intromission of influence in the political affairs of another state. If we regard all concealed or covert interventions as truly unethical and inadmissible, we should be consistent about it. We of the United States have not thought through how we feel about these questions.

There is an additional dimension to the record of covert action in Chile during the "in-between" time of my incumbency. That is the record of covert actions that were not taken, because I was opposed. There were a number of them,[25] but the two most important were related to proposals to lend covert support to the strikes by Chilean truckers, professional people, shopkeepers and others—strikes that brought the country to the brink of collapse both in October 1972 and in the precoup period in 1973.

The CIA station in Santiago favored U.S. financial support to the striking truckers, and I opposed it.[26] According to Jack Kubisch (who was U.S. assistant secretary of state for inter-American affairs at the time), the president's National Security advisor, Henry Kissinger, also favored subventions to the strikers—and Kubisch opposed them.[27] In Senate testimony, Karl F. Inderfurth, one of the Church Committee's senior staff investigators, commented: "Nathaniel Davis, U.S. Ambassador to Chile, and the State Department, had strenuously objected to any funding of the strikers. . . . . There's no question that the strikers were creating a climate in which a military coup appeared to be inevitable."[28] About the same time, according to the Church Committee report, the Forty Committee "authorized support for private sector groups, but with disbursement contingent on the agreement of the Ambassador and State Department. That agreement was not forthcoming."[29]

Reviewing my recent book in Commentary, Alvin H Bernstein, chairman of the strategy department at the U.S. Naval War College, criticized my position:

The covert measures Ambassador Davis permitted consisted solely of funneling some $2 million a year to the moderate opposition . . . and to the free press. He thought it justified to work covertly to keep Chile an open society but drew the line at underhanded operations designed to destabilize or disrupt it. Even the reader who instinctively believes that the U.S. should not bribe Congressmen, inspire violent kidnappings, or deceive its friends in a foreign country comes away from this book wondering whether Davis should not have been more troubled by the prospect of Allende, unimpeded, consolidating his Marxist grip. . . .

It would be more difficult for Davis to take the moral position he does against covert intervention in Chile if the Chilean military had not acted and a Marxist regime with ties to the Soviet bloc were now operating in South America. . . . An elected Communist president in the U.S. sphere of influence . . . is the nightmare of any believer in democracy. The perennial problem of how clean you can keep your hands in a dirty world endures because statesmen and administrators have a moral obligation to preserve our interests abroad, as well as to remain true to our domestic principles.[30]

So there you have it. This particular censure is friendly and mild; but the hard Left calls me the beast of Chile, while the hard Right calls me the fink of Santiago.

I ought to end with an assessment. I wish I could point to a great array of positive accomplishments in Chile; but the real achievements seem more negative than positive: worse things avoided, rather than marvelous things achieved. If I were Alvin Bernstein, I suppose I could point to the removal of the presence of an elected Marxist president in the U.S. sphere of influence, at the cost of a few million U.S. dollars and no U.S. expeditionary force or even a CIA-organized coup. But I am not Alvin Bernstein, and the manner of Allende's going fails to stir my pride. I believe that the peaceful, constitutional, democratic road to socialism should be kept open—not blocked forever. It should not be necessary for those who share Salvador Allende's dream to accept the secret policeman's boot on the stairs at night, as a necessary price for the achievement of their economic and social values. Bloody revolution is not the only road to social justice as the Left conceives it. Socialism may not be the best or even a good way to order a society's affairs—but the ability of free citizens to *choose* socialism, or capitalism, or some other economic system, is beyond price. For these reasons, I believe that the ending of Allende's Chilean Way was a tragedy, not a triumph.

Allende and his colleagues and coalition partners took actions that unquestionably weakened his regime and jeopardized its successful continuance in office.[31] His Chilean political enemies of many stripes—and the military officers who ultimately carried out their "pronouncement"—also played crucial roles in bringing about the end result. I do take some pride in the fact that the overthrow of the Allende government was truly not the doing of the United States. So, I am back to negative accomplishments.

I am happy that I do not wear John Peurifoy's laurels as the architect of a CIA-run invasion and coup in a Latin American land. I am glad that the Perón–Braden political shoot-out of 1945 did not find its repetition in Chile, with the banner of anti-Americanism nailed ever-more-firmly to the mast of Chilean pride. I take satisfaction that Chile did not become another Cuba, with U.S. economic sanctions and military hostility driving the country into an ever-tighter Soviet embrace. I am happy that U.S.–Chilean nationalization disputes did not follow the Peruvian road at the time of the IPC case, the Mexican road at various times, or the road followed in so many other Latin countries. I am also gratified that we were less eager to recognize the

Chilean junta after the coup than we gave the appearance of being in Brazil in 1964.

I did not act alone in these matters; but I was on what I believe to have been the right side, and I influenced the outcome. I make no claim to have held back the sea with my finger in the dyke or to have been a David vanquishing a Goliath in Washington with deadly aim. The sea came crashing and roaring over our dyke; and a loyal diplomat does not smite his chief with a smooth stone shot to the forehead. I shall always be grateful that I was given the chance to know Salvador Allende, Eduardo Frei, and other extraordinary personalities of that fascinating land, which seems to have issued forth with flair and talent beyond its ration. I was not a victim, as one reviewer of my book has concluded. I was fortunate to have been an actor in one of the great dramas of our time.

NOTES

1. *Clarín*, October 21, 1971, p. 4.

2. Richard R. Fagen, Letter to Senator J. William Fulbright, reproduced in Laurence Birns, *The End of Chilean Democracy* (New York: Seabury Press, 1974), pp. 166–67.

3. Letter of May 25, 1973, from Foreign Service Inspectors William E. Knight, E. Gregory Kryza, and Charles E. Finan to Inspector General Thomas W. McElhiney, p. 1. This letter was declassified on December 31, 1977.

4. Henry Kissinger, *White House Years* (Boston: Little, Brown, 1979), p. 681; Seymour M. Hersh, *The Price of Power: Kissinger in the Nixon White House* (New York: Summit, 1983), p. 294.

5. Richard Nixon, "U.S. Foreign Policy for the 1970s," *Building for Peace: A Report to the Congress,* February 25, 1971, p. 54.

6. Elmo R. Zumwalt, Jr., *On Watch* (New York: Quadrangle, 1976), p. 323.

7. Philip W. Bonsal, *Cuba, Castro, and the United States* (Pittsburgh: University of Pittsburgh Press, 1971), p. 156.

8. Nathaniel Davis, *The Last Two Years of Salvador Allende* (Ithaca, N.Y.: Cornell University Press, 1985), pp. 28–32.

9. Ibid., pp. 76–77.

10. Ibid., pp. 102–03.

11. Ibid., pp. 104–05.

12. *P.L. 93-475,* Laws of 93rd Cong., 2nd sess., October 26, 1974, 22 U.S. 2680a.

13. U.S. Congress, Senate, Select Committee to Study Governmental Operations with Respect to Intelligence Activities, Book I, *Foreign and Military Intelligence.* (Washington, D.C.: Government Printing Office, 1976), pp. 311–15.

14. This question is examined in Davis, *The Last Two Years,* pp. 308–20 and 348–49.

15. U.S. Congress, Senate, Select Committee to Study Governmental Operations with Respect to Intelligence Activities, Book I, *Foreign and Military Intelligence* ton, D.C.: Government Printing Office, 1975), p. 2.

16. Davis, *The Last Two Years,* pp. 345–48.

17. Ibid., pp. 346–47 and 361–63.

18. Ibid., pp. 350–61.

19. U.S. Congress, Senate, *Covert Action in Chile, 1963–73.*

20. Davis, *The Last Two Years,* pp. 309–10 and 326–27.

21. Ibid., pp. 319–20, 327–29 and 334–44.

22. Ibid., pp. 336–43.

23. Ibid., pp. 334–35.

24. William V. Shannon, "The Politics of Death," New York *Times,* August 3, 1975, Section 4, p. 15.

25. Nathaniel Davis, "U.S. Covert Actions in Chile, 1971–1973," *Foreign Service Journal* (November 1978):13; Davis, *The Last Two Years,* pp. 308–10, 324–27, and 332.

26. Davis, *The Last Two Years,* pp. 324–25.

27. Ibid., p. 328.

28. U.S. Congress, Senate, Select Committee to Study Governmental Operations with Respect to Intelligence Activities, *Covert Action,* Vol. 7, (Washington, D.C.: Government Printing Office, 1976), p. 22.

29. U.S. Congress, Senate, *Covert Action in Chile, 1963–1973,* p. 30–31.

30. Alvin H. Bernstein, "Clean Hands," *Commentary* (July 1986):68.

31. Davis, *The Last Two Years,* particularly pp. 402–05.

7

Ambassadors in Foreign Policy

C. Neale Ronning
Albert P. Vannucci

This volume began with the general premise that, during the ambassadorial postings under study, something of lasting importance occurred for both U.S. foreign policy toward the country and region and for the Latin country itself. Two historians, three political scientists, and a career Foreign Service officer have examined the role played by six ambassadors.

In his chapter on Dwight Morrow, Richard Melzer describes the brief and only diplomatic assignment of a very talented and well-connected Wall Street banker. After years of futile U.S. pressure, Morrow was sent to Mexico in 1927 to resolve a host of differences and restore good relations between the two neighbors. Morrow was selected for his great skills as a negotiator; his assignment was greatly complicated by the fractiousness of Mexican politics at the time. Morrow brought considerable energy and talent to the task as he saw it; he reported directly to the president and largely ignored the State Department. Projecting a very high profile both in Mexico and back in the United States, Morrow accomplished the desired reconciliation, in large measure. He assisted the consolidation of Mexican President Calles's power, against an array of centrifugal forces; and he helped to defuse a number of potentially explosive outstanding issues between the two governments, including those involving foreign oil interests and land reform. However, the highly visible manner in which he did all this soon undermined his efforts, and he left Mexico—and public service—after three years.

Melzer assesses Morrow's term quite favorably. He describes a breakthrough tour, which constituted a departure from the past and a precursor of future advancements in U.S.–Mexican relations. Indeed, he relays the opinion that Morrow helped to lay the groundwork for the Good Neighbor Policy, that his "demonstrations of goodwill and deep respect for Mexican sovereignty [are] qualities that all U.S. envoys should emulate in laying the groundwork for effective diplomacy."

The study by Louis Pérez of Sumner Welles's brief but frenetic service in Cuba offers both interesting similarities and dramatic differences. Like Morrow, Welles was sent as a proven troubleshooter, in an attempt at a new and less heavy-handed approach to improve seriously strained relations. Welles, too, pursued his assignment vigorously; but, unlike Morrow, he found a seriously disintegrated domestic political situation. And most differently from Morrow, after only five days, Welles concluded that the head of the government to which he was posted had to go. Employing extraordinary pressure, he effected the imposition of an inept, illegitimate, and short-lived replacement. The collapse of his "solution" presented the ambassador with a potentially calamitous situation. Sent to restore order and U.S. influence, he had orchestrated quite the opposite. Welles then abandoned his own aversion to military intervention, and attempted—unsuccessfully—to have Washington concur. Failing to sell that radical solution, Welles set about— on his own—to promote "conditions of continued instability and disorder." Pérez describes the great skill with which Welles exploited differences among both government opponents and supporters. In an extremely volatile and vulnerable setting, the U.S. ambassador was able to quickly topple the government once again. But Pérez concludes that Welles's most "lasting impact was to move Batista from the shadows of the political arena into center stage." If so, his was indeed a Pyrrhic victory.

Spruille Braden in Argentina offers some strong similarities to Welles in Cuba. Both were well-experienced, self-confident career diplomats sent to domestically unsettled countries at times when relations with the United States were difficult. Shortly after their arrivals, both came to the conclusion that their missions called for them to remove the governments in place. Both set about their tasks with energy and speed and publicity and effect. Within three months, Braden's crucial efforts contributed to such a deterioration in Juan Perón's position that he was removed from all of his government posts and sent into exile. Unlike Machado and Grau in Cuba, however, Perón proved to be very resilient. Not only did he return to power within days, but he went on to meet and overcome Braden's subsequent efforts (from Washington) against him. By the middle of 1947, Perón was in an unassailable position, and Braden was in retirement. Albert Vannucci finds explanations for Braden's behavior in his identification with one faction within the State Department, his closed belief system on Perón, and the negative and inflexible national image that he held of Argentina. Vannucci makes much of these as factors in Braden's inability to see Argentina's ripeness for social revolution, and the true nature of Perón's emergence.

Adolf Berle arrived in Brazil five months before Braden arrived in Argentina. Like Braden, Berle was caught up in policy and personality disputes in Washington, his posting to Brazil was in partial compensation for the acceptance of his "resignation" as assistant secretary. And also like Braden—and Welles, as well—he arrived with a very sharply focused set of perceptions about the situation in his host country. One crucial difference was that the preeminent twentieth-century political figure of Brazil was completing a decade and a half of rule—rather than just beginning his career, as was the case in Argentina. Fifteen years of Vargas's rule had brought fundamental changes to Brazilian politics, society, and economy—and conflicting interpretations in Washington. Eight months into his assignment, fearing that promised elections would not take place, Berle acted on his own initiative to deliver his famous September 29, 1945, speech—"the atomic bomb that ended *Queremismo.*" Neale Ronning details the reasons for Berle's action: his paternalistic attitude; the influence on him of Vargas's opponents; the ambassador's legalistic and North American concept of democracy; and his irritation, which he shared with many in Washington, at the increasing nationalizations of the *Estado Novo.* Interestingly, the only person in the U.S. government with whom Berle discussed his plans was Spruille Braden— who was, by that time, an assistant secretary and the principal author of a recently released "Blue Book" on Argentina. One month to the day after Berle's speech, the military demanded and received Vargas's resignation.

In addition to examining this stunning and unilateral action, Ronning also looks at another curious incident: Berle's subsequent efforts to counter the State Department's request to obtain greater access for U.S. oil companies. Still acting independently, and only days after greatly facilitating Vargas's retirement, Berle now assumed the position of defending Brazilian sovereignty. In this issue, he achieved partial—but temporary—success. Soon thereafter, Berle resigned, 13 months after his arrival. His successor was much more sensitive to directives from Washington, and advanced the U.S. oil policy until the arrayed opposition in Brazil made it impossible.

With regard to Berle's overall conduct—and certainly as reflected in his notorious speech—his service shares with Braden's earlier one the appearance of several qualities. Ronning conveys the assessment that Berle's short stay contributed to aborting Brazil's best hope for democracy, a hope that has yet to be fully realized.

Jan Black's study differs from the preceding ones in that its subject is not only still alive but an active contributor to assessments of his work. Lincoln Gordon's service is singular in this volume for its longevity—more than twice the duration of any of the others—and for the intellectual background that he brought to his first and only posting. There are also parallels with several of the previous studies. Like Welles, Berle, and Braden before him, Gordon arrived "in country" at a time of massive political uncertainty, and he had clear preconceptions about the situation. In Gordon's case, his views were shaped by a career as professor and economist; he was also the author of the economic chapters of the proposed Alliance for Progress. Gordon took up his assignment in the fifth year of Brazil's post-Vargas democracy and only two months after Vice-President Quadros had become chief executive. Quadros articulated quite a different route for his country's future than the one envisioned by Gordon, and the "extraordinarily confident" ambassador did not retreat from advancing his own.

In several respects, Gordon's tour bears the closest resemblance to Spruille Braden's: the personal and political disdain for the head of government (or de facto head, in Perón's case); the maneuvering with the military to encourage their withdrawal of support from that head; and the promotion to assistant secretary—ostensibly as a reward for a job well done, but soon terminated when developments were reassessed. Jan Black describes a publicly critical and overbearing ambassador who relied on his well-known connections in the White House, rather than directions from State. Black presents the militarization of Brazil, which began during Gordon's term and was described by him in his famous telegram as "a great victory for the free world," as a harbinger of the wave of military governments that would sweep over the continent and begin to recede—and then, tentatively—only after two decades.

The final study is the most unique. Written by the subject himself, it raises a host of important and disturbing questions. With Welles, Berle, and Braden, Nathaniel Davis shares having a career in the Foreign Service. He differs dramatically from them in the importance he places on the duty of a chief of mission to be a "loyal agent"—that is, to implement policy emanating from Washington, whether or not he agrees with it. Davis reports that there was a clear "two-level" policy in place when he arrived in Chile. He recounts the serious inherent difficulties in keeping the two elements separate, the covert aspect secret, and the whole policy understood throughout the U.S. government. He claims to have contributed assessments from the field that quieted the interventionists in Washington. He credits his Morrow-like display of amiability with making the best of the difficult situation; avoiding dramatic public feuds (unlike several of the ambassadors in this study); and enabling the continuation of military cooperation, economic aid, and a host of educational and cultural exchanges.

Davis emphasizes that there were no coup plans or activities by anyone in the embassy during his posting; he is deeply pained that such plans were ordered in 1970 and kept secret from State, Defense, and the previous ambassador. He describes that policy as not only disloyal to his predecessor, but fatally flawed. Maybe an ambassador might have to be removed—he counsels—but never deceived. Davis discusses the $6 million anti-Allende campaign that was conducted during his post; he describes it as the continuation of a decade-long effort, directed more at keeping a viable opposition "afloat" than at destabilizing the government. Davis then refers to the harsh criticism of his service received from all along the political spectrum. It seems unlikely that anything he has written here will finally lay to rest the continuing controversies that surround the demise of Salvador Allende. However,

Ambassador Davis has contributed significantly to a greater understanding of our subject here, the U.S. chief of mission.

What conclusions can be drawn from this collection of studies? At least six general and tentative observations suggest themselves. The first and most obvious is that ambassadors can be important determinants of U.S. foreign policy. We have seen repeated instances when an individual aggressively pursued his "own" policy, based on his personal predispositions and interpretations of developments—whether or not these were shared by his staff and colleagues, his superiors at State, or his connections in the White House. Far from being mere functionaries, the subjects of this study did indeed often behave like the "manipulative elite" of which Professor Robert Isaak speaks.

It follows, then, that the assumption alluded to in the introduction—that the individual variable can rank highly, even in situations of noncrisis—seems to be borne out. True crises existed during the service of Welles, Gordon, and Davis. In the case of Welles, the crisis was at least partially of his own making; Gordon assisted the realization of the one that occurred during his tenure, while Davis did much less so. But interestingly, some of the most determinative behavior was played by individuals who were serving in times that were difficult and confused—to be sure—but that by no means qualified as crises. Acting more as individuals than as State Department representatives, Morrow, Braden, and Berle helped to shape events in significant ways. The studies here corroborate the expectation that, with regard to Latin policy, individuals qua individuals may warrant a higher ranking than normally accorded.

Second, there is also evidence to support giving the external environment greater importance in U.S. Latin policy than Kegley and Wittkopf (in *American Foreign Policy*) and others generally do. The first two studies, for example, took place during the interwar years, when the United States had retreated home after its great adventure in Europe. That—as well as a feeling of having been chastised by futile efforts at coercion within the Western hemisphere—helps to explain the conciliatory missions on which Morrow (successfully) and Welles (unsuccessfully) were sent. Their missions stand in high contrast to Braden and Berle's postings, which occurred at the end of World War II—when the United States was riding high, as the savior of the world. Not only is there no evidence of instructions to pursue conciliatory measures, but arrogance—and, at times, belligerence—even went undisavowed. Indeed, in the more egregious of the two instances—that of Braden—it was rewarded with promotion. The last two studies bracket the U.S. trauma in Vietnam. Lincoln Gordon's deportment in 1964 is far more reflective of a self-confident superpower than Nathaniel Davis's in 1973.

Third, these studies reveal that U.S. policies were seldom clearly established and communicated. Rather, individuals seem to have been sent with general instructions—such as to improve relations or resolve a particular outstanding issue—but not provided a comprehensive and coherent policy statement. As a result, the chief of mission had a luxurious expanse within which to move; he could read his minimal mandate—as well as a communication from any source—pretty much as he liked. Clearly, an individual in a position such as this could and should not be tightly restricted. More than one of the subjects here, however, had a tether long enough to strangle himself and to choke relations between the two governments.

Fourth, there is a striking disparity between the two studies that begin and end this volume and the five that come between. Dwight Morrow and Nathaniel Davis are palpably different from the others, in attitude and demeanor. Their conduct indicates a respect for—rather than a desire to replace and remake—the individuals and cultures found. These striking differences suggest that there may be something akin to "judicial temperament" at work, and that it should be an element in making appointments. Nominees who are conscious of their biases and predispositions, and who make the effort to overcome these in their reporting and conduct, offer a different set of diplomatic possibilities than do persons such as some studied here who have been described as belligerent, arrogant, and condescending. This may be especially salient if, as it seems, there are almost always some intergovernmental issues that are amenable to resolution. *If* an ambassador wishes to pursue these issues, he can find some bases for cooperation and for enhancing the prospect of better relations, without extraordinary effort.

A fifth and related consideration is the importance of distinguishing between short- and long-term interests. Most generally, it is in the interest of the United States to have foreign relations that facilitate the promotion of common interests and the resolution of differences. The maintenance—or, at times, establishment—of such relations always occur in the context of what preceded. Latin governments and publics alike have proven their sensitivity to and vivid recall of past treatment. Therefore, it could be crucial for a chief of mission to thoroughly know the history of U.S. relations with his country of assignment and to acutely feel the role he plays in the writing of the next chapter. So many times in these pages, we have seen behavior that severely damaged what was already a fragile nexus. Sumner Welles, for example, fully realized his ambitious short-term goals. He succeeded in removing two presidents and installing two others. But the chain of events that he helped set into motion led, two decades later, to a complete rupture and the most difficult relationship that the United States has had to manage in its long inter-American history.

Finally, these studies seem to call for a word about the propagation of certain convictions held within U.S. society. North American faith in electoral democracy has often plagued Latin American, and U.S. ambassadors have played their part. With few exceptions in the past, the holding of elections in Latin America has been little more than a legitimizing ritual through which a minority of privilege has been able to maintain its position. In U.S.

policy, faith in that legitimizing ritual is expressed through intervention in the name of democracy. Berle's dramatic action can serve to illustrate. He clearly wrestled with the problem; in the end, he was seemingly guided by faith that the electoral process would eventually bring about results such as those he perceived as having been achieved in the United States. There was little in the history of electoral politics in Brazil to suggest that this would be the case, and Berle himself was aware of this. Thus, in the end, he seems to have been moved more by faith than by analysis.

In spite of eloquent rhetoric in support of electoral democracy, North Americans can quickly lose faith in the electoral process in Latin America when the results of elections threaten their interests or objectives or muddy their preconceptions. Thus, Washington set out to undermine elected governments in Brazil and Chile, where the validity of prior elections had not been questioned. Ambassadors have been active and even enthusiastic participants in this process.

The promotion of electoral democracy (when it serves an interest) is a reflection of a more general attitude or orientation within U.S. society—that the United States knows what is best for Latin Americans and must, at times, even save them from themselves. Quite clearly, Welles, Braden, and Gordon—and, to a lesser extent, Morrow and Berle—believed that they knew better than the leaders of the countries to which they were accredited what was best for the people. It is difficult to see how they could have acted as they did, without such a belief.

Clearly, more than a few insights can be taken from a close examination of the past conduct of U.S. ambassadors in Latin America. And lest anyone assume that the issues raised here no longer apply: In a recent biography, Salvadoran President Napoleon Duarte observes that, during the early 1980s, "The U.S. ambassador became more powerful than I was."

Selected Bibliography

Aberbach, Joel D., Robert D. Putnam, and Bert A. Rockman. *Bureaucrats and Politicians in Western Democracies*. Cambridge, Mass.: Harvard University Press, 1981.

Acheson, Dean. *Present at the Creation: My Years in the State Department*. New York: W. W. Norton, 1963.

Allison, Graham, and Peter Szanton. *Remaking Foreign Policy*. New York: Basic Books, 1976.

Ambrose, Stephen E. *Rise to Globalism: American Foreign Policy, 1938–1980*. 2nd ed., rev. New York: Penguin Books, 1981.

Bacchus, William I. *Foreign Policy and the Bureaucratic Process*. Princeton: Princeton University Press, 1974.

———. *Staffing for Foreign Affairs: Personnel Systems for the 1980's and 1990's*. Princeton: Princeton University Press, 1983.

Ball, George W. *Diplomacy for a Crowded World: An American Foreign Policy*. Boston: Atlantic-Little, Brown, 1976.

Barnes, William, and John Heath Morgan. *The Foreign Service of the United States: Origins, Development, and Functions*. Washington, D.C.: Historical Office, Bureau of Public Affairs, Department of State, 1961.

Berkowitz, Morton, P.G. Bock, and Vincent J. Fuccilo. *The Politics of American Foreign Policy*. Englewood Cliffs, N.J.: Prentice-Hall, 1977.

Berle, Adolf. *Latin America: Diplomacy and Reality*. New York: Harper & Row, 1962.

Berle, Beatrice Bishop, and Travis Beal Jacobs, eds. *Navigating the Rapids 1918–1971; From the Papers of Adolf A. Berle*. New York: Harcourt, Brace, Jovanovich, 1973.

Black, Jan Knippers. *United States Penetration of Brazil*. Philadelphia: University of Pennsylvania Press, 1977.

Bliss, Howard, and M. Glen Johnson. *Beyond the Water's Edge: America's Foreign Policies*. Philadelphia: Lippincott, 1975.

Bloomfield, Lincoln P. *The Foreign Policy Process: Making Theory Relevant*. Beverly Hills: Sage, 1974.

————. *In Search of American Foreign Policy*. New York: Oxford University Press, 1974.

Bohlen, Charles E. *Witness to History 1929–1969*. New York: W. W. Norton, 1973.

Bonsal, Philip W. *Cuba, Castro, and the United States*. Pittsburgh: University of Pittsburgh Press, 1971.

Braden, Spruille. *Diplomats and Demogogues—The Memoirs of Spruille Braden*. New Rochelle, N.Y.: Arlington House, 1971.

Burch, Philip H., Jr. *Elites in American History: The New Deal to the Carter Administration*. New York: Holmes and Meier, 1980.

Campbell, John Franklin. *The Foreign Affairs Fudge Factory*. New York: Basic Books, 1971.

Cline, Howard F. *The United States and Mexico*. New York: Atheneum, 1973.

Coplin, William D., Patrick J. McGowan, and Michael K. O'Leary. *American Foreign Policy*. North Scituate, Mass.: Duxbury Press, 1974.

Crabb, Cecil V., Jr. *The Doctrines of American Foreign Policy: Their Meaning, Role, and Future*. Baton Rouge: Louisiana State University Press, 1982.

————. *Policy Makers and Critics: Conflicting Theories of American Foreign Policy*. New York: Praeger, 1976.

———— and Pat M. Holt. *Invitation to Struggle*. Washington, D.C.: Congressional Quarterly Press, 1980.

Davis, Nathaniel. *The Last Two Years of Salvador Allende*. Ithaca, N.Y.: Cornell University Press, 1985.

Denny, Brewster. *Seeing American Foreign Policy Whole*. Champaign: University of Illinois Press, 1985.

DeRivera, Joseph H. *The Psychological Dimension of Foreign Policy*. Columbus, Ohio: Merrill, 1968.

Destler, I. M. *Making Foreign Economic Policy*. Washington, D.C.: Brookings Institution, 1980.

————. *Presidents, Bureaucrats, and Foreign Policy; The Politics of Organizational Reform*. Princeton: Princeton University Press, 1972.

————, Leslie H. Gelb, and Anthony Lake. *Our Own Worst Enemy: The Unmaking of American Foreign Policy*. New York: Simon and Schuster, 1984.

Donovan, John C. *The Cold Warriors: A Policy-Making Elite*. Lexington, Mass.: Heath, 1974.

Downs, Anthony. *Inside Bureaucracy*. Boston: Little, Brown, 1967.

Duarte, José N. and Diana Page. *Duarte: My Story*. New York: Putnam Publishing Group, 1986.

Ekirch, Arthur A., Jr. *Ideas, Ideals, and American Diplomacy*. New York: Appleton-Century-Crofts, 1966.

Esterline, John H., and Robert B. Black. *Inside Foreign Policy: The Department of State Political System and Its Subsystems*. Palo Alto, Calif.: Mayfield, 1975.

Fagen, Richard R., and Wayne A. Cornelius, Jr., eds. *Political Power in Latin America: Seven Confrontations*. Englewood Cliffs, N.J.: Prentice-Hall, 1970.

Ferrell, Robert H., ed. *The American Secretaries of State*. New York: Cooper Square, 1965.

Frankel, Charles. *High on Foggy Bottom*. New York: Harper and Row, 1969.

Fox, Douglas M., ed. *The Politics of U.S. Foreign Policy Making*. Pacific Palisades, Calif.: Goodyear, 1971.

George, Alexander L. *Presidential Decisionmaking in Foreign Policy*. Boulder: Westview, 1980.

―――― and Juliette L. George. *Woodrow Wilson and Colonel House: A Personality Study*. New York: Dover Publications, 1964.

Graebner, Norman A., ed. *Ideas and Diplomacy: Readings in the Intellectual Tradition of American Foreign Policy*. New York: Oxford University Press, 1964.

――――. *An Uncertain Tradition: American Secretaries of State in the Twentieth Century*. New York: McGraw-Hill, 1961.

Greenstein, Fred I. *Personality and Politics*. Chicago: Markham, 1969.

Gregg, Robert W., and Charles W. Kegley, Jr., eds. *After Vietnam: The Future of American Foreign Policy*. New York: Doubleday-Anchor, 1971.

Halperin, Morton H., and Arnold Kanter, eds. *Readings in American Foreign Policy*. Boston: Little, Brown, 1973.

Harr, John Ensor. *The Professional Diplomat*. Princeton: Princeton University Press, 1969.

Hermann, Margaret C. with Thomas W. Milburn, eds. *A Psychological Examination of Political Leaders*. New York: Free Press, 1977.

Hersh, Seymour M. *The Price of Power: Kissinger in the Nixon White House*. New York: Summit, 1983.

Hilsman, Roger. *To Move a Nation*. New York: Doubleday, 1967.

――――. *The Politics of Policy Making in Defense and Foreign Affairs*. New York: Harper & Row, 1971.

Hoffman, Stanley. *Gulliver's Troubles, or the Setting of American Foreign Policy*. New York: McGraw-Hill, 1968.

――――. *Primacy or World Order: American Foreign Policy since the Cold War*. New York: McGraw-Hill, 1978.

Howland, Hewitt H. *Dwight Whitney Morrow: A Sketch in Admiration*. New York: Century, 1930.

Hull, Cordell. *The Memoirs of Cordell Hull*. 2 vols. New York: Macmillan, 1948.

Ilchman, Warren F. *Professional Diplomacy in the United States 1779–1939: A Study in Administrative History*. Chicago: University of Chicago Press, 1961.

Janis, Irving. *Victims of Groupthink: A Psychological Study of Foreign-Policy Decisions and Fiascoes*. Boston: Houghton Mifflin, 1972.

Isaak, Robert A. *Individuals and World Politics*. North Scituate, Mass.: Duxbury Press, 1975.

Johnson, Richard A. *The Administration of United States Foreign Policy*. Austin: University of Texas Press, 1971.

Kegley, Charles W., Jr., and Patrick J. McGowan, eds. *Challenges to America: United States Foreign Policy in the 1980s*. Beverly Hills: Sage, 1979.

Kegley, Charles W., Jr. and Eugene R. Wittkopf. *American Foreign Policy: Pattern and Process*. 2nd. ed. New York: St. Martin's Press, 1982.

Kennan, George F. *American Diplomacy, 1900–1950*. New York: New American Library, 1951.

——. *Memoirs.* Boston: Little, Brown, 1967.

——. *Realities of American Foreign Policy.* Princeton: Princeton University Press, 1954.

Kissinger, Henry. *American Foreign Policy.* 3rd. ed. New York: Norton, 1977.

——. *White House Years.* Boston: Little, Brown, 1979.

LaFeber, Walter. *America, Russia, and the Cold War 1945–1975.* New York: Wiley, 1976.

Leacacos, John P. *Fires in the In-Basket: The ABC's of the State Department.* Cleveland: World, 1968.

Lindblom, Charles E. *The Policy-Making Process.* Englewood Cliffs, N.J.: Prentice-Hall, 1968.

Lovell, John P. *Foreign Policy in Perspective.* New York: Holt, Rinehart, and Winston, 1970.

McBride, Mary Margaret. *The Story of Dwight W. Morrow.* New York: Farrar and Rinehart, 1930.

McGann, Thomas F. *Argentina, the United States and the Inter-American System 1880–1914.* Cambridge, Mass.: Harvard University Press, 1957.

May, Ernest R. *"Lessons" of the Past.* London: Oxford University Press, 1973.

Mayer, Martin. *The Diplomats.* New York: Doubleday, 1983.

Mennis, Bernard. *American Foreign Policy Officials: Who They Are and What They Believe Regarding International Politics.* Columbus: Ohio State University Press, 1971.

Morgenthau, Hans J. *In Defense of the National Interest: A Critical Examination of American Foreign Policy.* New York: Knopf, 1952.

Morrison, Joseph L. *Josephus Daniels: The Small-d Democrat.* Chapel Hill: University of North Carolina Press, 1966.

Mosher, Frederick C. *Democracy and the Public Service.* New York: Oxford University Press, 1968.

Nathan, Richard P. *The Plot That Failed: Nixon and the Administrative Presidency.* New York: Wiley, 1975.

Nicolson, Harold. *Dwight Morrow.* New York: Harcourt, Brace, 1935.

Osgood, Robert E. *Ideals and Self Interest in America's Foreign Relations.* Chicago: University of Chicago Press, 1953.

Oye, Kenneth A., Donald Rothchild, and Robert J. Lieber, eds. *Eagle Entangled: U.S. Foreign Policy in a Complex World.* New York: Longman, 1979.

Packenham, Robert A. *Liberal America and the Third World.* Princeton: Princeton University Press, 1973.

Parenti, Michael, ed. *Trends and Tragedies in American Foreign Policy.* Boston: Little, Brown, 1971.

Pérez, Louis A., Jr. *Cuba Between Empires, 1872–1902.* Pittsburgh: University of Pittsburgh Press, 1983.

——. *Cuba Under the Platt Amendment: 1902–1934.* Pittsburgh: University of Pittsburgh Press, 1986.

——. *Intervention, Revolution, and Politics in Cuba: 1913–1921.* Pittsburgh: University of Pittsburgh Press, 1978.

Peterson, Harold F. *Argentina and the United States, 1810–1960.* New York: State University of New York Press, 1964.

Roett, Riordan, ed. *Brazil in the Sixties.* Nashville: Vanderbilt University Press, 1972.

Ronning, C. Neale (ed.). Intervention in Latin America. New York: Alfred A. Knopf. Inc., 1970.

———. Law and Politics in Inter-American Diplomacy. New York: John Wiley and Sons, Inc., 1963.

Rosenau, James N., ed. Comparing Foreign Policies. New York: Sage/Halsted Press, 1974.

———. Domestic Sources of Foreign Policy. New York: Free Press, 1967.

———. National Leadership and Foreign Policy. Princeton: Princeton University Press, 1963.

———. Public Opinion and Foreign Policy. New York: Random House, 1961.

Rourke, Francis E. Bureaucracy and Foreign Policy. Baltimore: Johns Hopkins University Press, 1972.

Rubin, Barry, Secrets of State: The State Department and the Struggle over U.S. Foreign Policy. New York: Oxford University Press, 1985.

Salter, Sir Arthur. Personality in Politics: Studies of Contemporary Statesmen. London: Faber and Faber, n.d.

Sapin, Burton M. The Making of United States Foreign Policy. New York: Praeger, 1967.

Simpson, Smith. Anatomy of the State Department. Boston: Houghton Mifflin, 1967.

Smith, Robert F. The United States and Cuba: Business and Diplomacy, 1917–1961. New Haven: Yale University Press, 1960.

———. The United States and Revolutionary Nationalism in Mexico, 1916–32. Chicago: University of Chicago Press, 1972.

Smith, Steve, and Michael Clarke, eds. Foreign Policy Implementation. Winchester: George Allen and Unwin, 1985.

Spanier, John. American Foreign Policy since World War II. New York: Holt, Rinehart, and Winston, 1980.

———, and Joseph Nogee, eds. Congress, the Presidency and American Foreign Policy. New York: Pergamon Press, 1981.

Steigman, Andrew L. The Foreign Service of the United States: America's First Line of Defense. Boulder: Westview, 1985.

Stillman, Edmund, and William Pfaff. Power and Impotence: The Failure of American Foreign Policy. New York: Random House, 1966.

Stimson, Henry L., and McGeorge Bundy. On Active Service in Peace and War. New York: Harper & Brothers, 1947.

Stoessinger, John G. Crusaders and Pragmatists: Movers of Modern American Foreign Policy. New York: Random House, 1966.

Stupak, Ronald J. American Foreign Policy: Assumptions, Processes, and Projections. New York: Harper & Row, 1976.

United States, Commission on the Organization of the Government for the Conduct of Foreign Policy. Washington, D.C.: Government Printing Office, 1975.

Vocke, William E., ed. American Foreign Policy: An Analytical Approach. New York: Free Press, 1976.

Waltz, Kenneth N. Foreign Policy and Democratic Politics. Boston: Little, Brown, 1967.

Warwick, Donald P. A Theory of Public Bureaucracy: Politics, Personality, and Organization in the State Department. Cambridge, Mass.: Harvard University Press, 1975.

Welles, Sumner. *Seven Decisions That Shaped History.* New York: Harper & Brothers, 1950.

――――. *The Time of Decision.* New York: Harper & Brothers, 1944.

Wesson, Robert G. *Foreign Policy for a New Age.* Boston: Houghton Mifflin, 1977.

Wilcox, Francis O. *Congress, the Executive, and Foreign Policy.* New York: Harper & Row, 1971.

Wilson, Joan Hoff. *American Business and Foreign Policy, 1920–33.* Lexington: University Press of Kentucky, 1971.

Wood, Bryce. *The Making of the Good Neighbor Policy.* New York: W. W. Norton, 1961.

Woods, Randall Bennett. *The Roosevelt Foreign Policy Establishment and the "Good Neighbors."* Kansas City: Regents Press of Kansas, 1979.

Index

About the Editors and Contributors

C. NEALE RONNING is Professor of Political Science at the Graduate Faculty of the New School for Social Research. He has also taught at Princeton, Tulane, Johns Hopkins School of Advanced International Studies, Columbia, and the Ohio State University. He is the author of several books on Latin America, including *Law and Politics in Inter-American Diplomacy* and *Intervention in Latin America*. Dr. Ronning holds a Ph.D. from the University of Minnesota.

ALBERT P. VANNUCCI is Associate Professor and Chair of Political Science and Coordinator of International Studies at the University of Pittsburgh at Johnstown. He is the recipient of a 1985 Chancellor's Distinguished Teaching Award. He has participated in a number of briefings and in the scholar-diplomat program at the U.S. State Department. His articles and reviews have appeared in the *Journal of Latin American Studies,* the *American Political Science Review,* and *Perspective.* Dr. Vannucci holds a Ph.D. from the Graduate Faculty of the New School for Social Research.

JAN KNIPPERS BLACK is Research Associate Professor of Public Administration at the University of New Mexico, where she also teaches in the Department of Political Science. Previously, she was Senior Research Scientist and Chairman of the Latin American Research Team in the Foreign Area Studies Division of American University. Author of *United States Penetration of Brazil,* Professor Black has authored, edited, or coauthored more than two dozen books on Latin America and on U.S. foreign policy. A former Peace Corps Volunteer in Chile, Dr. Black holds a Ph.D. in international studies from the American University.

NATHANIEL DAVIS is Alexander and Adelaide Hixon Professor of Humanities at Harvey Mudd College. Dr. Davis served for 36 years in the U.S. Foreign Service, including postings as U.S. Ambassador to Chile, Guatemala, and Switzerland; Assistant Secretary of State for African Affairs; Director General of the U.S. Foreign Service; and Senior National Security Council Staffer. He has published widely on contemporary international relations. His most recent book is *The Last Two Years of Salvador Allende.* Dr. Davis holds a Ph.D. from the Fletcher School of Law and Diplomacy.

RICHARD MELZER is the Director of Instruction at the University of New Mexico–Valencia Campus, where he teaches United States and Latin American History and Political Science. He has read at least one conference paper or had at least one manuscript published every year, save one, since 1974—a total of eleven papers, seven articles, and one book. Dr. Melzer holds three degrees in Latin American History, including a Ph.D. from the University of New Mexico.

LOUIS PÉREZ is Graduate Research Professor of History at the University of South Florida. His most recent book is *Cuba under the Platt Amendment, 1902–1934.* He has published articles in the *Hispanic American Historical Review, The Americas,* the *Journal of Latin American Studies, Cuban Studies/Estudios Cubanos, Latin American Research Review,* and the *American Historical Review.* Dr. Pérez holds a Ph.D. from the University of New Mexico.